A Marital Puzzle

REVISED EDITION

Transgenerational Analysis in Marriage Counseling

by Norman L. Paul M.D. and Betty Byfield Paul M.S.W.

WITH A FOREWORD BY James L. Framo, Ph.D.

Gardner Press, Inc.
New York & London

To VAN and CINDY

GARDNER PRESS, INC.
19 UNION SQUARE WEST
NEW YORK, NEW YORK 10003

All foreign orders except Canada and South America to:

AFTERHURST LIMITED
CHANCERY HOUSE
319 CITY ROAD
LONDON, N1, ENGLAND

Library of Congress Cataloging in Publication Data

New York: Gardner, 1986
Gardner,

CURRENT PPD: 8509

Paul, Norman L.
    A marital puzzle: transgenerational analysis in marriage counseling /
Norman Paul and Betty Byfield Paul.
Rev. ed. Gardner, 1986

ISBN: 0898761271   86-20560

Contents

Foreword

OVER THE YEARS I have never ceased to be surprised and intrigued by the kind of singular emotional intensity which permeates the bonds of intimately related people. Among the various human events which arouse this intensity, there are few to match those which occur between married partners, a relationship which can incite the deepest passions in the human realm. *A Marital Puzzle* represents a first in the marital therapy literature—an entire book of selected verbatim transcripts of treatment interviews of a severely distressed couple. The interpretative comments by Norm and Betty Paul, interspersed between the clients' verbatim statements, are especially valuable. Although Norm Paul was the therapist in this case who was fully there for the couple and who struggled through the impasses with them, it was Betty who was the inspiration for the book, its organizer and guiding force.

$N = 1$ presentations have become rare in the mental health field, but their value has been underestimated. Unlike the group statistical method, which conceals as much as it reveals, intensive examination of a single case over time can be a more accurate portrayal of phenomenological reality. This approach is another form of the scientific method whereby the therapist finds and discards clues, makes hypotheses, and confirms or rejects them on the basis of evidence as it accumulates. Detailed transactions of treatment sessions have great value: they open the reader to the intricate maze-work of psychotherapy; they allow one to follow the maneuvers of the therapist who weaves through the mass of material, illuminates the themes; and does the detective work of finding out where the pieces of the puzzle fit. There are many articles written for students on how to conduct a therapy interview, and even papers on termination; the Pauls have attempted to describe the indescribable "dirty middle" phase or ongoing *process* of therapy, the part very few therapists write about.

Norman Paul endeavors to help people get to know unknown parts of themselves, and learn more how they experience themselves. He encourages clients not only to make research projects of themselves, but has them objectively study their own marriage as well as how they parent their children. To accomplish these goals he utilizes a variety of imaginative, creative techniques, such as superimposing clients' faces on parents' faces via video, crossconfrontation (playing excerpts from emotionally charged treatment sessions from other families and couples in order to elicit emotional states which were hidden), the showing of sexually explicit films (to help people connect with dissociated aspects of their sexuality), and audio and videotape playback. The difference between the way we see ourselves and how we are seen by others Paul calls the "credibility gap," and by observing self on videotape playback one can narrow that gap. All these techniques are designed not only to gain access to the self, become an expert on the self, but also to be able to put oneself in the place of the intimate other. Empathy is a key concept of Paul's work.

The theoretical rationale of Paul's work rests on the premise that marital problems are but the surface manifestations of attempts on the part of the spouses to work out conflicts from their family of origin *through* each other. This intergenerational approach takes its place alongside the work of Bowen, Boszormanyi-Nagy, Williamson, Whitaker, and Framo. Paul's great contribution is the development of innovative methods of making trans-generational forces more visible. He demonstrates in this case how the fantasies and images of marriage, derived from the family of origin, can lead to estrangement and anguish between partners. The couple in this book deal with such universals as low self-esteem, exaggerated dependency, despair, losses, sexual difficulties, and alienation from the family of origin. The case of "Cindy" and "Van" shows the pain of marital distress, the lost opportunities, the grief, the regrets, yet at the same time reveals the pleasure of re-discovery and enrichment of a relationship.

I felt sad at the end of the story of this couple, even though the follow-up ten years later showed that the positive changes held up. It was like saying goodbye to people with whom I had been on a journey and we had all experienced the powerful insides of ourselves.

James L. Framo, Ph.D.
San Diego, California

Preface

A Marital Puzzle was conceived in May 1973 as an attempt to provide some new insights into the problems in marriage. We offer this book to those interested in understanding a transgenerational perspective of marriage. Our thesis is that the quality of one's relationship to members of one's original family forms the unrecognized backdrop for the success or failure of one's marriage, which includes the functioning of one's children.

Our aim, as it evolved during our collaboration, is to show, through a detailed study of one marriage in trouble, the process of the resolution of a serious marital crisis. The material for this study is taken from the tape recordings of the interviews, coupled with a commentary on the rationale for the various kinds of techniques used. We have attempted to illustrate that there are many sides to a marriage and that sex and love can't be isolated from the relationship of the partners, nor can a child's existence be regarded as an entity independent from the marital relationship.

We are indebted to the Hoopeses for permitting us to present to the public their story and their struggle in achieving a new marriage. (Obviously identifying data have been altered to preserve appropriate anonymity.)

Dr. Norman Paul, their family psychiatrist, provided the interview material and his techniques for this book. He has used these techniques in the treatment of marital and parent-child disorders over the past fifteen years. Their use has evolved principally from a desire to evolve more effective approaches for the understanding and resolution of problems that exist between spouses and between parents and their children.

Betty Byfield Paul, a psychiatric social worker in a large suburban public school system, conceived of and implemented the style of presentation. Her daily work in elementary schools has made her increasingly aware that marital difficulties and their relationship to the development of children is an area of growing concern to the community at large.

Acknowledgments

WE ACKNOWLEDGE with gratitude the help we have had from our numerous friends and colleagues who have assisted us through provocative discussion. We wish to make special mention of those who have criticized this manuscript. These were Joan Goldsmith, codirector of the Institute for Open Education, Antioch Graduate Center; Dr. Clifford E. Barbour, president emeritus, Pittsburgh Theological Seminary; Fred Rogers of "Mr. Rogers' Neighborhood" and his wife, Jo-Anne Rogers; Dr. Douglas Bond, professor of psychiatry, Case-Western Reserve School of Medicine; Norman Law, director of design, Arthur D. Little, Inc., and our children, Marilyn Paul and David Paul.

Both Harriet Weiner and Roberta Ornstein provided dedicated secretarial and research assistance. Harriet Weiner's help and insight in the editing of the explanatory comments were invaluable. In addition, she wrote the first draft of what developed into "An American Fairy Tale."

The Jared Coffin House of Nantucket, Massachusetts, provided the necessary solitude for the birth of this book in a setting that underscored the importance of the historical perspective.

Special thanks are due to Eric Swenson and Sherry Huber of W. W. Norton for their encouragement and support.

Introduction

BY NORMAN L. PAUL, M.D.

INITIALLY I was trained to work with adults and children individually. My primary orientation was psychoanalytic and was associated with some training in group psychotherapy. My first questioning of the focus on individual psychotherapy started during my first-year residency. It occurred during a supervisory hour with a senior psychoanalyst who commented in the course of another resident's presentation that "it was desirable that the patient should have a good relationship with the therapist." I wondered why this should be so (I didn't dare say this aloud, lest I be subjected to ridicule), even though I was familiar with the rationale that the transference reaction to the therapist could enable the patient to work out his conflicts and better understand his feelings. It is obvious to me now that my initial qualm about the relationship to the therapist was related to the budding notion that it is more important for a patient to have or develop a good relationship with members of his family than to have one with his therapist.

Gradually, over the years, I have come to believe that although a person can be viewed as a "psychiatric patient," labeled with a diagnosis that is commonly used by psychiatrists, operationally the "patient" is a person whose life experience is such that he has been rendered ignorant of the emotional facts of his own life. For whatever reasons, he lacks a precision of knowledge applicable to himself about the array of feelings that are normal to experience. Also, he doesn't know what a fantasy is and that it is generated in *his* own head. To label such ignorance primarily as a psychiatric illness not only demeans the human being, but casts him in a role from which it is very difficult to extricate himself.

The psychiatric patient unwittingly finds himself in other difficulties. Because he has suffered both the indictment of being labeled a psychiatric patient and the negative attitudes others display toward deviance, his sense of personal security is further compromised. His ignorance about behaviors, observed by others, generates a belief, a faith that the traditional psychiatrist has the expertise to assist him in achieving a comfortable sense of self-esteem. More often than not he will feel a sense of stigma which is usually perceived and reinforced, usually unwittingly, by members of his family, i.e., parents, siblings, spouse, and even children. He often becomes more and more dependent on his psychiatrist, instead of less and less.

In association with this escalating dependence on his psychiatrist, the patient often has difficulty in thinking for himself. He feels unsure about his competence to make decisions about himself, and finds himself deferring to the judgments of the therapist. Because he has not been encouraged to develop a capability in conducting a dialogue with members of his own family, he often finds himself feeling variably estranged from them—he is "crazy" and "immature," with the implicit inference that the others are "sane" and "mature."

My Dilemma with Joseph Y

(An illustration highlighting my transition from a traditional psychiatrist to a family-oriented psychiatrist.)

I believe that each of us represents a composite of experiences since birth, and that these experiences, emotionally laden and then forgotten, are continually influencing our present functioning. How such unrecognized experiences were decoded and thus made understandable is seen in my therapeutic struggle with Joseph Y.

The decoding of what one is told and particularly what one is not told represents in large part the detective work involved. To be aware that there are data which one couldn't even suspect at the beginning of contact with a client necessitates the capacity to entertain a degree of uncertainty within oneself which at times can be quite taxing.

In March 1960, I was consulted by a twenty-year-old man, Joseph Y, upon the urging of his mother. The presenting problem was that his mother felt that he was unresponsive to her desire that he behave "like other boys." She feared that he was mentally ill and might have to be placed in a mental hospital, as his father had been in 1946. The first time I saw Joseph, he exuded intense anxiety, felt that his body was shrinking in size, and that people everywhere looked at him maliciously. He had no sense of self-worth. He was quite unkempt. He lived at that time with his forty-two-year-old mother and his nineteen-year-old brother Donald, who was attending college. Both boys were unmarried. Joseph was working as a stock clerk in a department store. In that first meeting, he related his problem specifically to the fact that his father was mentally ill, and had been continuously hospitalized for the preceeding fourteen years, having undergone a prefrontal lobotomy.

In an explosive torrent of rage directed first at his father, and then at himself, Joseph exclaimed, "He made me sick inside," and "He's always in me." He said that all his difficulties stemmed from his poor relationship with his father, and that his poor school performance in the second grade began shortly after his father's lobotomy. At that time, in 1946, his father had returned home for a brief period of convalescence from the lobotomy. While at home he and Joseph got into an argument over a television program. The argument between the two continued until the father suddenly had a postlobotomy seizure, and was rendered briefly unconscious. Mother then rushed into the room and, in a state of panic, shoved Joseph out of the room, accusing him of having made his father "faint."

Shortly after, Mr. Y was rehospitalized while Joseph was encouraged by his mother to believe that he had triggered the seizure which had driven his father "crazier." This myth came to be regarded as established fact in Joseph's mind.

Over the next ten years, while his father was hospitalized at a local state hospital, Joseph would visit him once a year or once in two years, and developed the feeling that for him his father was dead. Joseph's guilt was intense. In 1956, when Joseph was sixteen years old, the hospital staff decided that it would now be prudent to attempt to rehabilitate Mr. Y and return him to the community. This coincided with Joseph's attending a local adolescent clinic because of increased confusion, poor school performance, and social isolation.

The state hospital negotiated with Mrs. Y to have her husband return home. He did so, without ostensible preparation of the family. Joseph's initial reaction to seeing his father at home was profound fright. He was confused about the seeming return to life of a man he felt was dead. He suddenly became suffused with both suicidal impulses and murderous feelings toward his father. His psychiatrist at the adolescent clinic became sufficiently alarmed by Joseph's reaction that he immediately telephoned Mrs. Y, who promptly called the hospital. Within a short period of time, after consultation between Mrs. Y and the hospital, Joseph's father was returned to the state hospital.

Shortly after this, during a verbal altercation between Joseph and his younger brother Donald, Mother interceded and stated adamantly that she wasn't "going to get rid of Donald for your [Joseph's] sake as I just got rid of your father." Within a few weeks Joseph was again overcome by overwhelming guilt and terror in relation to his father. One morning he woke with a horrified sense that he was becoming bald like his father. At the same time he began to experience a sense that his body was shrinking in size; he feared that he might disappear entirely.

During the next four years he consulted with four psychiatrists. He was periodically unemployed and leading a generally withdrawn, hermitlike existence, meeting with his psychiatrists only at the insistence of his mother. His response to psychotherapy was nil, as he began to realize that the hoped-for, magical disappearance of his problems was not materializing. Joseph was like a puppet, initiating very little on his own, and going out of the house primarily at his mother's direction.

The crisis in March 1960, dictating his mother's sending him to me, was related to his younger brother's receipt of a scholarship to a prestigious university. At that time Joseph had begun to feel that people were talking about him and singling him out for derision because he was Jewish.

During the following year I saw Joseph twice weekly in an attempt to focus primarily on his relationship with his father. The purpose was to assist him in discriminating his fantasies from what was real. This was extraordinarily difficult, because as he focused on his father, he concurrently expressed murderous rage toward his mother, as well as his own suicidal preoccupations, his sense of nothingness, and his enormous envy of his brother. As he became increasingly aware that his rage toward his father obscured his sadness, pain, and longing for the father that he had had before his sixth year, he shifted his focus onto his mother. He now began to feel murderous rage toward her.

In March 1961, because of the absence of improvement for Joseph socially, occupationally, and at home, I began to feel that it would be important for him to work out his feelings about himself in a context which would include other people. His pervasive sense of estrangement and isolation from the world at large was unremitting. His continuing conviction that he had driven his father crazy and his incapacity to relate comfortably to any peer dictated my referring him to a colleague, with whom he started on a course of group psychotherapy. I had hoped his concerns and sense of malignancy could be muted by relating to other group members, with whom he might begin to experience a sense of emotional kinship. I continued seeing him twice weekly in individual therapy.

In the group he seemed to be hallucinating at times during the initial weekly visits. After two months he was able to be drawn into group discussions, wherein he compared himself disparagingly with his college-educated brother, and began to share his distress whenever his mother pushed and coerced him to behave like other boys. As he began to take notice of several members of the group, he improved his grooming and began to muse about leaving home. In late November 1961, as he had become more aware of himself as a separate person, his anger and rage at his mother seemed to escalate. This would occur concurrently with his sense that when he was with her at home, his emerging sense of self and separateness would disappear, and he felt he was lapsing into nothingness. Because of the increasing frequency of raging arguments between Joseph and his mother, coupled with her description of his habit of hallucinating his father's presence late at night, screaming and inveighing against him, mother would call me daily to tell me that Joseph belonged in the same hospital with his father. It was in this context of escalating tension and acrimony in the Y household that I initiated conjoint family therapy. For in my own escalating sense of helplessness in coping with Joseph, I had come to question the wisdom of working with him alone.

And so, in early December 1961, I began to have meetings with Joseph and his mother. My operating hypothesis at that time was that both mother and son were reacting to each other on the basis of intense guilt and shame, experienced in themselves and projected onto the other, like a reverberating circuit. These feelings were regarded as a displacement of helplessness and responsibility for the husband-father's chronic hospitalization and absence from home. In January 1962, Joseph's younger brother, Donald, was invited to join these sessions. His participation proved most valuable, since he was able to present a less charged view of the interactions between his brother and mother. At times he would verify the validity of certain experiences Joseph had referred to, which his mother had denied. With the aid of such an alternative reality perspective provided by Donald, Joseph was increasingly able to see that what he had thought were fantasies had indeed occurred. Joseph began to experience himself as a real person.

It was extraordinary to observe that when Joseph and his mother were present without Donald, who would be absent because of examinations at college, that the two of them would often behave as if an imminent murder of the other or suicide of the self would occur. Without Donald present, it was as if mother's only relationship included an insane son who would imminently envelop her; the related verbal abuse and rage was most intense during these sessions. I used a gavel in an attempt to maintain order between these two people who had to be instructed repeatedly as to how to share time and space, very much as if they were in nursery school. I feared (and at times felt) that I could be drowned into a state of mutism or insanity by the escalating rantings and ravings. The gavel was most effective in setting limits and curbing the emerging nightmare. When such sieges would continue near the end of a session, I would indicate to both that since I was not a policeman, it was not my business to control their behavior. In such instances I would take from my desk two temporary care admission forms for a Massachusetts state hospital, and indicate that I believed that each of them should be admitted to the hospital where Mr. Y was located. I added that when each regained his own control and was released from said hospital, each could return to my office separately or together, where we could continue to disentangle each from the other. It was extraordinary to see that as I began to complete these forms for each of them, each immediately quieted down and became composed. They would then leave the office without any need for their being sent to the state hospital, behaving as if their prior craziness had not occurred.

In late spring 1962, in an individual therapy interview with Mrs. Y, she finally revealed to me her secret, which I could not have anticipated, and which surprised me. Although she had been seeing social workers off and on for the preceeding twenty years, since an attempted suicide after Donald's birth, she had never mentioned the secret to any of them. The secret was that she became pregnant by Mr. Y out of wedlock; the product of this conception was Joseph. She had attempted to abort him eight times, and failing this, had married his father. It took me about four months to persuade her to tell this to her sons. Though she feared recrimination from Joseph in particular, none was ever forthcoming from either son. Though there was no evidence that anyone would blame her for getting pregnant, her sense of guilt and shame had remained unrelenting over the years.

It became very clear also after she revealed the auspices of Joseph's birth why she was so reluctant and at times even insistent that Joseph not visit his father at the hospital, concerned lest his father spill the beans. After this disclosure by Mrs. Y, it was extraordinary to observe Joseph's gradual emerging sense of self. He then shared his fantasy that in some peculiar way he had felt that it was he himself who had gotten his mother pregnant with himself. He was thus reflecting the nonverbal vibrations that he had absorbed from his mother, whose resentment and blame toward her husband for her pregnancy had been deflected onto Joseph.

He added that he had felt that he was the one who had wrecked her life by her pregnancy with him, consummated by him. His mother unbeknown to herself had transferred her guilt about her pregnancy and marriage from her husband to Joseph. Things began to make sense to me and to them. As this happened, Joseph was shorn of his misdirected burden of shame and guilt. Gradually, his ability to relate to others improved.

In the summer of 1963, I decided that I had allowed myself to believe what I had been told by Mrs. Y and her sons, that the father was a total vegetable. He'd been on the back wards of the state hospital for seventeen years. I decided that I would like to have him come to my office; I had become acutely aware that, like Joseph, I had treated him as though he were dead. In spite of much reluctance and opposition from Mrs. Y, principally because of her shame about having a institutionalized husband, I pursued this plan, and on August 1, 1963, Mr. Y arrived with his two sons and his wife.

I remember very vividly being in my office and hearing them coming down the hall. I felt frightened, thinking Mr. Y might become beserk and attempt to harm either myself or somebody else in the office. I did feel that because the boys were tall and strong, I had attendantlike help available should the need arise. It was extraordinary meeting him. His bald head and the scars from the burr holes from the lobotomy were readily apparent. I noted that in many ways, he seemed as anxious and frightened as I felt. And then came an unexpected and bewildering session, which helped to change my subsequent professional life.

During this session, Mr. Y reviewed in some detail his life experiences, including his shock and dismay at seeing his own father die suddenly from a heart attack when he was eighteen years old. He also told of his continuing distress about being in the hospital over the years, and still wondered when he could come home. He spoke clearly, at times repetitiously. He evinced an emotional flavor of such depth that Mrs. Y was shocked to hear him make so much sense. Joseph indicated how much he had missed his father over the years, which embarrassed Mr. Y. I was shocked by the whole experience, insofar as I hadn't anticipated this quality of conversation and emotional expression from this man who had been on the back wards for many years.

They left the meeting pleased and bewildered. The following day I went on vacation, confused and depressed because I felt that I had allowed myself to be conned into believing something that was obviously untenable in light of what had transpired the day before in the office. This experience has had a profound effect on my thinking. It led me to believe that my job is to check out *for myself* how much of my client's perceptions dovetail with both what I can perceive and have to discover for myself. In this instance, it obviously required the presence of Mr. Y.

It became obvious to me that Joseph lived out his parents' sense of stigma, transmitted primarily by his mother's intense guilt and shame about her unwanted pregnancy. I had a fantasy in September 1963, after vacation, that maybe this man might be able to be rehabilitated at home and obtain a job in the community. This ill-founded fantasy was short-lived, insofar as after seeing him and his family for six more sessions, it became apparent that nothing much could be done for this distressed human being who had been segregated for so long in a mental hospital. Joseph continued to visit him, and was able to further develop a more compassionate relationship with him. Mr. Y died in the state hospital in 1970: Mrs. Y is now more comfortable living alone in a new apartment. Joseph Y is living alone and works as an assistant manager of a department in a supermarket. He feels more comfortable than he ever has felt before, and this includes being with his mother.

The Y family learned that taking the risk in discussing intimate secrets stripped these secrets of their diabolical power. Joseph's release is similar to Harry's in T. S. Eliot's *Family Reunion:*

Look, I do not know why, I feel happy for a moment, as if I had come home. It is quite irrational, but now I feel quite happy, as if happiness did not consist in getting what one wanted or in getting rid of what can't be got rid of but in a different vision. . . . Now I see I might even become fonder of my mother—more compassionate at least—by understanding. But she would not like that. Now I see I have been wounded in a war of phantoms, not by human beings—they have no more power than I. The things I thought were real are shadows, and the real are what I thought were private shadows.*

—HARRY

* *The Family Reunion,* by T. S. Eliot, pp. 102–103.

The result of seeing the Y family has taught me to try to be very dumb and to search for facts without thrusting my expectations into a family scene. My general posture is that until there is evidence that family members feel more comfortable about their lives and their interrelationships, some important information is still missing that could make the family scene more understandable. My general goal is for each family member to be able to cope more realistically with the uncertainties of life and have a sense of joy about being alive. This can occur if one is capable of sorting out the unpleasant, the tragic, and the pain, which, when accepted and then shared with some other in one's own life, preferably a family member, can imbue family members with a spirit of genuine love.

The Y family situation represents an extreme example of family disorganization and pain shared by each of its members. This family enabled me to begin to understand lesser types of family distress, and to search for newer techniques which would shorten the length of time necessary for troubled families to understand themselves and heal.

It is obvious that no human being grows up in a vacuum, but rather in some form of a family setting. A family has two general relationships, marital and parental. These have usually been treated as separate and marginally interrelated. However, both forcefully impinge in various ways on developing children for good and for ill.

It becomes apparent that the parenting process, as illustrated by the Y family and by many others, is directly related to the quality of the marital relationship. This, in turn, is related to the way the spouses cope with the subtle collision of two differing family life-styles, each derived from his original family and expressed through each spouse in the marriage. The marital relationship is the instrument by which the unique ways in which the spouses have related to the world are transmitted to the children. In trying to understand how this new family life-style is formed, we must ask the following questions: What are the elements in a marriage? How does a marriage work? How do two people fit together and what makes them stay together?

WE ARE PUBLISHING this version of *A Marital Puzzle* to make available in paperback form substantively the original version which was published in 1975 by W.W. Norton and Company. This new edition includes, in addition to the original book, a synopsis of two follow-up interviews with Van and Cindy. We decided that if it were possible it would be desirable to find out briefly what had happened during the years of 1973 to 1983. Chapter VIII presents this synopsis.

It had become evident to us after a time, that we had not described the process by which *A Marital Puzzle* had been created. This creative process was initiated by Betty Paul, who upon learning of the dramatic resolution of the Hoopses crisis in seven interviews suggested to Norman Paul that a detailed account of these interviews including the innovative interventions would represent a dynamic and exciting means of sharing a very unique and effective therapeutic approach. Betty Paul then proposed that by repeated and directed inquiry of Norman that she would enable him to analyze both his theory and style of intervention. She felt that Norman's collaborative and catalytic work with the Hoopses would be a communicable example of his basic orientation towards his clients, i.e. that his role is to enable them to learn and to process the "emotional facts of life." Betty Paul, through incisive interviewing skills, and careful observations via closed circuit t.v. thus helped to generate the contextual framework of *A Marital Puzzle*.

Reviewing *A Marital Puzzle*, and their work both together and separately during the last ten years made the authors think that a basic philosophical framework put forth in both versions of their book is uniquely expressed by T.S. Eliot's words in "Sweeney Agonistes." When Sweeney describes his perception of the context of life he says is . . . "Nothing at all but three things."

DORIS: What things?
SWEENEY: Birth, and copulation and death. That's all, that's all, that's all, that's all, birth, and copulation and death.
DORIS: I'd be bored.

SWEENEY: You'd be bored. Birth, and copulation and death.
DORIS: I'd be bored.
SWEENEY: You'd be bored. Birth, and copulation and death.
  That's all the facts when you come to brass tacks; Birth, and
  copulation, and death.

> —Page 80 The Complete Poems and Plays 1909-1950
> by T.S. Eliot published by Harcourt, Brace Co. New
> York, 1952

At times life is boring, and this book, in part, is about how
some humans cope with boredom—a challenge for everybody.

A
Marital
Puzzle

But, for the purpose of science, what is the actual world? Has science to wait for the termination of the metaphysical debate till it can determine its own subject-matter? I suggest that science has a much more homely starting-ground. Its task is the discovery of the relations which exist within that flux of perceptions, sensations, and emotions which forms our experience of life. The panorama yielded by sight, sound, taste, smell, touch, and by more inchoate sensible feelings, is the sole field of activity. It is in this way that science is the thought organisation of experience. The most obvious aspect of the field of actual experience is its disorderly character. It is for each person a *continuum,* fragmentary, and with elements not clearly differentiated. . . .

. . . I insist on the radically untidy, ill-adjusted character of the fields of actual experience from which science starts. To grasp this fundamental truth is the first step in wisdom, when constructing a philosophy of science.

—Alfred North Whitehead, *The Aims of Education*

An American Fairy Tale

ONCE UPON A TIME there was a girl, and her name was Sally. Sally had a Mommy, whose name was Meg and a Daddy whose name was Pete. Meg and Pete loved Sally very much and wanted only the best for her. They wanted Sally to grow up and be happy and to spend her life as painlessly as possible, and as they saw it, this meant getting married and having children. Now Meg and Pete were intelligent and attractive. They tried their best to teach Sally how to live. Sally knew they cared about her and she was grateful and she believed what she was told.

Whenever Pete and Meg instructed Sally on happiness, this is what Sally heard:

You can't be happy unless you are married.

No one will marry you if you aren't good.

You aren't good if you are sexually experienced.

Sex is unpleasant and dishonest before marriage. (What it was after marriage, they didn't say.)

If a man loves you he will marry you and never be mad at you and always smile.

And you will be happy ever after.

Even happier with a couple of children who will be just what you want them to be.

Sally really wanted to be loved, and she thought her parents' advice was reasonable. Whenever she got to know a man, she began wondering if he was The Man she would marry, and if he really loved her, but whenever the man started getting sexually intimate she panicked, because it meant he didn't respect her and he didn't think she was marriageable.

One day Sally met Joe, who was a nice young man. Joe, a college graduate, was beginning what was obviously going to be a successful career, and he loved children. He was fond of Sally too. They fell in love.

Now, Joe's parents, like Sally's, loved Joe very much and wanted only the best for him. They wanted Joe to grow up and be happy and to spend his life as painlessly, but as profitably, as possible. Their idea of the best was somewhat different from the idea that Sally's parents had. They felt that their boy should be free as long as possible and not settle down until late in life when he had exhausted all the world's possibilities. *Then* he would be ready to get married and have children. What was passed down to Joe was this:

Stay free as long as possible.
You don't have to marry in order to have sex.
You haven't lived until you've had sexual experiences.
Sex is fine and exciting before marriage. (What it is after marriage, they didn't say.)
Someday, you will meet the perfect woman to marry. She will always smile and never be mad at you.
And you will live happily ever after.
Even happier with a couple of children who will be just what you want them to be.

Joe was attracted to Sally, and thought that some day he might marry her. But not too soon. He wasn't ready. What he was ready for was sex with Sally. That didn't commit him to anything.

Sally, for her part, thought it did. She was quite happy to become Joe's lover, because she trusted him and felt that he would certainly marry her. But Joe never mentioned marriage.

Sally felt betrayed. Sometimes Joe saw her crying. She never told him what she was crying about, but he somehow felt it was his fault. This made him angry.

One day, he threatened Sally: Tell me or else. Or else I'll leave.

Well, thought Sally, here was the golden opportunity.

"I thought we were going to get married."

Oh, so that's it. "We are." Someday.

Oh thank God, he said we are.

Then they announced their engagement. He really cared for her. He didn't want to lose her. She didn't want to lose him. She knew she had to be married. He knew she was the one, and he was a gentleman. The timing wasn't quite right for him, but they would manage.

So they were married.

The morning after the ceremony, Sally woke up early. She looked at her left hand. There was a golden ring on it. A wedding ring. Journey's end. Sally and Joe lived happily ever after.

Or could they?

*   *   *

The story you are about to read is not a fairy tale. It is an account of what really happened to a couple, Cindy and Van, who started off in their marriage very much like Sally and Joe. Cindy and Van, like Sally and Joe, each had different images or fantasies of what marriage should be. (Fantasies, images, and daydreams are universal properties of human mental life. The basic challenge for each of us is recognizing the existence of our own fantasies. There are two classes of fantasies: those that we may be aware of, and those whose presence are inferred from certain kinds of behaviors.) Cindy and Van each believed, though, that because they looked good to the world, the marriage would end up being good for them. Many of us are caught in this dilemma.

After ten years of marriage, Cindy and Van found themselves in the middle of a severe marital crisis. They began to ask themselves some questions, and although they blamed each other, and at times themselves, they nevertheless sought some answers. They began a process of decoding their behaviors with normal skepticisms and some reservations about what would happen to them as a result of this "therapy." The therapy proved to be a journey, wherein each learned how much they hadn't known about themselves, their relationship, and their naïveté about the living process. This book will share with you the exact problem-solving process that involved them, their psychiatrist, and finally included a consideration of members of their families of origin.

During these seven original interviews, conducted over a

three-month period, they discovered together the underlying causes of their crisis. It slowly became apparent during these eleven weeks that their troubles were rooted in an unrecognized collision of two differing life-styles, derived from their respective families of origin. The principal focus of the seven interviews was to assist each spouse in becoming aware of both the manner in which each experienced himself, and how each related to the other. In addition, by the use of video- and audiotape, each became aware of the personal-historical and family-historical forces which helped to shape both their own self-image and their style of relating to one another and their children. At the end of the seventh interview, "therapy" was concluded by mutual agreement, as a trip abroad had been planned by the Hoopeses. The resolution of the crisis and an emerging sense of self and self-esteem was beginning to unfold and be expressed in increased marital harmony.

No plans were made at the end of the seventh interview for a follow-up. Because of the rapid and dramatic resolution achieved by Cindy and Van we solicited their participation for a series of follow-up interviews one year later. Excerpts from these are included.

This book was written to take the mystery out of marital counseling. In a broader sense, it is an attempt to illuminate the marriage relationship, and to provide a steppingstone to increased recognition of the multiple factors that contribute to both marital happiness and tension.

By sharing the exact words and reactions of this young married couple, you will have an opportunity to identify with one or the other marital partner, and with their original families. In this way you can begin to think about yourself in relationship to your own spouse, and how you relate to your own original family. This, in turn, will enable you to empathize with yourself, your spouse, and your children.

This case embodies some of the major difficulties we all experience in our lives. Some of the universal issues described here include: a poor self-image, effects of loss of a parent during adolescence, unrecognized estrangement from one's original family, and sexual difficulties.

It will soon become apparent that, as Harry Stack Sullivan

said, "everyone and anyone is much more simply human than otherwise, and more like everyone else than different." Sullivan, an eminent psychiatrist, further emphasized the importance of the integrity of one's inner experience, the need for a sense of personal security, the need for a sense of validation of both one's own being, and of the existence of a variety of feelings, such as joy and sorrow, pain and pleasure, and the need to love and to be loved.

Developmentally, these human needs can first be met in a child by empathic dialogue between the child and the parent. Such dialogue becomes the prototype of the dialogue necessary for a successful marriage, and the effective rearing of one's own children. Failure or absence of empathic dialogue in a marriage leads to conflict and tension.

The Conflict of Two Family Histories

The concept of marriage as the collision of two family subcultures can account for most tensions and conflicts within any marital relationship. These "subcultures" consist of the patterns of behaviors, memories, habits, and expectations which a spouse acquired in his original family. We might call these aggregated patterns a "gut-culture," a fundamental way of being-in-the-world. It is in this original family field of interactions and interplay that an individual develops his values about life, which contribute to an image of what he or she desires in a prospective mate. This image, often embodied in daydreams, naturally tends to idealize the image of the projected spouse. It is in the uncompromising determination that this image must be realized, coupled with one's difficulty in being able to understand both the sources of such images in oneself, and in the other, that the seeds for future incompatibility are sown.

Incompatibility is defined here as any area of marital conflict. This can include choice of vocation for either partner, choice of where to live, how to dress, how to sleep, when to have sex, what kind of sex, how many children, etc. Marital incompatibility exists if either or both partners feel a conflict exists. An example of this is a woman who wants to step out of her housewife role, get a college degree, faced with a husband who can't see how such activities would make her a better wife, or even a happier individual. The husband believes that she would have no problems if she'd simply settle down to being a housewife. His real problem lies in his inability to recognize her needs, independent of his own. His not conceding that a conflict exists is a problem in itself.

As the interview process unfolds, Cindy and Van each become aware that what each had experienced in their family of origin sensitized them to behave within the marriage in a manner which unwittingly recreated many features of what they had already lived through in their original homes. Their relationship replicated the sense of entrapment that each believed they had escaped from when they left their original families.

Everybody's Credibility Gap

> Go, said the bird, for the leaves were full of children,
> Hidden excitedly, containing laughter.
> Go, go, go, said the bird: human kind
> Cannot bear very much reality.*

The role of the family therapist is to encourage each spouse in becoming an expert on himself, and a lesser expert on the other spouse. During the process of the initial seven interviews, Cindy and Van were exposed to a variety of innovative techniques, each of which was designed to catalyze both their awareness and an exchange of unrecognized feelings and images. These stimuli were designed to sharpen their recognition of the contrasts between the way each saw himself and was seen by the other. This difference is called a credibility gap. The inner image of how each looked to the other was challenged by observing the black and white image of himself on the closed-circuit TV monitor. There is a delay between the videotape recording of each spouse and the playback to the couple. The playback permits each spouse to put into perspective what has transpired and to see for the first time pieces of behavior which they might have missed.

Why does each spouse tend to project his or her shortcomings

---

* "Burnt Norton" by T. S. Eliot, *Four Quartets* (New York: Harcourt, Brace and World, Inc., 1943), p. 14.

onto the other partner? It seems that blame emerges whenever one's self-image of good will toward the other is not perceived as such. A closed-circuit television picture of a person confronts him with his own credibility gap; for example, the difference between his image of benevolence and its surprising absence to himself when viewed on the television monitor.

Apart from any other consideration, we are faced with the immense difficulty, if not the impossibility, of verifying the past. I don't mean merely years ago, but yesterday, this morning. What took place, what was the nature of what took place, what happened? If one can speak of the difficulty of knowing what in fact took place yesterday, one can I think treat the present in the same way. What's happening now? We won't know until tomorrow or in six months' time, and we won't know then, we'll have forgotten, or our imagination will have attributed quite false characteristics to today. A moment is sucked away and distorted, often even at the time of its birth.*

Credibility gaps exist for each one of us in a variety of ways. Escalation of marital tension and conflicts derive in large substance from the fact that each individual is generally unaware that he has a credibility gap. This gap includes an imprecision of one's recollection of events, and especially of the transactions between oneself and one's spouse. This often leads to recurrent conflict, since neither can remember how and who made a decision. This often leads to a contest as to who has the more accurate memory.

To avoid such conflict arising in the marital counseling setting, the interview in its entirety is recorded on audiotape for a couple. They are instructed to take the tape home, to listen to it separately or together, so as to begin to see how and when each unwittingly provokes the other, each allows himself to be provoked, and how the marital encounter is similar to the marriages of their respective parents. Thus the audiotape playback here becomes an experiential mirror of what had happened. It permits the couple to move beyond the moment and to see how each contributes to the collision of wills.

The collaborative enterprise between a couple and a marital counselor involves assisting each individual to become aware of the myriad forms of his own credibility gap. Each of us, under the

* *Writing for the Theatre* by Harold Pinter in *Evergreen Review 8* (1964), p. 81.

best of circumstances, can only have a glimmer of awareness as to how we are perceived by the other. During Cindy and Van's therapy, extensive use was made of both audio- and videotape recordings of them and of others, which were then played back to them. A person's typical response to these tapes is one of surprise, and at times shock, that he sounds or is seen in such an unexpected way. The use of delayed closed-circuit television playback, as well as audiotape playback, had the effect of letting Cindy and Van see their respective styles of communication. This includes an individual's own style of listening, including the nonverbal messages that one actively, unbeknown to oneself, transmits to the other. Finally, a person can become aware of how his manner of presenting his observable self tends to be patterned after parents, siblings, or even grandparents.

The discovery that one is always actively communicating to the other spouse via one's behavior results in lessened blame of the other. It gives one somebody new to work on, i.e., oneself.

The innovative techniques used with the Hoopeses in addition to playback via closed-circuit television of both speaking and listening poses, include the use of audiotapes from other families who had previously agreed to the use of the tapes, with their personal anonymity preserved. These tapes capture emotionally charged experiences which are regarded as basic and significant in everyone's life; i.e., grief, loneliness, anger, and frustration. All too often, we tend to neglect these emotions. Cindy and Van were no exceptions. The tapes used were designed to bring out emotional states they had hidden from themselves. They were encouraged to share these feelings and related memories with each other. In addition, sexually stimulating movies are shown to couples, sometimes to each separately and sometimes with both present. The reactions of each spouse to the sexual stimuli, presented on film, provide the marriage counselor and the couple with an opportunity to sort out which spouse has which problems, and to clarify each person's attitudes and desires about sex. This unscrambling of feelings and behaviors are part of the decoding operation. A major problem in a marriage is the difficulty to imagine being the other—a male being a female, with a female's experiences and memories, and vice versa—and thus there is an inability to hear what resides in the other's head and heart. A major aspect of the collaborative enterprise includes teaching each spouse to listen, not only to his own inner being, but also to tune in to the frustrations, desires, and aspirations of the other.

Astonish me.*

The Myth of Self-Will

There is a myth which is present in each of us. Generally it develops in adolescence, especially when we feel that our parents are not particularly responsive to our state of being, which tends to happen fairly often.

This myth is the major self-conning operation—the belief that when we grow up and are married, we will in no way be like the parent of the same gender. Further, every mistake our parents made will be righted with the next generation. Our own marriage will be flawless where our parents' marriage was flawed; our child-rearing will be perfect in every respect, especially since our own upbringing was imperfect. Our children will feel no pain. All will be well.

Occasionally we may become aware that we are replicating an unrecognized pattern, based on the way our parents functioned in their own marriage. With this dawning awareness comes an exquisite sense of quandary, of wondering "How could this be? I didn't will it this way. I willed it to be different."

Usually, when an individual becomes aware that his or her dreams of being different haven't come about, this recognition leads to intense anguish or hurt. We become acutely aware that we were unable to control our actions, regardless of our deepest desires. Generally, we can forget this for the moment and go on to other things.

We are all less aware, less conscious, and less able to control our lives than we like to believe. Paradoxically, awareness of this dilemma is the first step in resolving it.

---

* "Diaghilev," in *Scandal and Parade: The Theater of Jean Cocteau* by Neal Oxenhandler (New Brunswick, N.J.: Rutgers University Press, 1957), p. 47.

So we beat on, boats against the current, borne back ceaselessly into the past.*

Because there is generally an incompatibility between research and practice, it will be obvious from the data that follows that we could have explored in greater detail many of the points touched on, which would have provided a richer, more complete understanding of the forces dictating the lives of the Hoopeses. Short cuts were taken based on intuition and prior experience, with the primary emphasis on the part of the therapist that the couple's need for information about themselves as it was related to their problems of the moment was of paramount importance. The need for more data and refinement of theories was judged to be secondary. Our belief is that one new case understood from a different point of view can shed further light on the marital puzzle.

* *The Great Gatsby* by F. Scott Fitzgerald (New York: Charles Scribner's Sons, 1953), p. 182.

A Suicidal Attempt and an Affair

But before I ·treat a patient like yourself I need to know a great deal more about him, than the patient himself can always tell me. Indeed, it is often the case that my patients are only pieces of a total situation which I have to explore. The single patient who is ill by himself, is rather the exception.*

—REILLY

Orientation

ON THURSDAY, SEPTEMBER 7, 1972, Van Hoopes called me at my office for an appointment for himself and his wife. He said, in a manner suggesting no great urgency, that they had some marital problems. I described my approach as family-oriented, that I required a family chart, one for him and one for his wife. The chart was to include for each the names of parents, dates of birth and dates of death, names and dates of birth and death of siblings of each parent, their own dates of birth, and names and dates of birth of their children. In addition, I asked that on these charts, there be included reference to incidence of prior disease and treatment where known of family members, including oneself. He said that much data could not be readily obtained; I said complete these charts as best possible.

I indicated that I get involved with each person's credibility gap, which was the difference between one's inner self-image and the observable self; this phenomenon dictated the use of closed-

* The Cocktail Party, by T. S. Eliot, pp. 114–115.

circuit television playback. And, insofar as I am intent on assisting each spouse in becoming more of an expert about himself, these sessions are audiotaped on two tape recorders, one that becomes their property for review at home and the other which becomes my record of the session, to be preserved in my files. I stated that memory for what happens in these sessions without recourse to the audiotape is usually imprecise and, for maximum benefit, it is desirable that they save and listen to their tapes, as they represent the actual process of what transpired in the session. That each has an opportunity, on playing the audiotape at home, to hear how one sounds to the other, how one allows oneself to be provoked by the other, and in turn how one provokes the other.

I stated that the fee is $60.00 per hour which is prorated, that there is a videotaping charge of $20.00 and, in the event a videotaped segment of the session is saved, a charge will be made based on the cost of the tape to me.

He stated in a desultory manner that he was interested in pursuing this course of action, that it sounded expensive, and when could I plan to see the two of them. We agreed to meet on September 21, 1972.

The Cast of Characters

VAN Blond, lanky, 6', meticulously dressed, looking ten years younger than his stated age. He is conspicuously blasé, detached. His face is generally immobile. He seems to take pride in speaking distinctly, in an almost clipped way: a mode of speaking designed to control any feeling he might have. His hand gestures, too, are controlled and smooth, and somewhat mechanical, like a puppet's. When he looks at Cindy, he often seems bewildered by what she says, as if he is surprised that she is capable of talking at all, and even more surprised and bewildered to find himself with his wife in this office setting. He can't quite believe it's happening to him. He and Cindy are both visibly tired.

*   *   *

CINDY About 5'5", neatly dressed, well built, and with frosted brown hair, expressive brown eyes. She appears withdrawn. At the beginning of the session her face is drawn, elongated, tired, drawn, elongated, tired, but by the end it changes remarkably, getting rounder, fuller, with more color. Today, she is physically exhausted, and rarely speaks above a whisper. She is most voluble talking about Van when she reaches a crescendo of outrage. She seems as if she is ready to surrender what last vestige of hope she had, both for herself and for her marriage. At the end of the session, when Van says he is interested in coming back, she is disbelieving, even though he has taken the initiative.

*   *   *

Cindy and Van together are what one would call an attractive couple, if one saw them at a cocktail party.

FAMILY CHART
VAN HOOPES

MATERNAL
MOTHER   Matilda Evans, 1918
SIBS   George Evans, 1925

PATERNAL
FATHER   Van Hoopes, 1902
SIBS   one sister

Van Hoopes, September 3, 1940
SIBS   Dorothy Marshall, August 15, 1941

CHILDREN
Brian (adopted), April 28, 1966
Mary Lee, September 7, 1967

MEDICAL HISTORY
FATHER   hospitalized for depression, 1955
SELF   Psychotherapy, 2 years, 1965–67

FAMILY CHART
CINDY HOOPES

MATERNAL
MOTHER   Linda Clark King,
           September 6, 1922
SIBS   Karen Lindler, 1902
       Frank Clark, 1904
       Morgan Clark, 1908
       Nancy Clark, 1913
       (two other sibs died)

PATERNAL
FATHER   H. Frank King, March 2, 1918
SIBS   Harold J. King, 1914
       Bonnie Lee Pucci, 1910
       Bernice Cranston, 1912
       Mabel Ivers, 1920
       Andrew King, 1925 (d. 1937)
       (one other sib died)

Cindy Hoopes, November 15, 1941

SIBS   Dalton Johnathan King, September 4, 1944
       Michael Robert King, March 9, 1948
       Malcolm James King, June 5, 1949

CHILDREN
Cathy (adopted), July 28, 1966
Mary Lee, April 7, 1967
Brian, May 24, 1970

   Van and Cindy enter and Cindy hands Dr. Paul the family charts and a blank cassette audiotape.

DR. (Looking at preinterview charts) Your first name is Cindy?
CINDY. Uh-huh. Cindy Clark.
DR. Is that a nickname?
CINDY. No, that's it.
DR. That's it. You were born where?
CINDY. In Monongah, South Dakota.
DR. How do you spell that?
CINDY. M.O.N.O.N.G.A.H.
DR. And how much schooling have you had?
CINDY. A college degree.
DR. From where?
CINDY. South Dakota University, in Vermillion, South Dakota.
DR. And your . . . your date of birth is November 15, 1941.
       [*This is a search for identifying data, an attempt to think immediately in terms of where she came from, how much schooling she has, etc. I am trying to get a sense of who she is. Is Cindy a real name? Was there a tendency to infantilize her from the beginning?*]
VAN. (He's been watching her) Will you be all right?
       [*I wonder why her husband is concerned about her. His question comes immediately after I asked her her date of birth. That can be viewed as an indirect expression for my attention, because that's his first utterance.*]
CINDY. No, I feel like I'm going to faint.
       [*She says this in a very anxious, almost panicked way.*]
DR. From what?

CINDY. I . . . live as fast as I can.

DR. Want a glass of water?

CINDY. No, I think I'm okay.

VAN. Why don't you put your head down?

CINDY. No. I . . . I think I'm okay.

DR. Have you had this problem before?

CINDY. I think I'll be okay.

DR. Okay.

(Pause)

DR. (To husband) And your name is Van?

VAN. Right.

DR. Do you have a middle name?

VAN. Yes, Howard.

DR. And you were born where?

VAN. Mobile, Alabama.

DR. And how much schooling, and from where?

VAN. Ph.D., Rhode Island University.

DR. In what department?

VAN. Social work.

DR. And what would you say is the problem you people are having?

VAN. When I ask people that, they pause and wonder. Hearing you ask that makes me also pause for a moment.

> [*The husband projects himself into the therapist's position. This suggests that he's going to be very resistant to getting involved with himself and his own accountability for whatever problems they have.*]

CINDY. I don't have to pause; I know. We're both bleeding to death; we can't help each other.

> [*The contrast between these two people is made very clear by this response. She expresses herself vividly. She's concerned about the death of a marriage.*]

DR. From what?

CINDY. My husband's in love with another woman, and he's bleeding because he wants her, and I'm in love with my husband and I am bleeding because I want him.

> [*Very clear: the problem. Very common with many couples.*]

DR. Umm. Do you know the other woman?

[*I want to get real information from her.*]

CINDY. Yes, very well. Jennifer Clauson.

> [*She knows her name, so I go back to the husband to ask details about her.*]

DR. Is she married, or . . .

VAN. No, she's single.

DR. And how old a gal is she?

VAN. Twenty-three.

DR. And how long have you known her?

> [*I begin to wonder what triggered this off and what pain avoidance is involved. I believe that affairs stem from unrecognized sexual or gender conflicts existing in either spouse. As an example, a husband's unrecognized intense concern about potency can provoke his wife into having an affair.*]

VAN. Three years.

DR. Three years. And how long have you been involved with her?

CINDY. Three years.

> [*It should be noted that when the question was directed to Van, Cindy responded for him. It is obvious that she is very envious and concerned about her husband's involvement with this other woman. At this point I begin to wonder if Cindy promoted Van's involvement.*
>
> *Other forces dictating this could be a history of early death of a parent in Van's background. For example, if a man's mother had died when he was three years old, it is likely that he would, unbeknown to himself, become jealous of his own son for having a mother beyond the age of three. This is a form of transgenerational envy.*]

VAN. Ohh, uhhhhhh . . . things were fairly intense this summer.

> [*Van suggests here a reluctance to consider the fact that it's been going on for three years. In his own mind, did it only become a conspicuous involvement this previous summer?*]

DR. Meaning what? You lived out of the house, you lived with her, or what?

VAN. Oh, no, no. Intensity regarding discussions about what possible future relationship might be . . . sexual involvement . . . That's it.

DR. So where are you now? You living at home or . . . ?

VAN. Yes. I've never contemplated leaving per se, getting out of the house or anything like that.

> [*My interest here is to find out what the reality of this extramarital relationship is. Does it include the prospect of divorcing his wife? Is he out of the house now? Or, what is very often more subtle, is he, by virtue of his sexual involvement with this other woman, attempting to provoke his wife to take the initiative in wanting him out of the house? Here we get involved with the issue of passivity on the part of, in this instance, a man whose behavior can be viewed as a stimulus for his wife to take definitive action of one sort or another.*
>
> *Because of what I sense to be his tenuous participation in the session, at this time I decide not to challenge his evasive description of his relationship to Jennifer. I feel that it would be easy to lose Van. (I generally find men more hesitant, more fragile in confrontations, and more often blocked in both recognizing and articulating their feelings. They require a special kind of empathetic support.)]*

DR. How did you feel in your own head as you were juggling these two scenes?

VAN. Well, for a considerable part, I guess, of the summer, it was like living two lives, and then, uh . . . last week in May? . . . we, went down to Maine for a week.

DR. We who?

> [*I, therefore, gently pursue the reality of the situation, as well as his feelings. It seems that he was more interested in pursuing than in being pursued, as we can see in his skittish responses to Cindy's desiring him. She wants him, but he's not interested. It is interesting to note his reference that it was like living two lives. This suggested to me the question of whose two lives he was living*

*within himself. It is very common for a man who is
married and seeing a mistress to feel that he is two distinctly unrelated people.*]

VAN. The family. Cindy and I and the two kids. And it was, uh,
during that time that, uh, the issue came to the surface and
the cards were sort of on the table. So, uh, it was at that point
that I think, things had reached the point where they had to
be talked about, discussed, and looked at.

[*It is apparent that in May Cindy precipitated a crisis.
It's unclear, and has never really been cleared up, how
this confrontation came about. I further reality-test what
was so significant about the confrontation which emerged
in May 1972, insofar as the secret relationship had
been going on for three years.*]

DR. Why then? I mean, this had been going on for three years.

VAN. Well, the relationship which Jennifer and I had began with
a . . . it was more of a friendship, uh . . .

[*Here is further information.*]

DR. How'd you meet her?

VAN. Well, she was a secretary of mine.''

DR. Where?

VAN. Rhode Island University, where I teach.

DR. Okay. You teach what down there?

VAN. Social casework. And uh, I could, I don't know if you want
a history of that.

DR. Just briefly.

[*My inquiry is directed to ferreting out reasons for
Van's attraction to Jennifer.*]

VAN. Yeah. Well, uh, I guess mainly from that point I think I
mentioned rather early that I wanted Cindy to get to now
Jennifer because I thought she was an interesting person,
kind of a unique individual . . .

[*It becomes clear that Van is extraordinarily naïve,
viewing her in a most idealized fashion for her alleged
maturity. On the other hand, he found in her someone
whom he could teach, who could work for him, and
who probably began to view him in more of a father-*

idealized role.]

DR. In what way? What was so unique about her?

VAN. Oh, she sort of at times, I guess my impression would be she was twenty-two going on thirty or something like that, or at least it was the way in which she dealt with things, uh . . .

> [*I am seriously trying to find out how he perceived his comment about Jennifer being nineteen going on thirty. My thoughts also include curiosity about why he wanted his wife to get to know Jennifer . . . what is so unique about her? Especially, I wondered what was he attempting to promote between the two women?*]

DR. She was aging fast, or . . . ?

VAN. Well, she had a maturity that was beyond her chronological years. The way she related to people, the way she dealt with things, it was unique, I think, at least in my experience. Uh, that created a bit of an upset for Cindy—she felt very threatened by what I was saying.

> [*His naïveté is further expressed by his seeming incredulousness as to why his wife would find his idealizing Jennifer as being very threatening. This jealousy reaction would be normal, it seems to me. So then the question becomes: Why was he attempting to get his wife to become quite jealous of the attractive attributes of Jennifer?*]

DR. Yeah?

VAN. I guess the way I said it probably was the threatening part. It had to do with . . . I find Jennifer a very attractive person, and I'm not quite sure what that means, and uh, where that's going, or what our relationship can or cannot be . . .

I don't know if I said that exactly right, but it's something to that effect.

> [*It's interesting that his detachment, so to speak, is expressed as he turns to Cindy for approval and says, "I don't know if I said that exactly right, but it's something to that effect." This suggests that they have been through this many times before, and he has gotten himself into*]

the position of being a Peck's Bad Boy and looks for
reinforcement of that from his wife.]

DR. This is going back some time?

VAN. Yeah, well, this was, gee, about at least two years ago, I
think. I can't remember exactly.

[*It's interesting, too, that he's fuzzy about the time re-*
lationship.]

CINDY. Three years ago.

[*Here it becomes a question as to whether Cindy is the*
one who remembers points in time in this situation, as
well as being the memory bank for events that have
stressed their marriage.]

VAN. Well, at that point Cindy said, "Look . . .

[*Van seems to agree with Cindy's delineation of the*
time when this affair or involvement began, and begins
to address himself to what she says.]

DR. That was the time when Cindy was pregnant with Mary Lee?

[*I interrupt, looking at the family chart, and note that*
the time of the involvement seemed to coincide with
Cindy's pregnancy with Brian. Questions that are gen-
erated in my mind at this point include: Who wanted
the baby? How was the decision made to have the
baby? What was the level of sexual satisfaction during
the pregnancy?]

CINDY. Yes.

VAN. Yes, that's the time when she was pregnant.

CINDY. And also, he was working on his dissertation, and would
be away from the home seven days a week.

[*I wondered: Why was it necessary for him to be away*
from her while she was pregnant? Did he have an aver-
sion to seeing her pregnant?]

The rest of the session was involved with my at-
tempt to find out some of the reality of his pro-
fessional activities at the moment, insofar as he indi-
cated earlier his identification with the therapist, which
suggested this was an area of considerable importance
to him. I wonder at this point whether his work in mar-

riage and the family is designed in some ways to achieve some kind of control over other people. Basically I'm curious as to how he orients himself to his clients.]

DR. And you do what, marital counseling now?

VAN. Yeah. Uh, most of the stuff I do is marriage and family work. I also do some consulting and I do some supervising of people.

DR. This is at Rhode Island University?

VAN. No. Consulting is at Hampden Family Service Agency; the supervision is at Millerville Community College. Then I have a private practice, and teaching at Rhode Island University.

DR. Uh, you two probably weren't getting along too well before that, I would suspect.

[*My suspicion is based on my experience that the seeds for affairs usually include unrecognized areas of incompatibility before the affair blossoms forth.*]

CINDY. I thought we were . . . I thought we had a perfect marriage.

VAN. Yeah, that's the puzzling thing.

DR. (Disbelief in his voice) The perfect marriage?

CINDY. Yeah, I thought we did.

VAN. I don't know what that is, but . . .

[*Note the contrast of perception. Van is less sure about their relationship, indicating a fuzziness in his ability to think about what the relationship is about. His frequent use of the words "I think" indicate his dependency on Cindy to make decisions for him and the family, as if he were the child-husband.*]

CINDY. I wasn't happy, but we were functioning as the perfect American couple.

[*Her remark suggests that they think the appearance of perfection is what counts. From the outside, things looked fine. Perhaps, in some sense, that is the nature of a Perfect American Couple, like a Perfect American Car: a high-gloss finish, and the innards of dubious integrity.*]

VAN. Our relationship I think worked . . . I'm not sure, I tried to do a lot of thinking about that; I think our relationship worked in, uh, the fact that I'm sort of, the kind of guy who, uh, in many ways is dependent on Cindy to make decisions or to run things, and I just sort of fit in. As our relationship worked, it was kind of uh, I let her do some of the things that I probably should have ► ► ► * responded to, or made decisions about, but we had a kind of a balance, that was working. There were no crises in our relationship, there were only external crises. Because of the pregnancies, and so forth.

> [*He betrays some recognition of his passivity again, which meets his needs to allow her to seize the more dominant and expressive role for the two of them, but at the same time let him feel that things were working.*
>
> *It is of interest to note that here the stresses on the marriage, for instance, a pregnancy, were not seen by him as related to the relationship, but as related to events external to the relationship. It is, however, commonly agreed that pregnancies are part of a marriage and not external crises. It seems that the crisis was seen as external because it was Cindy who was pregnant. (This distancing of their wives' pregnancies is often observed in prospective fathers.) A pregnancy is an expression of the marriage relationship. At the same time, it affects the relationship.*]

DR. But something wasn't working, that's for sure.

VAN. Yeah, I think . . .

DR. Did you want to have kids?

> [*In every marriage, even though there may be a consensus on the desirability of having children, experience has shown that the existence of a baby converts the two-person relationship of a husband and wife into a triangle; two's company, three's a crowd.*]

VAN. Did I? We struggled with that for a couple of years, uh . . .
   I was resistant. It was seven years after we were married, I

---

* ► ► ► indicates beginning and ◄ ◄ ◄ indicates end of segments that were videotaped for later playback.

think, and we . . . at Cindy's insistence, uh, well . . . maybe that's true, always, but Cindy sort of raised the issue and said, "Look, you know, what are we going to do about this?" I had not finished my doctorate work. I was sort of saying, "Let's wait for a little while longer," plus the fact that uh, Cindy had difficulty in becoming pregnant, so that resulted in our adoption, which is another kind of decision to make. So we went through the adoption . . .

> [*Van reveals that his reluctance to have children was finally overcome by Cindy's desire. The question raised in my mind: How did he anticipate becoming a father? This would be related to what kind of fathering he had had. I begin to think about the desirability of confronting Van later as to his relationship with his father. His doctoral work seems to have been used as a distraction in some ways from actively considering having a child.*
>
> *I begin to wonder at this point how Van felt about women. Here he suggests that woman is the stronger, the more powerful figure. So I wonder about the pattern of the relationship between Van's father and mother. This is pivotal, because Van's ultimate identification is with a man, his father. If his father was seen as passive in relationship to his mother, Van will be likely to see himself as passive in his own marriage. His affair could be a means to distract himself from his growing sense of passivity, from wondering about his boyishness or his potential effeminacy.*]

DR. How do you know it was her difficulty?

> [*My sense about Van was that he abdicated responsibility for a variety of different issues, including decision making, and here I'm wondering whether in some ways he was abdicating again his own responsibility in Cindy's inability to get pregnant. Very often the whole conception issue is used as a battling ground to see who really wants to have the child and who doesn't. In many instances the infertility has been known to be an expression of marital and sexual incompatibility, witness the*

number of pregnancies that occur after a child has been
adopted—as happened here. It could be that fear of
becoming a parent contributes to marital incompati-
bility.]

VAN. Uh, tests.

DR. Where?

VAN. Well, in Vermillion, South Dakota, and then a gynecologist
in Providence.

DR. Yeah. Cindy, what's your version of what's been going on?
Between the two of you.

> [*I am attempting to get Cindy to describe the quality of*
> *their relationship which existed before the affair.*]

CINDY. Uh, I felt like my husband has been living a double life,
and I've allowed him to have his other world, because I
thought that world was what he needed to function in the
professional world, and when he stopped giving me emotional
support, then I got suspicious of all his professional . . .

> [*She makes it very clear that she has been placed in the*
> *position of allowing her husband to do things in the*
> *outside world. Her controlling behavior has been in*
> *effect reinforced by his desire to have her support him*
> *in his profession. In such marriages we have no idea*
> *what shifts have occurred since the marriage. When did*
> *she begin to be placed in the decision-making position?*
> *How much of this was provoked by Van's passivity?*]

DR. How does he show you this emotional support?

CINDY. How did he?

DR. Yeah.

CINDY. Well, from intercourse, and from wanting to be around
me, and then all of a sudden no intercourse, and if we did,
he couldn't have an orgasm, and then there was no . . .
every time he was around me, it wouldn't take anything for
him to fly off the handle; he was extremely irritable at the
children, and I just always felt like when he was home he
didn't really want to be there. He was so tense, and uh, the
weekends were the only time I was around him, anyway. And
they were just too tense for him. ◄ ◄ ◄

> [*Cindy was involved in a barter arrangement with Van:*

in exchange for her permission to have him pursue his professional activities in the outside world, he was to provide her with emotional support. Cindy experienced sexual intercourse and some pleasant social exchange as emotional support. She indicates that he has had some potency problems. This too makes me wonder about the issue of a death. Unresolved mourning has been related, in my experience, to changes in sexual behavior, including impotency, premature ejaculation, as well as abstinence. This then helps to clarify his need for an affair, because if he was unable to consummate an orgasm, his doubts about his masculinity would become intensified necessitating his becoming involved with another woman. Cindy's juxtaposition of his irritability with the children with his lack of potency suggests how troubled he was with his difficulty in his sexual encounters with her.]

(There is a knock on the door.)

DR. Just a second. The technician I think just arrived . . . (He leaves the room.)

CINDY. When you sit and hear us, can you believe it's us?

VAN. Ah, no, it's a weird feeling, it really is. I've heard the same things so often.

CINDY. Oh, God, Van . . . was it worth it?

VAN. I'm really weary this morning. Are you?

> *[There was a crisis that night, during which Cindy experienced a sense of having died. (See following pages.)]*

CINDY. I am so sick and so numb. I don't know what the hell happened last night, but . . .

> *[Her comments about being sick and numb suggest she continues to feel a state of dying of her soul.]*

VAN. Well, I don't either.

CINDY. I thought I died. I thought I, I, I almost died last night. I'm so afraid to die. I am so weak today thinking about how close I came to dying last night. Was it a dream or did I almost die last night?

VAN. I don't know what's going to happen to you.

CINDY. I woke up today and I thought I had died. The only time I felt like that in my whole life was when I was on the operating table dying and I just thought I died just like last night. (She sighs)

> [*The crisis is associated in her mind with the time that she had an almost fatal automobile accident in the fall of 1965 which apparently had terrified her. Some of her feelings about death and dying were reactivated the previous night.*]

VAN. It's the weirdest thing.

(Dr. Paul re-enters the office.)

VAN. Both of us are exhausted today; it was a very difficult night.

> [*Van initiates reference to a difficult night. The details of this then emerge.*]

DR. What happened last night?

CINDY. ▶ ▶ ▶ I think I tried to kill myself.

DR. How?

CINDY. And I feel like I almost did die.

> [*Cindy makes it very clear that the previous night her preoccupation was with dying. She is still in a fog as to whether she tried to commit suicide or not.*]

DR. How?

CINDY. Well, I don't remember.

VAN. I never could get you to be clear about that.

CINDY. I never could quite remember. All I know is that I ate, I ate like a stuffed duck, until 12:00 yesterday. Just a little bit. And I got so nervous about 5:00 because I was going to a group, and I took a Librium.

DR. What group?

CINDY. Uh, faculty wives. And he had a client, and the kids were, were screaming, and I knew that when I left last night he was either going to call Jennifer, or go see her, and I thought: I've got to go out, but I don't really want to go out because this is going to give him another opportunity to be with her, so I took a Librium, and I've been having . . . ah . . . severe menstrual cramps and bleeding these last three days. I have the IUD and it's really giving me a bad reaction, and so I thought to myself at 7:00 I had these severe cramps and I was passing blood clots.

> [*Her anxiety as she recreates the events of the day before is specifically related to Van's being free to talk to and see Jennifer. There is an allusion to a sexual encounter.*
>
> *Cindy reveals an intense bodily reaction to frustration and despair, i.e., severe menstrual cramps and bleeding and an adverse reaction to the IUD.*]

DR. Were you pregnant?

CINDY. Well, I felt like I was having a miscarriage. Anyway, I took two Pamprins, or something . . .

VAN. Is that what it was?

CINDY. . . . that I bought at the drugstore.

DR. Yeah.

VAN. I never could get you to tell me how much alcohol you took.

CINDY. And then when I got . . . I was trying to get through the night at the fashion show, and the commentator kept saying, blue eyes and blonde hair are in this year. And this little model looked just like Jennifer. And I just looked up and I was sitting there and I started shaking and I thought, "He's with her right now, he's with her right now," and I had six women that I had to pick up, and I kept saying, "How can I get rid of these six women and get home? I want to get home. I'm going to catch him with her." And I walked in the door, and he left his lights on upstairs, and I go on upstairs, and I see the telephone's moved into his easy chair. And I said, "You just talked to her, didn't you?" And I poured myself a straight shot of bourbon. And that's the last I remember. I kept thinking, "This feels so good, I just don't ever want to wake up. I just. . . ." And I can remember feeling the stinging going in my arms, and the only time I felt like that was when I was on the operating table and I knew I was dying.

> [*She is preoccupied with blue eyes and blonde hair, suggesting her fear of losing Van to Jennifer. She feels she can do nothing about it except to blot out the pain of the vision of Van and Jennifer through the use of*

*drugs and alcohol. (It is interesting here that many sui-
cidal persons indicate in their bodily and emotional reactions that they are more intent on eliminating the
pain of intense despair, than actually killing themselves.) There is an obsessive quality in Cindy's need
to catch Van with Jennifer. The critical question: What
are the elements that dictate her excessive concern
about the other woman? Why should an attractive
woman like Cindy become so despairing of her own life
if she imagines losing her husband to another woman?
Does this mean that for her the value of her own existence is totally related to being Van's wife? If she loses
Van, what are the implications, in addition, to her
sense of femaleness?]*

DR. From what?

CINDY. I had a tubal pregnancy that ruptured, and I had hemor-
rhaged from . . .

> *[We find out that there is a direct connection in her own
> mind between the events of last night and the tubal
> pregnancy, which is an emergency, in which without
> immediate medical attention, a woman can die.]*

DR. Where were you hospitalized?

VAN. Roger Williams Hospital.

DR. In Providence?

VAN. Yeah.

CINDY. That's the last I remember, I was saying, "Oh, this feels so
good, I just want to die."

VAN. I heard you walk out of the house, and when I found you,
you were out in the middle of the yard throwing up.

CINDY. I don't remember that—

> *[After her state of consciousness evaporated, we have
> reference to an altered state of consciousness where
> Cindy was totally unable to remember what had tran-
> spired after the statement, "This feels so good I just
> want to die," which occurred both after the tubal preg-
> nancy seven years before and last night.]*

VAN. I picked you up and carried you back in, and then from
that moment on I walked you around and poured coffee

down you, and tried to figure out what you had taken. I couldn't believe that you had that much booze in that short amount of time. You had no motor control whatsoever. You couldn't stand up, you couldn't control anything.

> [*Her behavior as described by Van is an indication of her confusion and, in a sense, her being dead to herself. She seemed to have been totally drunk at the time, without, as Van put it, "any motor control."*]

DR. Have you attempted suicide before?

> [*I ask this bluntly.*]

CINDY. Oh, no, no, I know I didn't think about it last night, it was just that I was nervous—

> [*It's interesting that after describing what had happened the previous night, which from all evidence suggests an unrecognized suicide attempt, she denies the evidence and indicates that she was just "nervous."*]

VAN. That was my concern, that you had done something stupid . . .

CINDY. Oh, God, no, I wouldn't have done anything stupid. But I'm scared to death how close I felt last night. That I was dying.

> [*On further reflection, Cindy denies conscious intent to commit suicide, at the same time revealing a sense of being in an uncontrolled state where life was slipping away from her.*]

DR. (To Van) Had you been talking to Jennifer last night?

VAN. Yeah, I called her. So, I told Cindy when she came home.

> [*Van makes it very clear that there was sufficient provocation for Cindy to believe that her marriage was slipping away further. This compounded by her menstrual and IUD concerns led to her suicidal behavior. It wasn't just a suspicion about Jennifer in Cindy's head. It was blandly confirmed here by Van, as if it were a natural thing for him to tell Cindy about his conversation with Jennifer. This suggests that the two of them have up until last night achieved some kind of equilibrium about Jennifer where Cindy had permitted and expected him to have some contact with her. Perhaps*]

*on the threshold of coming to see me, anxieties in Cindy
skyrocketed, so that she tried to put the brakes on this
affair. Thus a crisis was created just before their appointment. The fact that she got to the office indicated
that there existed some hope in herself to give this therapy a ghost of a chance.]*

DR. Yeah . . . Cindy, how do you get along with your mother?

*[Right at this point, after Cindy describes what can be
regarded as her sense of futility and failure as a woman,
I begin to wonder about what model she had for being
a wife, an adult female, and mother. Thus, I now get
involved with asking about Cindy's mother.*

*Also, I'm trying to dilute the intensity of her pres-
ent anxiety and concern about her marriage by intro-
ducing a personal historical perspective. This is the first
step in what will be an attempt to get each one of them
involved with the influences of the original nuclear family as it is related to the crisis of the moment.*

*Why did I get involved with Cindy and her mother,
rather than with Van and his father? It would seem
logical to focus on Van, rather than on Cindy, because
he is the one who is involved in the apparent problem
of a three-year affair. My intent here is to focus on
more of the background figures dictating the affair of
the moment, and this has to do with Cindy and her
mother. I want to find out how Cindy's femininity was
viewed by her mother.]*

CINDY. I just went home recently, and I thought I got along real
well with her. It's kind of a . . . I can't really deal with
feelings, but I think I get along real well with her.

*[It's interesting to note how easy it was for Cindy to
shift from the crisis of last night to talking about the
problems with her mother. Here, she again indicates
she can't deal with strong feelings, as was evident the
previous night.]*

DR. What do you mean you can't deal with feelings?

CINDY. I can't tell her where I'm at, as far as I have different views
on religion, and I . . .

> [*Now she says she also could not express her feelings to her mother about their differing opinions on religion.*]

DR. What's her view, and your view?

CINDY. God is damning me for this life I have. Somehow . . .

DR. God is what?

CINDY. Damning me.

DR. You? What life?

CINDY. That my husband is having an affair.

DR. Which she knows about?

CINDY. I couldn't have children; it was God's punishment. God knows something about me that I don't know.

> [*The inference here is that without her being able to hold her position vis-à-vis her mother, her mother's indictment of her in terms of eternal living damnation stands unchallenged. Herein lies the suggestion that from her mother's point of view there is something basically defective about Cindy, as if she were an agent of the devil. Cindy's prior inability to conceive and Van's affair represent evidence of the Lord's retribution. And the basic flaw in Cindy is only known to God. Cindy indicates that she feels that she's been a bad person, and because of the intensity of the damnation and its pervasiveness in Cindy, she can't even begin to understand what she did that was so bad. She is fighting the indictment tacitly, and at the same time seems to accept it. Otherwise one would suspect she would have challenged Van much sooner about the affair.*]

VAN. When we were in Maine, and the issue came onto the table, Cindy called her parents and told them.

> [*I wonder why Cindy called her parents and told them what was happening, in view of her mother's perceiving her as a subject for damnation. Did Cindy feel that they would come and rescue her? Or was she indicating her willingness to accept the indictment, lock, stock, and barrel?*]

DR. They live where now?

CINDY AND VAN. South Dakota.

VAN. And subsequently, a week after that, she went home to stay with them for a week. They're very conservative, and they felt for a number of years that we've moved away from the church, and therefore whatever happens is . . .

> [*Cindy still has the need to go home, knowing they're conservative, and knowing that both of them felt that in her move away from the church she is evincing deviant, disaster-prone behavior.*

DR. Was she pregnant with you when she got married?

> [*I ask this question, which again would seem to be very much unrelated to what is going on. I'm trying to take some heat off of her, knowing that she attempted suicide the previous night, which could be viewed as the extremity of being damned, the annihilation of the self. I was wondering why Cindy should be so intensely damned for not having children, and on a hunch wondered further if, in effect, her mother had been projecting her own guilt about her conception of Cindy onto Cindy.*]

CINDY. Was I pregnant?

> [*It's interesting that Cindy's immediate response to my question, which seemed to be specific, is the question, "Was I pregnant?" as if for the moment she was her mother.*]

VAN. No, was your mother pregnant with *you?* That's a question mark. She says no, but . . .

> [*Van's response indicates an immediate understanding that the question was directed to Cindy, presumably because she would be the one to know about her own mother's life.*]

CINDY. I think she was.

> [*Cindy clarifies that she thinks her mother was pregnant with her, Cindy being the first of four children. Cindy becomes more animated as she describes clearly an encounter that she had with her mother in 1966, when she and Van were planning to adopt a child, when Cindy was twenty-five years old.*]

DR. That's why you're damned.

CINDY. But I asked her, and I said to her when we were adopting,

I said "Mother, the birth certificate, when I got my birth certificate . . ."

DR. Yeah?

CINDY. I said, "Mother, you were pregnant, weren't you?"

DR. Yeah.

CINDY. And another funny thing was the way they eloped, and she looked at me, and she almost slapped me, and she said, "How dare you think that I'd be that kind of a person?" She said, "Don't ever think that of me!" And I said, "Well, Mother, I just wanted to make you feel good that I always felt love and security, and had I . . ."

> [*Cindy's recollection of her query about her mother's premarital conception of herself appears associated with an attempt to indicate that she would be accepting of her mother having conceived her out of wedlock.*]

DR. Yeah.

CINDY. Well, anyway . . . she said, "Don't you ever think that of me again. I could never have been that kind of . . ."

> [*Mother's own guilt still persists; she reacts in a manner belligerent to Cindy. It seems that Cindy's loving response was unacceptable to her mother because of her mother's continued anxiety and lingering self-condemnation. Thus Cindy's being damned by her mother could be viewed as her sharing her mother's self-damnation.*]

DR. Did your father tell you, or could you talk to him about it, or what?

> [*I'm trying to find out what kind of a father she had, whether she could communicate with him. It soon becomes clear that he's even less accepting of her than her mother. She can at least challenge or talk with her mother, but Cindy feels that her father still remains totally uncommunicative. Thus it appears that Cindy grew up in a setting where even though she had parents, she is an emotional orphan. When she said (on page 55) that she can't "deal with feelings," it now becomes more apparent that this difficulty has been lifelong. No one in her original family had been able to indicate to her an acceptance of certain distressing feelings which recur-*]

rently develop; not just within Cindy, but within every child.]

CINDY. Oh, heavens, no!

VAN. Her father is not the kind of man who one deals very well with.

DR. Why, what kind of man is he?

VAN. Uh, he is affectionately and sometimes fearsomely called by his associates . . .

DR. (Interrupts to talk on phone) I'm sorry. Go ahead. (To Cindy) What does your Daddy do?

VAN. He's in the oil business.

CINDY. Oh, he's the president of an oil company.

DR. Where? In South Dakota?

CINDY. Yeah.

DR. Yeah, big man type?

VAN. Ah, he's a big general.

CINDY. Yeah.

VAN. He is big in stature, and tremendously powerful, and he thoroughly loves power.

CINDY. He's a poltician and is acting as . . .

VAN. He uses strong-arm techniques.

DR. Are you scared to death of him?

CINDY. Yeah.

> [*Now we get a picture of Cindy's father. It is interesting that Cindy focuses on his occupational and community activities. Van adds a picture of Cindy's father's style of interpersonal relationship, focusing specifically on his being a devotee of power, and using strong-arm techniques. Is Cindy's fear of her father patterned after her mother's fear of him? To me, the father seems to be someone that Cindy could rarely communicate with, so that when she talked with her mother she probably was exposed to attitudes that, though expressed by her mother, also reflected those of her father.*]

DR. Is it that you don't know how to deal with feelings, or you haven't got any feelings?

CINDY. Oh, I've got feelings.

DR. Yeah.

CINDY. But I never . . . at home, one time I told my mother that I hated her, and I was punished for two weeks, I couldn't have feelings at home, and Van won't let me fall apart. Every time I wanted to fall apart, he says (snaps fingers), "Damn it! My whole life I've dealt with parents who fall apart. You be strong. Don't you fall apart," but . . . I don't know how to fall apart. ◄ ◄ ◄

> [*When Cindy indicates that the one time she told her mother she hated her, she was punished for two weeks, it becomes clear to me that when she talks about how she can hardly show her feelings anywhere, she is referring to expressions of feelings of distress, hurt, and hate. These feelings are not acceptable to either her parents or to Van. This suggests that neither her parents nor Van can tolerate such feelings within themselves. I wondered whether she tried to kill herself because she knew that her feelings of anger toward Van were not going to be accepted by him. For it does seem that the blandness Van expressed earlier would indicate that expressing her anger would only have served to distance him further, leading to increasing levels of frustration for both of them.*
>
> *It becomes clear, too, that in Cindy's mind "falling apart" means to cry. This evokes the image of someone in pain; she felt that she was stifled in the expression of what hurt her—she was stifled by Van (in bed as well as out), who could be viewed as dealing with her as her parents had dealt with her. She's supposed to be strong, which evokes the image of sturdiness, smiling on the outside, looking good, well packaged, because there was no one in her life able to bear the feelings stimulated in themselves when confronted by her pain. Here we also have some beginning insight about Van from Cindy. Apparently he felt that he had dealt with people in his earlier life—his parents—who were complaining, crying, or guilt-inducing to such an extent that he could not cope with them. Therefore, he wanted to be married to somebody who would be dif-*

ferent, somebody who would not "fall apart."]

DR. You don't know how to fall apart? You're falling apart inside all the time.

CINDY. Yeah. When I'm alone I cry and it feels so good.

> [*Cindy can only let her pain out when she's alone, but this then reinforces her inner sense of aloneness in a marriage.*]

DR. How are the kids faring in this zoological preserve?

> [*I'm curious about their awareness of the effect of this marital incompatibility on their children. In inquiring about the children I am trying to enlarge upon a transgenerational perspective.*]

VAN. Hmmm.

CINDY. Not well, but Van can't see it. I mean, things are coming out, like when I was in South Dakota, they drew some pictures, and in one picture was where Mommy and Daddy were holding hands, and playing and having fun together, and one was a picture of lions, that's where Mom and Daddy were fighting.

> [*It is interesting that their pictures showed Mommy and Daddy playing and having fun, and then later a couple fighting. These pictures suggest that the children were aware of a change in the relationship between Van and Cindy. Focusing on a transgenerational perspective is critically important. It makes clear that Cindy's inability to obtain from her parents an acceptance of her distressing feelings would naturally lead to the desire to have this lack of acceptance compensated for by her husband, leading to my question: Did she think she might be wanting too much from Van?*]

VAN. I don't understand why you said I can't see it.

CINDY. Oh, I mean that . . . you're not around the children so you don't know how they're reacting . . . The children and I have been competing in fighting for Van, and when Van walks in we all want to grab him and have him.

DR. Do you think you might be wanting too much from Van?

CINDY. Um-hum. Now I do.

DR. I mean before.

CINDY. Yeah.

DR. Here's what I want to do. What I do, often I play tapes from other families, either audiotapes or videotapes. Anything that I play has a legal release on it to protect the identity of the people on the tape. The tape you will hear can be reproduced on your audiotape. The point is really to try and capture relevant pieces on the audiotape of a process which you can tune into, which can give me a quicker rundown as to who's got what kind of problem. And that's my job, to try and unscramble—who's got what problem.

> [*I decide to play the Haas tape here so as to dilute their sense of uniqueness in terms of their prior experiences with their families of origin. This particular tape was selected because it vividly and graphically demonstrates how a daughter's marital incompatibility was related to her lifelong feeling of being stifled in the expression of her anguish and anger to her mother. This technique is a way of providing distance for Cindy and Van from the immediacy of the charged incompatibility and crisis of the previous night.*
>
> *This tape is played now to provide a piece of validating experience for Cindy that her desire to get too much from Van could be rooted in experiences with her parents that antedated her marriage. I want in addition to learn if the feelings expressed on the tape will reawaken in Van some experiences he had with his parents.*
>
> *It will also provide a valuable means wherein they both will be able to identify through their perceptions and responses to this tape similar experiences from their own lives, hitherto unexpressed. Then later, after they share with me what they heard and what they felt, I will be able to sort out who has what difficulty, in terms of expressing certain unpleasant feelings about his own being in time and space.*]

CINDY. Right.

DR. Okay. Now, this particular piece, a tape of a mother and a daughter. It's not necessarily designed to focus, Cindy, on you and your mother, but it's really a model of any two-person relationship. It can be you and Van, it can be Van and his father. As you listen to it, what I'm interested in, is what relevant pieces of your own experience are triggered by hearing this. Because what is going on between you two, as far as I'm concerned, though it's real in terms of the two of you, its historical sources go back into your premarital scene, whatever it was. And I'm interested in trying to establish what are the points of relevance between what happened before and what's going on now. A little bit about this tape you are about to hear. This is a gal, who's forty-one, and her mother is sixty-four. The forty-one year old, the daughter, has been married for about twenty years, has four kids, three of whom have seen child psychiatrists off and on over a period of time. The marriage is crummy. And she goes to this friend of mine, who is the third voice on the tape. He sent me this tape. It took him about nine months to persuade her to bring her mother in; she was scared shitless. Her mother would drop dead, or her mother would just totally reject her; she was scared to death. So what you're going to hear are excerpted pieces of that first meeting. It's about ten minutes but I'm going to let you hear just two pieces of it, and then we can pick up what's relevant to your scene, both of yours, not just you [Cindy]. What are the things that you find most distressing to hear? I mean, anything that you say in terms of picking up on it is relevant to me, so that I'll know better what is going on. Now, I have found that when these tapes are being played, what happens with most people as I have observed their eye movements, they will look at me looking at them listening to the tape. And to the extent that they are watching me watching them, they cannot attend more fully to the tape. So what I do, I leave the room and I clock it, or I listen in through the door to hear when the thing's over, then I'll come back in. I'm more interested in your reactions, than your trying to mastermind what you think I want you to hear.

CINDY. Uh-huh.

VAN. Yeah.

DR. Okay. The sound is a little bit off for about five seconds. You got another tape?

VAN. No.

DR. The other side [of their audiotape] can be used?

VAN. Yes.

DR. Okay.

VAN. You're interested in what . . . anything we respond to . . . ?

DR. Yeah. That's similar to what you hear here. Or you may get some little screwy ideas, anything.

VAN. Okay.

(Dr. Paul plays the Haas tape and leaves the room.)

──────────── **Transcript of the Haas Tape** * ────────────

Excerpt 1, near beginning of interview, playing time 4 minutes.

THERAPIST. Well, let's see if we can talk about these feelings, and uh where you two people are missing each other, and feelings that your daughter has not really been free to share with you. So, uh, with just that brief kind of introduction . . .

DAUGHTER. Yeah (laughs nervously).

MOTHER. (Nervous cough)

THERAPIST. See what it is that, uh . . .

DAUGHTER. (In a very low, quick voice) Well, I think that my mother said that I uh, for several years, for many years she felt that I, probably longer than she's certainly been aware of, maybe longer than I've been aware of, because uh, for a long time, almost as far back as I can remember, I've been uh— afraid to speak my feelings.

MOTHER. (She comes on very growly, a tough old lady's voice) I don't know why; I can't feel . . . I mean I didn't feel that way. To me, I felt it . . . uh, well, let's say, uh, not too long after you got married. That's when I, uh, began to uh, uh realize it. Before that I didn't, whether it might have

* From *Exploring Therapeutic Encounter*, Walter Haas et al. For information regarding the recording of and professional commentary on this therapy session, see Bibliography, p. 301.

been so, but I didn't realize it anyway.

THERAPIST. Well, Mrs. ——, she, uh says that she's always felt this way.

MOTHER. Yeah, I say, I didn't realize it.

THERAPIST. Why don't you ask her about it . . .

DAUGHTER. (Nervous laugh) heh heh . . . heh heh heh . . .

THERAPIST. . . . instead of saying I didn't know.

MOTHER. (Laughing) I don't know how to begin! I mean, this thing is so new to me, and I didn't uh, feel that way. In fact, I always felt we had a close relationship. See? Because I always felt, uh, I don't know how she felt about it . . .

THERAPIST. So what's she . . .

MOTHER. (Cuts him off) But I always felt I could speak to her freely . . .

THERAPIST. Oh, I don't doubt that, but what's happening now?

DAUGHTER. What do you mean, you mean this moment?

THERAPIST: Yeah.

DAUGHTER. Well, now my mother's talking, I mean, and I'm quiet.

MOTHER. I'll tell you . . .

THERAPIST. Did she, uh, did she hear your feelings?

DAUGHTER. When I said that I always felt . . . ?

THERAPIST. Yeah.

DAUGHTER. Well, she heard about it if she wanted to hear it.

THERAPIST. What did she do?

DAUGHTER. She, uh . . . that's the end of it. I know about her feelings though.

MOTHER. I don't know about it. You tell me, I feel . . .

DAUGHTER. (A little more forcefully) No, then you went on to say that not why did you feel this way, or how did you feel this way, how did you feel, or what . . . you wanted to talk about how you felt, that you always felt that you had a close relationship (her voice dies away here) . . . this is typical, this is uh . . .

MOTHER. (Steam-rollers over her again) Yeah, well I . . .

THERAPIST. Why are you smiling when you tell her that?

MOTHER. (Laughs) 'Cause it's difficult, I guess, for her to say.

THERAPIST. See, you've got a big grin on your face as you're telling her this.

DAUGHTER. I know, well, I guess it's easier than (inaudible) . . .

THERAPIST. Well, tell her uh, how it makes you feel . . .

DAUGHTER. I'm covering up my being upset, that's why.

MOTHER. I feel (unclear); say whatever you want to me . . .

DAUGHTER. No, I . . .

THERAPIST. Now, you're saying to your mother, uh, you didn't hear my feelings, you're always talking about your feelings instead rather than mine, and as you're telling that, uh . . .

DAUGHTER. Well, I guess I'm doing that because I feel very strongly, and I . . . it's easier for me to smile than show my strong emotions.

THERAPIST. Well, let's see if you can now.

DAUGHTER. Well, but at any rate (dodging the point) I thought that if, if uh, here I am a woman forty-one years old, and I'm still in many ways your . . . not child, I'm always your child . . . I'm still a baby. That I haven't gotten over so many feelings that I had for all my life, and this is why I got to Mr. Haas, and this is why my children have many unhealthy aspects, and this is why my second marriage, which you didn't even know about, has not been that easy. Uh, because of things that happened to me, uh, as a child. This is the obvious. Mainly, I guess, I've always felt I never had a mother, and I felt like an orphan. And, uh, I felt very lonely, and upset by that, and you know, that uh . . . so I would be a good girl, and I would be a sweet girl, and I'd be a quiet girl, and I'd do everything because I wanted to make sure I would have a mother. And I never would really tell you how I felt, or if I felt angry at you or anything; I never would tell you this because I was afraid I would lose you. I mean emotionally.

MOTHER. Yeah, I know what you mean (still gruff).

DAUGHTER. That you couldn't take it, and that, that I would never, never have. And, of course, if you fear somebody so much and fear the loss of them so much, you eventually begin to hate them. It's like a . . . you know. So a lot of my emotion is love, and a lot of it is a lot of hate, against you for all this, uh, this feeling of being alone and an orphan all my life. So the reason you're brought here, so finally at the age of forty-one I can get rid of this horrible feeling, so you and I can have a better relationship—hopefully—if it can't be, well then that's the way it will be, but at least I can live as a human being with my children and my husband in a healthy way.

MOTHER. I mean, to me it's very new, all this. I knew that she had some resentment, in uh, in her uh, I don't know, I can't tell you how many years. (The light is beginning to dawn; she is somewhat gentler.)

Excerpt 2, after 45 minutes, playing time 5 minutes

MOTHER. That's one thing, I wouldn't, you can say everything else, and you may be right . . .

THERAPIST. Let's uh, let's. I see what you're saying.

MOTHER. I don't want to be blamed. And then she said I wrote her a letter that time, and I *never* outside of one time . . .

DAUGHTER. (Interrupts, inaudibly)

MOTHER. You were in Columbus, that I ever wrote you a letter.

THERAPIST. Okay. We've got forty-five minutes past now, we've got about ten or fifteen minutes more. Uh, we can't miss the golden opportunity—or can we. Now, if we stop at this point, we'd have to say, uh, it's a draw.

DAUGHTER. Well, she's been beating me down all my life!

MOTHER. Oh, no . . .

DAUGHTER. Oh, Mother, I've been so beaten down by you (laughing hysterically) that it's . . .

THERAPIST. But you see, you permit it here, again. You see you've said . . .   you've tried to say, but you don't really say it . . . Mother, uh you . . .

MOTHER. (Coughs nervously)

THERAPIST. You never cared enough about me; you've neglected me. And you don't carry it very strongly at all. You feel it but you don't carry it directly to her. Then, look what's happened. She's completely turned it around; you don't care enough about her, you not only neglect her, but you neglect your children. And so I say all right, you've got a draw; you've both accused each other. You accuse her of neglecting you, and she turns around and says you've neglected me and you even neglect your children. Are you gonna let it pass?

DAUGHTER. Mr. Haas, I cannot say any more than I've said, because this is . . . of course it shows the pattern up very, very clearly, Mother, then this is, of course this is the obvious thing, that is uh, exactly what went on here in this little . . . it's the same thing that went on since I've been a baby. Is that I *never* . . . you . . . I was always the one at fault, I was always your mother, I was al . . . everything was always done to me, not . . . and I always had to jump to *your* tune. Always! Forever and ever (crying). And it's still being done right now.

MOTHER. (Incredulous) That you jump to my tune even *now?* What are you talking about?

DAUGHTER. Yes, emotionally. Emotionally! Right now!

THERAPIST. It doesn't have to be. It did before. But why do you let it go on right now?

DAUGHTER. I'm afraid of her . . .

MOTHER. Oh, that's . . .

DAUGHTER. That this will be the end, that's what.

MOTHER. It won't be the end. It's never the end with me! As far as I'm concerned . . .

DAUGHTER. I don't feel that, Mother.

MOTHER. Well, I can't.

DAUGHTER. Because . . .

MOTHER. What can I do to make you feel differently? Teach me. I'll do it. That's all I ask.

DAUGHTER. I don't feel that.

THERAPIST. (To daughter) Your mother made all these mistakes, and has been a difficult mother and an unavailable mother, but that doesn't mean that you can't complain more about it, and find out if she's still gonna be around tomorrow.

DAUGHTER. Well . . .

THERAPIST. She's saying that uh, she's not going to take a powder.

DAUGHTER. Emotionally I feel like you'd do it. I feel like you've always taken a powder . . .

MOTHER. Why, why I'd be there for anything you wanted.

DAUGHTER. Yeah, but it's always been in an angry way, you never, it's always . . . it's always . . . you're right there, sure you're right there, but it's always in anger, it's never in softness or sweetness. I can hardly even ever remember . . .

You know, of all the good that . . . I don't ever remember any warmth, or someone hugging me.

MOTHER. Are you kidding me?

DAUGHTER. I don't remember that. I always remember that I was so afraid of you that I couldn't do anything.

MOTHER. Then you are only remembering (slowly, pensively) . . . the . . .

DAUGHTER. I'm remembering my fear!

MOTHER. You are only remembering the bad things.

DAUGHTER. I'm remembering my constant fear!

MOTHER. My God! We used to be *so close!*

DAUGHTER. We never were, Mother. That's a myth. That's a myth. Don't you believe it.

MOTHER. Well then, I don't know.

DAUGHTER. It's a big myth, cause I was so frightened of you, all I could do is kinda keep out of your way and be good all the time, 'cause I was so scared!

THERAPIST. What did you feel like doing instead to her or with her?

DAUGHTER. A couple of times I felt like killing her!

THERAPIST. Tell her how furious you were.

DAUGHTER. I had such hatred, that if I ever let loose with my feelings, I felt like I'd murder you, because I hated you . . .

MOTHER. Well, I'm sorry you did, because I, I just don't understand this at all. This is something . . . all right, there are times when I know that I . . . but my God . . . I don't know what you call neglect . . . uh . . .

DAUGHTER. Emotional neglect.

MOTHER. Emotional neglect?

DAUGHTER. Oh, you always took care of me. I had shoes, and . . .

MOTHER. Oh, you had more than that.

DAUGHTER. I always felt that . . .

MOTHER. Much more than that. Much more.

DAUGHTER. Yeah, I was shifted off to other people.

MOTHER. Who?

THERAPIST. She feels you shouldn't have these feelings.

DAUGHTER. Well, whether I shouldn't have them or not, they're there.

MOTHER. When did I ever shift you off? (belligerent)

DAUGHTER. Well, forget about it . . .

MOTHER. No, no . . .

DAUGHTER. I've gotta talk about this . . .

MOTHER. Come on (goading) . . .

DAUGHTER. Because my feelings are there. Because otherwise I wouldn't have kids who have all kinds of problems. Where do you think they get it from, out of thin air? Because I'm screwed up!

MOTHER. (Interjects something)

DAUGHTER. You know I'm screwed up, Mom?

(During the playing of the tape, Van and Cindy have the following reactions to the voice of the mother:)

VAN. That's Big Daddy.

CINDY. Sure is.

> [*These spontaneous responses occurred while Dr. Paul is out of the room.*]

(The tape ends, and Dr. Paul returns.)

DR. What'd you think about that? How did you feel about that?

CINDY. (Visibly shaken) I identified so strongly with her. I was . . . But that's my father.

DR. ▶ ▶ ▶ That's your father?

CINDY. That's not my mother; that's my father. And that's exactly what I'm feeling and I'm saying. That was me on the tape with my father, and that was . . . that was too painful to . . . I'm, I'm very . . . (tearful)

DR. What?

CINDY. I really know what she's feeling.

> [*Cindy makes it very clear in her reactions to the tape that she identified completely with the daughter, and that the woman could be a stand-in for her father. The obvious inference from Cindy's intense identification*

here was that her father failed to validate Cindy's be-
ing by not accepting the long-standing intensity of her
frustrations. It tends to intensify Cindy's desire to have
Van compensate for what she did not get from her
father.]

DR. Van, what did you think of that? How did you feel about
that?

VAN. It was difficult for me to identify with the daughter. I guess
I ended up identifying with the therapist. I stopped and
thought about that for a minute. Both my parents didn't
function that way at all. They did not come on like gangbusters; they were very much more mild mannered. Uhmmm.
My father dealt with things by pulling into himself, rather
than by crushing people around him. In many ways he was a
very passive man, who, uh, couldn't deal with feelings, just
like this woman couldn't deal with feelings, the mother.

> [*I shift to Van abruptly, being concerned that Cindy's*
> *voluble expression of her feelings would distance Van*
> *further. This concern is confirmed in Van's reply when*
> *he distances himself from the material on the tape by*
> *identifying with the therapist. He does not personalize*
> *his relationship too much with Cindy, often sounding*
> *too verbal and intellectualized. Notwithstanding this,*
> *Van does get involved in a brief description of his*
> *parents. It becomes clear that his father, by pulling*
> *into himself, looms as a figure who related meagerly*
> *with Van, and is shadowy in a way like Van. This*
> *style contrasts sharply with Cindy's whose intense con-*
> *tact with her father seems more real and generated a*
> *more active sense of struggle in herself. Van provides*
> *some kind of a contradiction, that although his father*
> *was a very passive man who couldn't deal with his*
> *feelings, like the mother on the tape, it seems that*
> *his father's passivity led to a wall between Van and his*
> *father. Van continues to describe his father's life, in-*
> *cluding being orphaned, which explains his inability to*
> *relate to Van.*]

DR. What kind of work did your father do?

VAN. He worked in a fish market. He was orphaned at a very
young age.

DR. What age?

VAN. Probably six. Lived with an aunt, who was, uh, I think brutal to him, left school after the first grade and worked the rest of his life.

DR. And what kind of person was your mother?

VAN. Uh, my mother was a warm, kind of enthusiastic woman, who had sufficient troubles with her family, too, that probably set the stage for her being attracted to a much older man, like my father, who seemed solid and controlled. Her father was a guy who ran all over the place chasing rainbows and never found them; he's still doing that.

> [*I inquire of Van about his mother, and learn that the age difference between his mother and father was very different from the age difference between himself and Cindy. Their age difference is a little over a year; Van's parents had an age difference of sixteen years. His description of his mother makes her sound like Cindy; someone warm, enthusiastic, who had trouble with her family of origin.*]

DR. Where are they living?

VAN. They're both dead.

DR. Oh, you didn't have that down.

> [*Here I confront Van with the fact that he did not indicate, as he was instructed on the telephone in advance of coming to this session, that his parents were dead. This suggests that he feels in his mind and heart that they are still alive.*]

VAN. I didn't put that down? No.

DR. Oh . . .

VAN. Jeepers creepers.

DR. Mmmmmmm. When did your father die?

VAN. My father died in 1959. Or was it 1960?

CINDY. No, 1959.

VAN. 1959.

DR. Date?

VAN. I don't know.

CINDY. March the seventh, wasn't it?

DR. Of what?

VAN. '59.

CINDY. Yes. March . . . sometime in March.

[*It is interesting that it is Cindy who remembers the specific date of Van's father's death. The reason that I ask for specific dates is to help an individual focus his attention on the experience which occurs in a precise point in time. People live their lives, minute by minute, through time, on actual dates. Here it is Cindy who can provide more accurate data about Van's parents' deaths. The vagueness with which people will initially recount the date of death usually has to do with the sense of shock and bewilderment they experienced at that particular time. It is a momentary reliving of the shock of the death of someone to whom one was very attached.*]

DR. What did he die of?

VAN. Heart attack.

DR. They lived where, then?

VAN. Mobile, Alabama. That's where I grew up.

DR. And your mother died when?

VAN. My mother died in 1965. February.

DR. February what?

VAN. I don't know.

CINDY. It was very early, like the first or second.

DR. And you people got married when?

VAN. 1962. We moved to Boston in 1964 when I finished my master's degree, and . . .

DR. When in 1962?

VAN. 1964 we moved here . . .

DR. Yeah, but when did you get married?

VAN. In June. June 4.

DR. June 4.

VAN. 1962.

[*Here the vagueness of Van's recounting the date of his father's death is sharply contrasted by his ability to remember the date of marriage.*]

DR. How do you people feel being in here at this point?

[*I'm trying to find out how comfortable they feel being here before playing back the videotape to them.*]

VAN. I, I responded to your description of our house as being a zoological garden, I think, I sort of said this [referring to the office] looks a bit . . . in the same kind of classification, a bit hectic, but I feel comfortable with the machinery.

DR. What about you, Cindy?

CINDY. I am just so excited to be having somebody to hear us, that I don't even see the room. I'm just, I'm just so excited that I got my husband to come to you.

> [*It is interesting to note the difference between Van and Cindy. Van is more involved with his reaction to the immediate physical environment. Cindy is delighted to be able to be in any room with her husband and a third party who is available to hear them, suggesting that in some ways she felt that this type of encounter would never happen. Van's response to the description of his house as a zoological garden suggests that his perception is oriented toward physical entities, as I actually had been referring to their emotional chaos as being zoolike.*]

DR. How'd you do that?

> [*I get involved with Cindy's belief that she was responsible for both of them being here. This suggests either that Van was present as a passive participant, or that he was incapable of deciding for himself to be there at all.*]

CINDY. I don't know.

VAN. I thought it was my decision (laughing).

CINDY. (Laughing) Oh, I hope it was. I hope it was your decision. ◄ ◄ ◄

VAN. We had toyed with the idea, I'd been going through this business of, uh, it's my problem; if I can get my head straight, then our relationship will function. So I've been kicking around the possibilities of uh, getting back into therapy and resisting. Cindy has, I think, wanted both that, and also something for the both of us.

> [*It was interesting to see how Van then developed the idea that it's his problem, requiring individual psychotherapy. He clarifies his belief that the reason why their*

marriage does not work is because there's something wrong with his head. (The reality is that each of them makes a contribution to the marital incompatibility that currently exists. The important thing is for each to become aware more precisely what role each plays in making for the schism of the moment. Whatever roles each adopts have their historical roots. These roles are unconsciously programmed, based on patterns of inter-action in their original family system.) It seems, in part, that Van's thinking about "getting his head straight" is related to his guilt about his current affair. Van had had individual therapy for two years (1965–67) and his current belief is that more therapy will straighten the situation out. His willingness to par-ticipate with Cindy represents some concession to her, insofar as it seems as if it was she who desired "marriage therapy." (I like to think of it as marital self-education.)]

CINDY. No. I didn't want you . . . No, no way did I want you to have your own analyst. I felt like that was still more of you going out of the marriage and away from me, and not dealing with me and working with me. I wanted marriage therapy, I wanted people to hear me at the same time they were hearing you, and I wanted to work together. I didn't want you to continue going your own way.

> *[Cindy here makes it very clear that she viewed con-tinued individual therapy both as a means for Van to leave the marriage and as a sanction for him to avoid re-lating to and working with her.]*

DR. Well, I'm going to let you see yourselves, and find out what your reactions are, and then figure out what we can do.

> *[At this point I confront them with the fact that I'm going to use playback of parts of what had transpired earlier in this session.]*

CINDY. I don't understand that . . .

DR. What?

> *[During the phone interview before this session I had talked only with Van and informed him of the use of*

the videotape recorder, including subsequent videotape playback of parts of the session. I had assumed that he had told Cindy of this.]

CINDY. I didn't know you were taking our picture. Did you know that?

VAN. Yeah.

CINDY. Where's the camera?

VAN. The camera's right here.

[*I believe that Cindy's lack of awareness that I was taking their picture is related to her excitement about being here. Van was quite aware that the picture was being taken, and the camera was in full view of both of them.*]

DR. Now, well, what you get involved with here, as I told Van, is you get involved with what I call every person's credibility gap, which is the difference between how you feel inside about yourself and how you look to the other person. There are different ways of using this kind of information. You can see pieces of other people in yourself.

VAN. Uh-huh.

DR. You get a sense of, uh, what tactics each of you uses, either to turn on or turn off the other guy. The point about this whole operation, with all the tapes and so forth, is that I'm interested in each person becoming sort of an expert about how his or her head works. Rather than making the other guy a project, because I don't think that works; I haven't seen it work yet.

[*Because the human psychosensory apparatus, particularly the eyes and the ears, is focused on the other person, it's much easier to think of straightening out the other person instead of oneself. It is easy to use this natural human failing to ignore the fact that one's own behavior, of which one is unaware, has much to do with the way the other person perceives and reacts to oneself.*]

VAN. No, it doesn't.

DR. The thing that I'm sorta struck by, in listening to that [the Haas tape], it was interesting that you identified with the therapist, and I just wonder if that's been your role with Cindy.

> [*I get involved with the first direct interpretation vis-à-vis Van.*]

VAN. Yes, it has. And, we've talked about that in many ways. Yeah, well like last night, I sort of found myself again in a position of picking you [Cindy] up after you had collapsed, and I get angry about that, and frustrated by having to do that.

DR. But that may be the only way she can get a hold of you . . .

VAN. I know. I think that's probably true.

> [*It becomes a bit clearer here that Cindy's only way of making emotional contact with Van may well be to put herself in the role of being his patient, which, while it may annoy him, nevertheless indicates that he is being needed. It annoys him perhaps because it reminds him of his aversion to "falling apart."*]

DR. Okay, I want you to see yourselves, and then we can pace out what we do from here on. I'm going to leave you with yourselves for a few minutes. (He leaves the room.)

(There is videotape playback of pages 47–50, 51–60, and 70–74.)

> [*Segments are selected for videotaping to capture particularly emotionally charged reactions.*]

(After playback is concluded, Dr. Paul returns to room.)

DR. How do you feel about these people? What do you think of them?

> [*Why do I ask these questions? First of all, the image on the monitor represents the true observable self for both individuals. I want them to begin with the observable self, in order to then get involved with each one's own credibility gap.*]

CINDY. They're kind of interesting—

VAN. The guy looked shot. Ohhhhhh (yawning).

DR. In what sense?

VAN. Physically exhausted. Dark circles under his eyes, etc. (yawns again). He also (laughs) as you [Cindy] put it, is supercool.

CINDY. Supersophisticated.

DR. Detached.

CINDY. Yes.

VAN. You know, that hurts a little, but maybe that's true.

> [*The main sense of surprise at seeing oneself seemed to have occurred to Van, and was observable in the manner in which he described what he had seen. He sees himself as looking as physically exhausted as he felt from the events of the previous night. He is surprised to hear himself referred to by Cindy as "supercool," although he agrees that it is a valid observation. But when I described his appearance as being detached (which seems to me to be synonomous with "supercool") he finds that harder to accept. The question is whether he felt my view of him to be an indictment of him. Maybe "supercool" is a preferable term in view of his therapeutic stance with Cindy, whereas the word "detached" would suggest a noncaring involvement.*]

DR. (To Cindy) What do you think of her?

CINDY. She looks like she was extremely depressed. She's not got too much to be happy about. She looks like she's falling apart.

> [*Cindy makes more reference to her emotional state. This contrasts sharply with Van's focus on appearance, as if he were more image-oriented.*]

DR. She's spent her whole life doing that? Almost falling apart?

CINDY. Uh-huh.

DR. I'm thinking before Van.

VAN. I'm sorry. That was a question to me?

DR. No, I'm talking to Cindy. What kind of, uh, religious persuasion are you? At this point?

> [*Insofar as Cindy speaks about her falling apart, her prior references to difficulties with her mother about religion as well as feeling that she is being damned, I felt it was relevant to find out about her current religious beliefs.*]

CINDY. Nothing, really. I've almost totally gone to say there is no God.

DR. And what about you, Van?

VAN. I've moved from a position of being pretty conservative, to one of being pretty much uninvolved.

DR. Okay. Now, here's what I would suggest for you if you want to pursue this. I would suggest seeing each of you one time alone. Let me tell you my role in terms of what each of you tells me. Uh, there are some people who share the tapes with one another. Uh, I will not breach any confidentiality, what either one of you tells me, unless in my own mind I feel there is either the imminence of suicide or homicide, in which event I will tell the other person or the parents of whoever I'm seeing. I do not feel I have a right to keep certain kinds of information to myself in those areas. Uh, I have some reading material that can help you to plug into where my head is, and give you some kind of leverage as to where you people are, as I see you. There's a paper I wrote called "Parental Empathy," I don't know if any of you've ever seen it. Have you ever seen it?

> [*What I have in mind is to pursue more actively an exploration of the respective roles each has had in terms of the present marital crisis. My plan is to see each of them alone first before seeing them together. I couldn't see Van alone without seeing Cindy alone at some point, as he might feel that I was targeting in on him as the sole problem. Seeing Cindy alone is necessary to provide her support, in view of what happened the night before. I felt I could only find out how Van views his relationship with Jennifer by seeing him alone. I'm also thinking about getting involved with the question as to what abortive grief reaction might be causing the upset in his relationship with Cindy. In terms of seeing Cindy alone, my thinking is to find out what problems and conflicts she might have, other than those referred to above, and how they might contribute to the marital impasse. I'm also curious about what levels of sexual difficulties each might have. In seeing each of them alone I'll be better able to get valid information in this area.*]

VAN. I, I'm aware of it. Of the paper.

DR. You are. Okay. I'm going to charge you what it costs me to pull it together, it was a buck, and then there was another little piece of reading material called *Normal Adolescence*. Did you ever see that?

> [*The reason I give them the reading material is to convey to Van and Cindy that indeed this is a form of education, not treatment. The printed material is designed to help them cognitively in dealing with some of the concepts that I will be getting involved with in the subsequent sessions. It is also important for people to have certain tasks to pursue, failing which their expectation is that some kind of magical transformation will occur in the "treatment" setting.*]

VAN. Yes. Was that the Group for the Advancement of Psychiatry?

DR. Yes.

VAN. I've used it as a text.

DR. Okay. Well, what I would like each of you to do is to go through particularly chapter three, in terms of locating where each of you is sort of stuck in your respective adolescence. And that forms the agenda of what we get involved with when I see each of you alone.

> [I *clarify that I see what they're going through is a belated adolescence in certain respects. Adolescence represents a period wherein an individual begins to make a major shift in terms of his relationships, from the family to people outside the family. Marriage can be seen as the end point of an individual's adolescence. If there is any particular problem that occurs in a marriage, I see that as evidence that something went awry in the transition process that would normally occur and be resolved during chronological adolescence, but lingered instead over an extended period of time. Much of the process of mate selection has to do with unresolved problems of both adolescence and preadolescence. One tends to idealize the prospective spouse and to see him or her as a person who will help resolve those lingering*

problems. The marital incompatibility represents in many ways disappointment about what one had magically believed was to emerge as a reality in the marriage.]

And then, afterward I'd see the two of you together and tell you what I think, where to go. Generally, I'll tell you over time I have found that there are two things, two variables, that are related to improvement. Now improvement does not mean remaining married, in my mind. Improvement means that you're able to be a self, your own person, and have a strong sense of self. And in terms of this whole divorce bag, I'm convinced that before people get a divorce, they have some obligation to figure out the extent to which they are still emotionally hooked into their original nuclear family. Whether the parents are living or dead is beside the point. In other words, I think people have to achieve an emotional divorce from the original nuclear family, before they can make a viable marriage. It does not have to do with geographical distance from the family, because, like the way you're talking, Cindy, you know, being unable to accept a sense of prosperity, it's as if you've got your mother's head in your head.

[*The concept of mother's head in her head suggests to me that this introject forces her at times to behave like her mother without Cindy wishing to do so. The issue here is, how can that introject be neutralized so that she can become more comfortable being Cindy, rather than being guilt-ridden recurrently by virtue of antagonisms and frustrations she's had vis-à-vis her mother. In a sense Cindy is living out her mother's guilt about being pregnant with Cindy before marriage. It's curious to see how some of these issues transcend decades, and consume the potential for growth on the part of both parent and child.*]

And so the question then becomes, how do you get people unhooked? There are two things: one, getting the members of the original family unit in here, and second, listening to the tapes. The timetable in terms of how long this takes, I

don't know. I will not predict. Because when I start predicting
I load it. I operate from a very high degree of uncertainty. I'm
interested in facts, and getting things moving. The tapes are
to be saved, if you want to pursue this sort of thing, and
serially over time I may have you at home compare a tape a
month from now with one from this point in time. Because I
want you to make the judgments and observations as to what
is going on and what changes are occurring. In other words,
the focus is to lessen the dependency on what I think, because
if that continues over time we can't really finish until one of
us croaks. See? In brief, I'm just sketching out what this is
about. Do you people want to come back? I mean, what is
your sense about this whole thing?

> [*I attempt to make very clear my professional position
> so as to lessen the magical transference that usually oc-
> curs in one-to-one therapy. I work with the transference
> in a different way. I encourage them to help themselves
> by reviewing their tapes at home, so as to learn how to
> have a dialogue there. The more they are able to do this,
> the sooner they can get out of the office and live their
> lives more actively. They have to participate; the tasks
> are defined; questions can be asked. Here I'm making it
> clear that this is to be indeed a collaborative enterprise;
> that they have choice to return or not as they wish.
> Their desire to come back will be viewed by me as in-
> dicating that they will be willing to try to go along with
> the tasks I have outlined.*]

VAN.   I think I probably would have a better feeling for whether
or not we could work together after being able to finish the
evaluation part, in being seen individually and then back
together.

> [*Here Van makes a definitive statement, indicating to
> me that he is capable of taking the initiative in a way
> that he has not exhibited at any time previously. Cindy
> then goes along with his statement.*]

DR.   Okay . . . okay. So you want to come back for the evaluation part?

VAN. That's my feeling.

CINDY. Oh, I very much want to.

DR. Okay, now . . . I could see one of you next week on Wednesday, and the other would be, have to be the following week, on Tuesday. Usually the best hours of getting in and getting out of this area are after 10:00 and before 4:00. I would see one of you on Wednesday; it would have to be at 2:15, if you could finesse that. Usually the individual sessions are shorter.

VAN. I have a class. Can you make it at 2:15?

CINDY. Uh-huh. Yes, I can make it.

DR. Okay. Now, it's important for me, in order to operate in this thing, to have feedback when you feel I'm taking sides. Because, uh, if you feel I'm taking sides and you don't tell me, then the whole thing becomes dead. What about you, Van, in terms of, uh . . . ?

> [*I make very clear my need for feedback from each one of them. This is specifically related to the fact that my being a male often tends to make women feel that I'm going to be more inclined to side with the man, rather than be as impartial as possible.*]

VAN. Let's see, uh, somewhere around Tuesday afternoon . . .

(A discussion of possible appointment times follows.)

DR. You have, then, a copy of *Normal Adolescence?*

VAN. Yeah.

DR. Okay, then you can use your own. Uh, let me just get the "Parental Empathy" and . . . I think you ought to bring a tape that's just a little bit longer. (He leaves the room.)

VAN. (To Cindy) Well, I'm feeling a bit like you. I don't know if this is the right way to deal with things or the most helpful.

> [*Van indicates that he feels ambivalent about pursuing this approach. I'm thinking again about his desire for the more anonymous type of setting in individual therapy.*]

(Dr. Paul returns.)

DR. The statements go out after the first of the month. If you can't make an appointment please let me know twenty-four hours in advance; if you don't I'll have to charge you for the time.

I would say the sooner you get some of these things sorted out—not so much in terms of the marriage, but in terms of where you came from—the better opportunity you'll have of figuring out what to do with your respective lives. I'm not for marriage and I'm not for divorce. I'm just against dirty divorces, because I've seen too many of them. So that's where I am, so that you know where I am. Okay?

CINDY. Do you see us at all in trying to work out a . . . I feel we're still in a triangle, that she's still so much involved, you know. All week he's dealing with his feelings about her, and I don't feel he can deal with me. Where does she fit in all of this?

DR. She's a distraction.

CINDY. Are we supposed to put her in the back of our mind right now, or in the forefront?

DR. Well, generally if I say to Van that he ought to not see her or talk to her, he might feel that I'm taking sides against him. I do think generally that if it comes to a showdown for someone like yourself, I do advocate what I call a freeze-split, which means the guy and gal separate with a moratorium on the marriage, but not seeing the gal. So the guy can sort of figure out what's going on in his own head. We have a world that is, uh, replete with marvelous distractions.

CINDY. Yeah.

VAN. Yeah. It isn't an issue, really.

DR. It is for her. See, one of the things about a marriage, is when one of the two people feel an issue exists, an issue exists.

CINDY. He comes home at night and cries, and I know he's crying for her, so that's why I can't feel he can . . . turn toward me . . .

DR. Well, I think that in this operation that, uh, one of the things that both of you ought to be prepared for is, you may well be surprised as to what the real issues are. Okay?

> *[I am attempting here to get this couple to recognize that there will be uncertainties with which they will have to live. These uncertainties will pertain to what's going to happen in these sessions, what the role of the other*

A Marital Puzzle

> *woman will be, and whether or not they will get a divorce. I'm intent on having them suspend judgment about a definite future course of action. I want them to explore first what's going on inside themselves, principally in terms of the relationship between events that occurred before the marriage, and events that are occurring in the marriage at the present. The reference to exploration or the adventure that they're going to begin after this session is a preparation for what may well emerge.]*

VAN. Should we take our tape with us?

DR. Yep, this is your property, to be saved, and I don't know what kind of tape it is, but . . . if you get cruddy tape then it makes a problem when I have to dub it, and I just don't like dubbing tapes. I find that to be a glorious pain in the ass.

VAN. Yeah.

DR. Okay? So that you have the times?

VAN. Yes.

(They confirm the appointment times.)

VAN. Thank you.

DR. You're welcome. Use your heads, it's the only head you're ever going to have.

CINDY. Mmmmmm.

DR. 'By.

COUPLE. 'By.

> *[What is to unfold will be a personal adventure for each of the three of us.]*

> But the circle of our understanding
> Is a very restricted area.
> Except for a limited number
> Of strictly practical purposes
> We do not know what we are doing;
> And even, when you think of it,
> We do not know much about thinking.*
>
> CHORUS

* *The Family Reunion* by T. S. Eliot, p. 128.

Cindy's Story

DR. PAUL. You got a tape?

CINDY. It's pretty hot.

DR. Yeah. That's why I've got to move out of here one of these days. What did you think . . . this is the twenty-seventh of September, 1972. What'd you think of the meeting last time? Did you listen to the tape?

> [*I always ask for feedback about the previous session. This emphasizes my belief in continuity between visits.*]

CINDY. No. Our tape recorder's broken so we couldn't listen to the tape.

> [*She answers my two questions in a manner suggesting resistance to listening to the tapes.*]

DR. Did you read the stuff?

CINDY. Read the what?

DR. Didn't I give you some stuff to read?

CINDY. Oh, yes. Yes, I read that all.

DR. Did it make any sense to you?

CINDY. Yeah, very much. Especially about . . . the paper you did, uh . . . it really helped me to put together the fact that I have, uh, only really been feeling for myself and I really, for the first time, can ache for Van, and really understand where he's at too. My intellect tells me that. My gut doesn't. My intellect's really on top of things, and then all of a sudden my gut starts psyching up and I get heat flashes and all this and then I tell myself, "Have control," but my intellect and my guts aren't working out together.

> [*She makes very clear that the task that had the most*

impact on her was reading the paper, "Parental Empathy."]

DR. And, uh, your husband have any reaction to the meeting?

[*I change the subject, being concerned that on the basis of what Van said he wanted in the first session, i.e., more individual therapy, he might not return. Thus it's important to get a reading early in the session as to his response to the first meeting. Her account of Van's reaction will dictate how I deal with her during the rest of this session.*]

CINDY. Well, we just had a real difficult week. It started off badly because we were really so exhausted and it was a difficult time being here that early morning, and Van has been functioning on no sleep and no energy at all, and our very good friend died Friday, and that just really knocked him out.

[*Generally, people will discuss much more readily somebody else's reaction to a given interview than their own. Here we see this in the ease with which Cindy pursued Van's behavior. Actually, she doesn't talk about his reaction to the meeting, but rather to the difficulty she thinks he experienced. (Actually there is no evidence provided by Cindy that she and Van had either discussed the prior session or even alluded to it.)*]

DR. How old a person?

CINDY. He's thirty-three, he was thirty-three. He died from a brain hemorrhage sustained in an automobile accident . . . that really did a job on him.

DR. What was his name?

CINDY. Pete Beech. Peter Beech. He got his MSW with Van, and they were very close.

DR. And how'd Van take that?

[*The death of Van's friend is another crisis for Van and Cindy. I try to find out Van's reaction to his friend's death. This will help me in exploring more actively during the next meeting with Van his reaction to his father's death.*]

CINDY. Real hard. He's really been in a bad slump. In fact, I really . . . I overreacted and had a bad experience on Saturday night, and uh . . .

> [*She makes direct reference for the first time to herself, and a new crisis which just occurred, seemingly an over-reaction expressed last Saturday night.*]

DR. To what?

CINDY. The first student that Van . . . the first year that he was at Rhode Island University, the first threat in our life, was this young little Melissa, another blue-eyed blonde girl. But he handled that one better than he did this Jennifer, in that . . . he got . . . I liked Melissa, and we were invited to her wedding, and so, uh, we have somewhat kept a relationship going as a couple, with this young couple, and all the time the husband and I make a joke that Melissa and Van wanted to keep a relationship going and we allow it by being together as a couple.

> [*Here I wonder who really has the problem with Melissa, and blue-eyed blonde females. Is it Cindy's curiosity as to whether Van is still involved with Melissa, or was the need to continue the relationship with Melissa and her husband really dictated by Van? It remains unclear as to who has what problem.*]

DR. Yeah.

CINDY. Well, anyway, they came Saturday night. And I think I'm real cool and I think I'm with things and very much in control, and the subject got going about blue-eyed blondes. Melissa mentioned how she wished she had brunette . . . her hair was brunette like mine. I said, "Oh, Melissa, no, all the men find blue-eyed blondes sexy, not brunettes," and I said, uh, "Don't you, men?" And both of them said "Yeah, as a matter of fact we do." And then immediately I got this . . . "I'm gonna vomit. I just . . . I'm gonna vomit." And I jumped up and I walked out of the room and I said, "Excuse me," and I went in the bathroom, and Van immediately said . . . came and knocked on the door and said, "What is it?" and I said, "I'm falling apart. Just leave me alone for a minute." I said, "Change the topic of conversation."

[*Not uncommonly, individuals or couples will try to conduct their lives "normally" in spite of the fact that close friends or relatives have died. Having Melissa and her husband over the night after Van's close friend died represents an attempt to do just this. What subsequently transpired may well have been a displaced reaction to the fact of Peter's death. Cindy's recurrent obsession with blue-eyed blondes is curious.*]

DR. Let me ask you a question.

[*What I did here was exactly what Cindy had asked Van to do—to change to topic of conversation. Here I'm trying to dilute the intensity of her own feelings of inadequacy by exploring prior experiences that may have contributed to this sense of inferiority. There is also a question here that runs right through this, which is: Why is it that Van hadn't had an affair with Melissa, but did have one with Jennifer? Historically, it appears that the affair with Jennifer began in the context of Cindy being pregnant and Van working on his Ph.D. thesis, two additional stresses to an already precarious equilibrium.*]

CINDY. Yeah.

DR. Anybody in your family blue-eyed and blonde?

CINDY. No.

DR. Not a soul?

CINDY. No. We're all dark Italians, brown eyes, brown hair, brown skin.

DR. And did you envy somebody who was blue-eyed and blonde-haired in high school?

CINDY. In high school? No, not that I can remember.

DR. Or a teacher?

CINDY. No.

DR. "I'd like to be like her?"

CINDY. No, I never, ever felt like wanting blue eyes and blonde hair until Melissa and Jennifer entered Van's life, and he . . . his mother was blue-eyed blonde, and his sister is, and its when he first told me that the movie stars . . . he's only turned on by blue-eyed blondes. And then . . .

[*Van is blue-eyed and blonde.*]

DR. Why'd he marry you?

CINDY. I don't know. And then the two . . . his first fiancée was of my hair coloring exactly, and they broke up, and then he married me.

DR. His first fiancée was whom?

CINDY. Her name was Amy Carnel. They were engaged and he broke up with her.

DR. Why?

CINDY. It would be either marrying her or breaking up.

DR. Amy Carnel? C.A.R. . . . ?

CINDY. C.A.R.N.E.L.

DR. Well, how'd he get engaged, then?

CINDY. Well, they had started going together, it's really his first love. They went together through high school; they were very hot and heavy. They had kind of a savings account together, and he was a year older, and he went off to South Dakota to college, and she stayed in Alabama and then she came out a year later and joined him in South Dakota, and he had just decided that she really wasn't what he wanted.

DR. Do you think there's ever any chance of getting your daddy up here?

[*Here again is an abrupt change of conservation. My cue was picked up from the words "South Dakota," and trying to get her to focus her attention back on her family and where her family lives.*]

CINDY. No.

DR. Or don't you want to even take a chance on that. I get a sense you're scared shitless of that guy.

CINDY. Yeah, I am, but I also realize I don't need to deal with him.

[*I'm skeptical of this. Generally, such attitudes are associated with intense kinds of marital incompatibility. The denial of the need for a relationship with a parent will be expressed in marital acrimony, because the unrecognized antagonism to that parent will be displaced or shifted onto the spouse.*]

DR. I don't know.

CINDY. Well, I was home, the last two weeks, I tried to . . . I went home and told them about Van and me and where we were at, and I just . . . the way he is . . .

DR. Last two weeks when?

CINDY. A week ago last Thursday. My kid brother was involved in a bad car wreck, and it was touch and go for five days, so I went home.

DR. That's home.

CINDY. Two weeks ago Thursday.

DR. That's home.

CINDY. Yeah, that's home.

DR. So your heart is still out there.

CINDY. Yeah.

> [*Confirms the validity of my previous comment. "Home is where the heart is."*]

DR. You gave yourself away.

CINDY. I always say that, I know. It's good to go home, 'cause, boy, when I go home, I'm it. The whole town, the whole family, I'm it.

> [*Why home is so appealing.*]

DR. Uh-huh.

CINDY. I'm really the queen, princess. I have forty first cousins and I'm the only one who's left home. And I'm my grand-mother's favorite grandchild, and I'm the only grandchild with a college degree. And I go home, and the small town of Monongah, and all my other girlfriends got married, and they have children fifteen and sixteen years old, and I walk down Main Street and everybody is so excited to see me. I'm really somebody in my whole family, uh . . .

DR. You're really somebody.

CINDY. Yeah, I really am. And up here, I've decided that I don't fit in with this culture that my husband's placed me in.

> [*Here is a clear indication of abdication of one's own responsibility for what presumably would be a joint decision. If she doesn't fit in, why does she stick it out? She obviously misses the quality of attention and*

> *warmth that she has at home. Can Cindy accept her
> own responsibility for having achieved a family am-
> bition, that of obtaining a college degree? It's unclear
> why she was unable to marry somebody like other
> members of her family and friends, who live at "home."*]

DR. Which is what?

CINDY. A very sophisticated, intellectual bunch of snobs.

DR. You want to go back there?

CINDY. Yeah, I feel more comfortable with those kind of people,
and yet I don't. I really . . . I don't really think I can go
back there, and yet I feel that those are the kind of people
that are really genuine, and that I am more outstanding
than they. I'm a snob when I go back, and yet . . . I um, I
really can't explain it, I'm on top of things when I go back
there. And yet I see those people as really genuine, sincere
people, and the people here I think we're all . . . are play-
acting. I don't think anybody is really genuine, anybody is
really sincere. Everybody . . . all they're doing is just screwing each other and raising their kids in day-care centers, and
just . . . that's it. And I don't fit into that. And I can't sit
around and talk about the latest art show I went to, or the
latest opera, or what books I'm reading. I don't fit into that.

DR. You want to go back, then?

CINDY. I do and I don't. I don't really want to live back there, and
yet . . .

DR. You don't know where you belong.

CINDY. I really don't.

> [*She clarifies her ambivalence. It sounds to me like she
> can't go back there, because she's afraid of confronting
> her father, and it may be that it was her relationship
> with him which in large part drove her away from
> home.*]

DR. Van have any reactions to being here?

> [*Again, a shift in focus. I'm curious as to whether
> Cindy's ambivalence about being in the Providence
> area is shared by Van. My question permits the clari-
> fication of Cindy's ambivalence about being in this*

area, as well as being in this room, in treatment.]

CINDY. Well, he loved it here. Now he's really disgruntled with it, but he could never be happy in South Dakota.

DR. No, I'm thinking about being in this room.

CINDY. Oh, in this room? Oh, well. He has, uh, I'd call it a professional snobbishness to it that he really can't see himself as sick and hurting as he is. He just wants to impress you instead of just showing you some things about himself . . . and I felt like he was play-acting with you instead of really getting gutty with you. And I said, "I think you're tense with Dr. Paul. You're trying to impress him with who you are, as a professional," and I think he's very uncomfortable to let himself down. I don't think you completely convinced him that you're what he wants and needs. And I . . .

> [*It's clear that there's a competition as to whose brand of snobbery is preferable.*]

DR. Does he want to discontinue?

> [*I continue to find out more about Van through Cindy's perceptions. I am focusing on her perceptions of Van, because it is so difficult for her to dwell on her own situation without getting involved with the intensity of her "falling apart."*]

CINDY. Well, he can't discontinue, Dr. Paul; he is really sick. I mean Saturday night, I didn't finish my story, but Saturday night he flaked out . . .

DR. Which way?

CINDY. He absolutely was so destructive, he completely ruined his therapy room. He . . . he knocked all the bookshelves off the wall, he knocked all the furniture upside down, he was throwing books, he was throwing his lamps, he threw his clock, he was completely . . .

> [*It may well be that Van's destroying his therapy room was an expression of his anger and frustration toward his friend's death. In a follow-up interview on December 13, 1973, he was asked for further reflections about this destructive behavior. He said that "all this stuff . . . i.e., everything my father said was*

> *important that I had to do . . . get a good education
> and all that . . . wasn't the salvation I thought it
> would be."*]

DR. Was he drunk?

CINDY. Yeah. And mad at me.

DR. About what?

CINDY. Well, I hadn't finished the story . . . but I told Melissa. Melissa was talking about . . . the subject of affairs came up, because she's so threatened and so jealous of her husband, who's a pilot. And so she brought the subject up about affairs, and she said . . . right after the blue-eyed blonde business and I just came back thinking I'm in control of my jealousy business . . . that "God, you're lucky you're married to a man like you are. I wish I had a perfect husband," and I said, "Bullshit to that. This perfect husband is out screwing a little blue-eyed blonde college kid," and as soon as I said it, I mean . . . it was as much a shock to me as it was to the room. Of course, the cocktail glasses just froze, and her husband said, "Oh, come on, Cindy, you're drunk . . . get off that kick. Don't tease us."

> [*Cindy is unable to believe that anybody could be jealous of her. She has to dispel the illusion, and does so quite well.*
>
> *When Cindy's anxiety crescendoes, she begins to depersonalize. For her, it wasn't that the people froze; the cocktail glasses froze. All this shows the intensity of Cindy's alienation from her feelings of jealousy, anger, and inadequacy. This is in keeping with the kind of estrangement from oneself and one's surroundings one experiences when drunk.*]

DR. How much had you been drinking?

CINDY. I had three Manhattans, and no food.

DR. Since when? That day?

CINDY. Since food, you mean?

DR. Yeah.

CINDY. About eleven that day.

DR. In the morning.

CINDY. Yeah.

DR. So you must have been in rollicking form.

> [*Low-key comment without any judgmental implications.*]

CINDY. I really for the first time, when she was coming, I said to Van, "I really got to pour myself a drink in order to be cheerful and happy." Cause we'd been crying and dealing all day with the death of our friend . . .

> [*The difficulty in acknowledging and coping with their friend's death seemed to dictate using the evening with Melissa and her husband as a diversion.*]

DR. So what happened? At that point, there was a chain reaction.

CINDY. Of course there was a chain reaction. And Melissa looked at me, and she got tears in her eyes, and she's had Van on a pedestal for a long, long time . . . her father's having an affair right now, too. She came to Van originally to talk to him because of her father's affair, and how he could do it . . .

DR. Did Van have an affair with her?

CINDY. No, but he fantasized about it. That's the first girl who came home . . . in his new profession. I was married to this self righteous WASP and then zap! I had this college professor, who all the girls are hot-pantsing over, and this young girl and her friends came by our house one night to see Van, and that's when he first told me that she came by all the time and flirted with him, and it was, he said, a real turn on to have these cute kids come by and, you know, you got to understand it, and so forth and so on, and I was teaching at the time, so I . . .

DR. ▶ ▶ ▶ You were teaching where?

> [*Another diversionary maneuver, designed to neutralize the building anxiety about blue-eyed blonde "cute kids." This as also an attempt to find out a little more precisely what she's doing with her life.*]

CINDY. In Attleboro.

DR. Where in Attleboro?

CINDY. West Junior High School.

DR. Teaching what?

CINDY. Commercial arts.

DR. Yeah.

CINDY. And I know how kids are, and I had just finished being a college kid myself, so I said, "Yeah, but how far does it go with you?" And he said, "Oh, well, you know, you gotta allow me my fantasy life." So he . . . you know, he admits that he fantasizes about it . . .

> [*My attempt fizzles out. Her preoccupation recurs. Van's saying "You gotta allow me my fantasy life" suggests that he was testing to see how much Cindy could tolerate of the fantasy, and then perhaps at a later point would attempt the reality of a sexual affair.*]

DR. How was your sex life before?

CINDY. Well, I used to think it was good, but now that I think about it really, really think about it, and Van throws it to me . . . it really isn't good.

DR. Why?

CINDY. Well, he says that I am overdemanding and oversexed to the point that nothing he does is ever enough to satisfy me. And I think, I really see somewhat now, that a lot of the times when I asked for intercourse, it was asking for reassurance. I really wasn't turned on, and I really had no desire, and I was as tired as could be, but somehow, I needed to have intercourse . . . to have some kind of reassurance.

> [*The way she describes being overdemanding and oversexed suggests that she has accepted Van's perception of her, essentially a putdown, which implies that there is something abnormal about her. The kind of reassurance she was trying to get from Van via intercourse represented a need to touch his body to be in close contact with him, even though she knew that at best this was a reassurance that couldn't last. Does she believe that if she were blonde and blue-eyed, she wouldn't be carrying such labels, and that Van probably would be much more responsive to her? All of this seems to be a reflection of her perception of herself, which antedated the marriage and courtship, where her striving to be the center of attention, etc., may well have been a compensatory reaction to feelings of inadequacy that had been present for a long time.*]

DR. So that intercourse was in the service of reassurance that he cared about you?

CINDY. Yeah, it was really some way of getting him to show me . . .

DR. So it wasn't really an expression of love.

CINDY. No. We had worn each other out for three . . . two years, really three but two really tight years, of trying to get pregnant, so that we were having intercourse just like he was on stud service, you know, three times a week and with no pleasure and I'd just lay there and hurry up and get it over with and get up and brush our teeth.

DR. Yeah. And get me pregnant quick.

> [*Intercourse, in addition to providing reassurance, is also a means of becoming pregnant. The problem for them is where in the scope of their experience does intercourse become pleasurable for both?*]

CINDY. So just recently, I mean in about the last year, I was starting to get aroused at parties, at cocktails, and so forth, like I can remember in high school, and then I'd come home and I'd really be turned on. And I'd think, "Now how do I communicate to Van?" And there would be times when he couldn't have an orgasm, and I'd think, "Oh, no."

> [*This pattern seems related to her chronic frustration over Van's inadequate love-making. Thus, it is understandable that she would come to accept the indictment of being overdemanding and oversexed. This pattern becomes circular and self-perpetuating. Each becomes progressively more self-conscious, embarrassed, and skittish. Whatever communication they might have had is further sabotaged.*]

DR. When he couldn't?

CINDY. Uh-huh.

DR. How come?

CINDY. I don't know. He would work real hard and he never could.

DR. He couldn't get an erection, or he had an erection but couldn't . . .

CINDY. He had an erection but he couldn't ejaculate. And he

would tell me that it was . . . "Well, you know, you just can't get in the mood instantly," and I would come back with, "It's always got to be you, and your mood. It can never be my mood. It has to be your mood, and I just have to be around here and wait until it's your mood, but I can't . . ."

> [*It seems that if it isn't the man's mood and it's the woman's mood, then it will be kind of difficult at times for a lot of men to make love. Obviously the desirable kind of situation would be where there's a spontaneity between the partners, so that there can be a mutual turning-on experience. Also, there's a question of how much drinking Van had been given to before he attempts intercourse.*]

DR. He couldn't ejaculate . . . how long has this problem been going on?

CINDY. (Puzzled and distressed) Well, it's been going on since the Jennifer end of the picture. We figured out . . .

DR. Ummmmm. So he cracked up on Saturday?

CINDY. He really flipped.

DR. And did he recover Sunday?

CINDY. No, he was so depressed, so drunk, he wouldn't even talk to me. No, it was Sunday night.

DR. Sunday night.

CINDY. Sunday night, because Monday morning was the funeral.

> [*Is this what commonly happens on weekends before Monday funerals?*]

DR. And where was that?

CINDY. Where was the funeral? It was in Woonsocket (Rhode Island). He cried all the way home from the funeral, and he hasn't really spoken much to me since, uh, and last night, he got . . . uh, he's not sleeping, uh, he's walking the floor; at two in the morning I rolled over and he wasn't in bed, and I went upstairs and he was sitting nude on the couch, just staring out the window. And I got him to bed, and then at five he got up; he's just not sleeping.

DR. Is he suicidal, do you think?

CINDY. No. No, he's just . . . he's just exhausted. He's just so tired that he doesn't even know now how to sleep, and he's

really in a state of depression. And I don't know how to
handle it, because I . . . I really am aching for him. I say
to myself, "God, Cindy, you ask him for your own happiness.
You ask him to give up this person that he really loves and
really was needing and functioning with, okay, you ask him
to give her up, he did, and he's back into your marriage now.
And this is what you want? And I say, "I can't ask that of
him." My intellect tells me this, my intellect says, "You can't
take this man this way and destroy him." And I feel I'm destroying him. And yet, and then the other side of me, the gut,
all of a sudden it starts churning and saying, "Damn him for
crying in front of me! Damn him for being depressed in front
of me for her!" Why can't he . . .

> [*"How to handle it," i.e., him and his emotionality. Be-
> cause of the general lack of gut communication between
> Van and Cindy, she really doesn't know what's burning
> in him, and so she's left with the conclusion that it is
> his involvement with Jennifer. It should be obvious that
> Van might have been preoccupied, distressed, and cry-
> ing; all normal kinds of behavior attendant to the loss
> of a best friend. And yet, Cindy can't see this. Her re-
> action suggests that what Van wanted in Cindy, namely
> somebody who wouldn't fall apart, is a quality Cindy
> also wanted in Van.*]

DR. How do you know he's . . . that's the real issue?

CINDY. That is.

DR. I don't know.

> [*Here I focus precisely on Cindy's inability to tune into
> Van in any area other than sexual attraction to blue-
> eyed blondes. All of this dovetails with her previous
> remark: "God, Cindy, you ask him for your own hap-
> piness." This indicates very clearly that because she
> doesn't know much about Van, she feels she needs
> him mainly to buttress her own sense of inadequacy. I
> suspect that Van feels the same way about her. In this
> regard, Cindy and Van are locked in a no-win situa-
> tion.*]

CINDY. And that's why he won't talk to me, I don't know what he's feeling, and I'll say, "Are you not sleeping because you're thinking about her? ◄ ◄ ◄ Do you really want a life with her? What are you thinking? What are you feeling?"

> [*Cindy is obviously getting wound up about Jennifer. Here she is suggesting a desire to have the situation between her and Van resolved. But the way she is behaving seems to be provoking Van to leave her, and to be with Jennifer. This will ultimately confirm her sense of inadequacy and inferiority, and in addition, confirm the validity of her parents' judgment about God's indictment of her for being bad.*]

DR. Okay. Let's do this, if you want to and if you're up to it. There's kind of a bad noise outside. Uh, what I want to do is to have you see a film. Let me tell you a little bit about what I do. You heard a tape last time.

CINDY. Uh-huh.

DR. . . . And I use films, and I use sex films. The thing about the sex films that I use, either heterosexual or homosexual, is that it's not to be regarded by you as a mandate for any kind of behavior. As an example, homosexual flicks, which I'm not gonna use today, it doesn't mean that you're a homosexual, or you're a lesbian or have lesbian tendencies. All I'm interested in is what turns you on and what turns you off, because from that I can get a quicker rundown as to how you see yourself and your own sexuality, than try to go through a whole bunch of details, which would take a long time.

CINDY. Okay.

DR. And if you're up to it I'll show it to you.

CINDY. Okay.

> [*Here I begin a totally different tack. I use this film as a projective test to help pin-point areas of normal inhibition, and to evoke memories of both sexual encounters and sexual trauma. Cindy's reactions will provide me with an understanding of both the extent of her inhibitions and her level of sexual interest. The film, by presenting a casual heterosexual encounter, sanctions such fantasies. It further helps to clarify areas*

of discrepancies between fantasy and actual experience. In many instances, there will be a distinct reaction of sexual arousal. This will lead to a clarification of the difference between the ways a person will express his or her desire for an abandoned sexual encounter.

What I'm trying to do with Cindy via the film is to again dilute the intensity of her sense of sexual abnormality, and to provide positive sanction for fantasies of heterosexual encounter. Further, this technique attempts to undercut the level of prohibition and inhibition that has been put on her by her parents, and reinforced by social convention. The point of it all is to provide Cindy with an experience which will increase her sense of options in the way she can look at herself and her sexuality.]

DR. Okay? It'll be on the wall behind your head, and, when it's over do this. At the end of the phone here there's a button which says "Buzz." Just press it down.

CINDY. Okay.

DR. And then I'll come back and we'll discuss it. Okay?

CINDY. All right.

DR. How do you feel anticipating that?

CINDY. Well, I . . . I, it doesn't bother me. I went to that American Academy of Marriage Counselors meeting or whatever. There was a whole weekend of flicks.

DR. Oh, down in New York?

CINDY. Yeah. And after sitting in that for two straight days, I don't think you have anything new to show me.

DR. Well, this is a different way of looking at it.

CINDY. Right.

DR. Okay, so you'll buzz when it's over.

CINDY. Okay.

(Dr. Paul starts film and leaves room.)

▬▬▬▬▬▬▬▬▬ **Description of the Film** ▬▬▬▬▬▬▬▬▬

The film of an attractive young man and woman takes place in a pastoral setting. The general feeling is that of sexual playfulness, with slight gymnastic overtones. Moments of tenderness are few. The couple remind one of playful young animals romping in a field.

A handsome young man dressed in hunting clothes walks in a wooded area. He carries a gun and a pair of binoculars. Suddenly he spies something in a clearing nearby. He looks intently through his binoculars, and in a distance he sees a beautiful young woman who is sitting naked, sun-bathing. She is carefully smoothing sun lotion all over: her face, her arms, her breasts, her navel, legs, hands, genitals.

Then she lies down to sun herself. The hunter moves closer. He takes his penis out of his pants to masturbate. He holds his binoculars in his right hand and moves closer. The woman sees him, jumps up, and runs away, grabbing her dress as she goes. He catches up to her by a tree and fondles her breasts. She does not move away. They begin to make love. But she suddenly attempts to run away, but trips and falls. He kisses her mouth, and again fondles her breasts. She jumps up once again. She is trapped by him; finally they collapse on her sun-bathing blanket. She begins to enjoy his advances as he caresses her vagina and inner thigh. They kiss enthusiastically. The hunter then takes off all his clothes except his pants. She helps him with that. He bends down to put his penis in her mouth. While she kisses his penis, she rubs his testicles while he strokes her clitoris. She continues to kiss his penis tenderly. He strokes her neck, and then bends down to kiss her clitoris; she kisses his penis. Turning around he puts his penis into her vagina, while he kisses her on the mouth. She then turns over, and he puts his penis in her vagina from behind. He fondles her breasts and nipples, and this continues until he ejaculates on her pubic area. The last we see of them, they are lying peacefully on the ground together.

There is no group or anal intercourse depicted. In general, what is demonstrated are masturbatory gestures on both the man and woman's part, and a variety of positions for intercourse. The film is ten minutes long, and is in black and white, with no sound.

▄▄▄

(When the film is over Dr. Paul returns.)

DR. Let me just check your tape. Okay. What'd you think of this? Did you like what you saw there?

CINDY. Oh, yes, I loved the whole thing. I just . . . I fantasized
that so much, that whole experience, and the weirdest thing,
though, ► ► ► I kept seeing my face. I think she looks exactly like me. I kept saying, "That's my face! That's my face!"

> [*Cindy's reaction suggests that the film did provide her
> with an overwhelming sense of sanction for herself, so
> much so that she saw her face in the face of the woman
> in the film (whose face does not look like Cindy's).
> This suggests that Cindy's desperation for sex as a re-
> assurance was an attempt to leapfrog the prohibition
> about her sexuality, which was put on her by her par-
> ents. Her intensity about sex is a threatening stimulus
> for Van.*]

DR. Did anything turn you off about it?

CINDY. No, nothing. Three weeks ago when I was in South
Dakota, I laid out in the, the woods and masturbated for like
an hour . . .

DR. Yeah?

CINDY. And I could hear a man over the water—I was at my
folks' lake, and I kept thinking, oh, I wish he'd come around
me. I hunger for that. I would love the whole experience,
everything. I tried to get Van to make love to me like that
sometimes, and he . . . he can't do it, he . . .

> [*The reference to hunger suggests a desperation which
> could only become counterproductive.*]

DR. Why does he seem to be uptight?

CINDY. He's just real fast, brings me to my orgasm and then he
reaches his, there's no real playing and there's no real ex-
perimenting. Only twice has he used his mouth on me, and
that's when he was really drunk, and we were . . . a long
time ago. The next morning I was expressing how much I
enjoyed it and he was really embarrassed to even talk about it.

> [*It is obvious that Cindy and Van each have different
> kinds of problems in orienting themselves sexually.
> Cindy's perception of Van suggests that he is quite
> inhibited. I wonder how much of this derives from the
> intensity of his religious training. I also wonder what
> are the factors in Van's own past history that have ac-*

counted for his own inhibition in approaching Cindy.]

DR. Mmmmmm.

CINDY. And I just love that whole experience, that . . . one time I can remember I tried to get him to go to the woods and make love with me, and there was a cardboard box, and I said, "Come on, let's go to the woods and hide," and we did, but he just was hurrying too fast, and I kept thinking, "God, let's just relax and enjoy it." And he was so afraid that it . . .

[How much of Cindy's perception of Van's fear is a projection of her own?]

DR. Of what?

CINDY. Of getting caught; somebody seeing him. That's what he said. But when we were first dating and he was just so hot for me, and I kept trying to save myself, as my mother would say, and I kept trying to tell myself, "Now don't get turned on. You can't have intercourse until you get married." And he was always so hot for me. And he would just . . . we finally did have intercourse, ah, just a week before he gave me my engagement ring, and he just . . . he shook, he was so excited, his body was just trembling. It was the most exciting experience I ever had, too, though I didn't have an orgasm. I didn't even know I was supposed to from him. I had masturbated for a long long time, even as a young kid, but in intercourse I didn't know what I was supposed to feel. But he did, and I can remember how exciting it was seeing how excited he was. And then, after we got married, uh, our honeymoon night, I can remember that it was so nice to finally be in a motel and be in a bed, and not be in the front seat of a car. But for him, he wasn't that excited. And for me it was like the first time. But he wasn't excited anymore.

[What did she learn about sex and orgasms from her family and marriage course? It sounds as if there was a dissociation between knowledge acquired in a classroom and her ability to translate this into her actual feeling experience. Did she feel that orgasm was tantamount to becoming pregnant? Was her failure to have an orgasm related to her fear of doing the same thing her

*mother had allegedly done, i.e., becoming pregnant
before marriage? One can only speculate on other
reasons: she may have identified having an orgasm, the
culmination of sexual encounter, as a clear-cut indica-
tion of loss of purity; and perhaps in some way she
sensed Van's fear of her orgasm. (See Session V, page
200.)]*

DR. Did he say why?

CINDY. He was still tired, it was a rough day, a long drive to the
motel, and he was real angry, he got real angry, he couldn't
find his house slipper if I remember, and he was . . . in the
suitcase, he was trying to get the things out, he really got
angry, and it was awhile before I got him calmed down over
the house slipper before we even went to bed . . . I'm
really kind of frightened about my sexual drives; all of a
sudden they're coming out, I mean I'm really hungry to be
made love to. And I'm so hungry to have a real experience.
I was really involved with a boy in high school and he and I
petted heavily, and I was so turned on then, but the religion
was so deeply implanted in my mind, and that I had to
be such a good girl, that I would never let . . .

*[The incident about the slipper suggests that it was Van
who was frightened and skittish about going to bed and
making love.*

*But then she shifts abruptly to reveal that it is she
herself who was frightened. At the same time she says
she's hungry to be made love to.*

*Her high school involvement is a splendid ex-
ample of ambivalence.]*

DR. Or you'd go to Hell?

CINDY. Yes. And I would never let Duke go all the way with me,
and his mother and daddy worked, and we used to go to his
house and lie on his bed, and just make . . . well, I used
my hand and he used his. I never would let him enter me; and
I thought that this was keeping me a pure person. And I
often think back, I'm so sorry that I couldn't really enjoy
Duke and uh . . . we'd go to drive-ins and I'd come home
and I'd know that I probably had the smell of semen on me,

because we were, when he ejaculated it would sometimes go on my slip. And I'd think, oh, my mother and daddy are gonna know. But when I went to the doctor to get fitted for my diaphragm when I was, uh, getting married, it was the old family doctor, and I will never forget the feeling, and Van was at the house that weekend with us, of having him find out that I wasn't a virgin. That he was gonna tell my mother and father, and he was gonna know that I was really . . . sin . . . I had sinned, and . . .

> [*Cindy is terrified of the consequences of sin. Here we get a certain emerging feel of her terror of being damned and of her supposed loss of purity.*]

DR. Did he say anything?

CINDY. No . . . nothing. He was just so sweet, and, uh, so gentle.

DR. Your guilt was pretty intense.

CINDY. My *mother* thought it was *terrible* that I was fitted for a diaphragm. And Van and I had taken a course in college, "Marriage and the Family." And we had a book open, a textbook open, that we both were studying for an exam . . . he would come home with me on the weekends . . . the college wasn't far from my home, and he's from Mobile . . . so he'd come home with me on the weekends. And my mother picked that book up, where it was the anatomy of the male, and I had drawn lines, you know, and she just (snapped her fingers) . . . she went berserk.

DR. Why?

CINDY. "How dare you two look at those pictures before you get married; you're not even supposed to think about those things!" And when I told her I was going to be fitted for a diaphragm before we got married, she just had fits. She said, "You wait till after you get married to think about those kind of things." I said, "But mother, I don't want to get pregnant on my honeymoon." And she says, "Better that . . . better that . . . !"

> [*Mother's message to Cindy suggests that straight knowledge about sexuality and love-making will make her vulnerable to damnation.*]

DR. Than what?

CINDY. "Than to go to the doctor and get your hymen broken before your husband does it." And at that I went upstairs and just . . . I can still remember the guilty feeling of wanting to vomit because I had disappointed her . . . I wasn't the kind of person she really thought I was. And I felt so sinful going down the aisle in my white gown, seeing my mother and daddy . . .

> [*What does an intact hymen mean to Cindy's mother?*
> *This pattern of vomiting expresses in part Cindy's feelings of resentment and guilt about disappointing her mother. I wonder whether Cindy felt that she had sufficiently disappointed Van to account for his moves toward Melissa and Jennifer. (Cindy seems constantly overwhelmed by her basic sinfulness, as well as her ugly appearance.)*]

DR. A fraud.

CINDY. . . . Saying how proud they were of me, and thinking, "Oh, if they only knew."

> [*If they really knew, what would they do to her? I neglected to follow this up. Is this in part why she went to college and left South Dakota—to avoid a confrontation about sex with her parents? At her wedding, of what were her parents proud? That she was virginal? The requisite quality seemed to be a physical and emotional innocence, for which, it seems to me, pride is inappropriate.*]

DR. What a fraud I am.

CINDY. Yeah. (A pause.) Do you know why he told me about Jennifer? I don't think he would've ever told me, but twice this past month two men have tried to seduce me, and he stopped them. He nearly killed both of them.

DR. What do you mean, two close friends seduced you? You or Jennifer?

CINDY. Me. That's why he told me. He was so angry at me, or at . . . I don't know what he was really angry at. But, uh, his brother-in-law came to see us, and I have really had strong feelings for Scott for a long time, though, but I . . .

DR. This is who . . . brother, or . . . ?

CINDY. His sister's husband.

DR. Where does he live?

CINDY. He lives in San Francisco, and he's a, uh . . .

DR. What's his name? Scott what?

CINDY. Scott Marshall. He is, uh, an insurance underwriter.

DR. Yeah.

CINDY. And he came to our house, August, the second, the second before the last weekend in August. At the same week my mother came. They both arrived the same day. And he didn't know exactly what was going on as far as Van and me, but he knew that we weren't happily married, and Van went to bed early, and Scott and I just by chance, happened to be sitting in the kitchen, and it was about two in the morning. And my mother is in bed, as close to me as that door is to where I am.

> [*For Cindy, her mother is a symbol of heightened ambivalence about sexuality. The question is whether in part Cindy is acting out her mother's sexual hunger. Cindy is chronically trying to get her mother to accept her, Cindy's, sexuality.*]

DR. Yeah.

CINDY. And so . . . Scott is right here, and we're having this conversation, and all of a sudden he puts me in his arms and he kisses me, and he says, "You know, you and I for fourteen years have joked about our feelings, but," he says, "I really want to deal with you the way I feel about you," he says. "I've always loved you." And he says, "This isn't the time, or the place, but someday I want to deal with you and my feelings about you." Well, I just started to cry, and I grabbed him and held onto him so tighly. It felt so good to hear him saying things that I've been so hungry to hear from Van for so long. Well, Van walks downstairs and sees us embraced— fully dressed, sitting in the kitchen, at the kitchen table, and he went berserk.

> [*The word "berserk" is used here when Van encounters Cindy with Scott, and earlier Cindy referred to her mother's similar state upon seeing the textbook picture*]

of male genitals.]

DR. What'd he do?

CINDY. Well, he pushed Scott to the side, and he said, "I don't believe it. God!" That man . . . you know . . . he just went berserk. He was white as a ghost, he got in the car and drove off and left us, and he came back at 6:30. I don't think . . . I still don't know where all he went. He came back, and he said [to Scott], "You're a shit-face, and I don't ever want to see you again." And Scott said, "You've got to deal with me." And the whole time he's gone, I went downstairs and took a cold shower and I kept saying, "He's gone. I'm going up to Scott. I'm going to go up in Scott's room. I'm going to go up in Scott's room." And I kept saying, "No, my mother's here." Damn my mother for being there on that weekend.

DR. Always spoiling the fun.

CINDY. I'll always hate her for being there that weekend. And the first thing he said to me when he met me was, "Did you enjoy your screw?" And I said, "No, damn it."

DR. Is that what he wanted you to do?

CINDY. I said, "Is that what you want me to do," and he said, "No, that's why I came back . . . I wanted to catch you."

[*Van has a desire for revenge due to Cindy's incessant preoccupation about him and Jennifer. Both of these mutual "catching" interests seem to be displacements from parental figures of the other spouse. Van catching Cindy could be analogous to Cindy's mother catching her.*]

DR. Have you caught him with Jennifer?

CINDY. No. (Sighs) No, I haven't. 'Cause he's been pretty good as an undercover agent. I suspected it, and when I really got suspicious that he couldn't make love to me, was that weekend when we went to New York, that sex convention, 'cause the weekend before was the weekend he went with her, and he was with her in New York City that weekend. The next weekend is when we're turned on, and uh, I mean, you can't watch these kind of things eight hours, and we'd go back to our room, and I'd be hot-pedaling out of my clothes, and he just couldn't get an erection. And he didn't make love to me the whole weekend. And on the way back, driving back home to Attleboro, I said, "Van, you can't . . . you don't love me any more, do you?" And he said, "No, Cindy, I don't know where I'm at. I really don't know how I feel about you any more, but I need distance from you." He said, "You've got to give me time to find out where I am," and I said, "Is it another woman?" ◄ ◄ ◄ He said, "No, it's not another woman," and he started . . . that's when he really started lying to me. And that's when I really knew there had to be another woman. When he couldn't make love to me that weekend. There had to be.

> [*Cindy assumes that he can't make love to her because of Jennifer. It could be, however, that the sex films raised Van's anxiety about his own sexuality to a more intense level than usual. His denial that Jennifer was the cause of their troubles suggests his beginning awareness that there were anxieties in himself unrelated to Cindy.*]

DR. That's when you first knew about Jennifer?

CINDY. Yes. As far as the sexual involvement goes. I . . . he promised me a year ago that he'd never see her again, and when I talked to her she also promised me she'd never see Van again.

DR. How did you know they had been screwing around?

CINDY. Well, I got the . . . I got ahold of one hotel slip, with a . . .

DR. Doesn't mean anything.

CINDY. And he said they were. I don't know how much it is.

DR. Well, let me just tell you what I wonder about. Whether he has been chronically depressed because of this erection problem . . . not erection, ejaculation problem. It can be a symptom of depression. And it can really throttle a guy to get involved with another gal, to try to prove that he can do it. And, at times he cannot do it, and that sort of drives him bananas. I don't know what's going on; I'm going to try and find out what's going on, but what . . . I guess what I'm trying to say is that we don't know the whole story.

[*I'm trying to amplify the point that Van previously made about it not being another woman, and to dilute, at the same time, Cindy's belief that his statement was a lie to her. (Affairs can so readily and so effectively distract everybody from underlying issues which are critical.) The real question is whether Cindy could accept all the sex that she believes she is capable of accepting. Does her intense preoccupation and desire for sex render her incapable of functioning in the sexual encounter with as much abandon and verve as she believes.*]

CINDY. I know it. That's what's . . . that's the aspect that's destroying me, if he is having more sex, if he's really being sexy, and giving her all the sex that I have been hungry for, that . . . I can't take that. I can't imagine . . .

DR. If that's so, what are you going to do? Are you going to get a divorce then?

CINDY. No.

DR. What're you going to do? Sweat it out?

CINDY. That's what I said to him, I'll go out and find a young man to screw, if that's what it takes.

[*This approach certainly is effective in killing time and keeping people preoccupied as to who's getting more points, and at the same time digs a rut which circumvents any resolution of the fundamental problems.*]

DR. And what'd he say?

CINDY. I said, in fact, I said, "Is this what you're asking from me? You have Jennifer for your intellectual feedback. And I get a new man to screw me, because that's my only unhappiness."

[*Is Cindy also feeling inadequate intellectually? Does she feel that she has to compete with Jennifer in this area?*]

DR. Yeah?

CINDY. And he said, "No, I don't think that . . . that's viable." And I said, "Well, what is viable?" And he said, "You have needs to be met that I can't meet, and I have needs to be met that you're not meeting." And I said, "Yeah, well, you found your friend to meet your needs, do I go find me a friend to meet my needs? And then we stay happily married ever after?" He said, "No, that's not viable," and that's when I said

to him, "We're going to a therapist, 'cause I'm not gonna live
this way. If you won't let me go out and find me a lover I
can't let you have your lover. We've got to find out what's
going on." I don't want to leave him. I really love him. And
I . . . I really . . . I can't picture a better life. I really
can't. I've never visualized living without him.

> [*Cindy's inability to view herself as being capable of
> happiness beyond the turmoil of the moment suggests
> that she is eternally indicted by her preoccupation with
> sex. In effect, she really wasn't meant to be happy at
> anytime. This further suggests that she is living out her
> mother's shame about her mother's premartial concep-
> tion of her.*]

DR. Well, I would say that something's troubling him, but I don't
know where it is.

CINDY. Right now he says he's just dealing in losses; all his life he's
had to deal with losses. He's never had any good things happen to him. And I say, "Well, me and three kids are good
things to you. And . . ."

> [*Apparently, Van has a reasonably good understanding
> of what is strangling his capacity to function more ade-
> quately in a marriage.*]

DR. He can't see straight.

CINDY. No, he really can't. And oh, God is he depressed. I don't
know how he functions. He's seein' six clients today, himself,
and he's taught three classes. I don't know how he functions,
I really don't.

DR. I want you to see this, and I want you to tell me what you
think about this gal, and then I'll tell you where we go. Okay?

> [*My decision at this point to play back the videotape is
> to try and help Cindy get greater distance from the in-
> tensity of her preoccupation about the affair and sex;
> and to get more involved with Cindy, as she is right
> now.*]

CINDY. Oh! I didn't realize you were doing this again.

(There is videotape playback of Cindy talking about her sex life)

> [*Material on videotape is on pages 96–101 and 104–
> 111.*]

DR. What'd you think of that?

CINDY. I think she's got some sad stories to tell.

DR. Yeah? Anything else?

CINDY. She's never got to live the life she really wants to live.
> [*This statement indicates a desire to compensate for that in the marriage.*]

DR. Before she was married or after she was married?

CINDY. Yea-a-h. Both.

DR. Both.

CINDY. Both. And I also found myself pretty for the first time.

DR. First time in how long?

CINDY. I don't know . . . since I was in high school, and I saw the college queens and everything. I mean the high school queens, and the Miss Sweethearts, and everything. I've been asking Van for a long time, "Tell me I'm pretty, tell me I look . . . look nice!" And uh, today I saw myself in a way I'd never seen myself in a mirror.
> [*This makes me wonder whether she lost her sense of being attractive consequent to heavy petting with Duke, because she felt that such activities were the stepping stones to sin and eternal damnation.*]

DR. So that was pleasing to you.

CINDY. Yeah. It was fun to watch me. I think I talk like a South Dakota hick.

DR. I thought that she had a Southern accent. I want to find out from you how you would feel if I showed this to Van?
> [*My intent here is to show Van the intensity of her struggle, which antedates the courtship and marriage to him.*]

CINDY. I wouldn't mind.

DR. Any other reactions?

CINDY. No.

DR. How do you feel about being here today?

CINDY. I really feel good. It feels so good to have somebody to talk to. I wanted somebody to talk to.
> [*I'm interested to find out what she got out of this session. Her response confirms her need to have me assist her in sorting out the different pieces of what is confusing her ability to feel comfortable with herself. Her abil-*]

ity to see herself as pretty, after videotape playback,
which she greeted with surprise, suggests that she does
have a chance to become happier with herself.]

DR. You feel you're having a tough time with Van.

CINDY. I just go around the house all day long having conversa-
tions with myself, and I keep thinking, well, "Is it me? Is it
Van? Is it both of us?" I think the same things out loud, and
oh . . . I need somebody to hear what I'm saying. If I'm
crazy, or if I'm put together okay, or . . . my world's not
falling apart . . . I really feel so vulnerable right now for
an affair, I'm so hungry for some affection. And I'm so tired
of giving. I've given to my kids, and now I've got this weak
cryin' husband who I feel is crying for another woman, and I
feel I need somebody to tell me I'm worth something, and
somebody loves me, and somebody . . . somebody's caring
about me right now. My kids are draining me, and my husband's draining me, and I just feel like I'm gonna drop!

> [*The roles keep switching. Now she wants to be the*
> *supercool person who cannot stand Van's falling apart.*
> *She still has difficulty accepting that he may be falling*
> *apart not about Jennifer, but about his best friend's*
> *death last week. She has needs, because of her own*
> *narcissism, to relate everything in Van's behavior to her-*
> *self and what she is and isn't doing. Because of the*
> *imputed sinfulness that had been thrust upon her, she*
> *has to have somebody tell her that she is "worth some-*
> *thing." But whatever praise she can accept can't seem to*
> *neutralize the eternal indictment thrust upon her for her*
> *sexuality. Cindy and Van are both like young kids, and*
> *they are fighting about which one is going to take care*
> *of them. Each is looking for the other to be a parent*
> *who will validate the positive potential residing in each*
> *one.*]

DR. You're sort of exhausted.

CINDY. I am exhausted.

DR. Well, I can't tell you to have an affair, and I can't tell you not
to have an affair. I do think that that's something Van is
trying to push you into, as a means of assuaging his own

guilt. I will see Van what, next week, is it?

CINDY. Yes. Next Tuesday.

DR. Tuesday at 3:00. Should I check back with you when I talk with him about getting the two of you back in here?

CINDY. No, actually work with his schedule, because I'm very flexible; he has the tight one.

DR. Okay. I think that you may well be surprised as to what this is all about; so will Van.

CINDY. I hope. I really hope.

DR. Things are often not the way they seem.

CINDY. Well, I just haven't seen him so down. Even when his parents died; I've never seen him so down. And I have been taking the blame because I thought it was because of me, and I asked him to give up something important to him. But I refuse to feel guilty. But yet I still feel for him, because he's so miserable.

> [*Cindy's feeling of love and duty for Van depend on his being so miserable because, in effect, he now expresses in his behavior the inner misery she has experienced for such a long time. She is presenting her self as an equivocating little girl, where she is stuck because of the indictment of sinfulness. Concurrently, Van could become more easily responsive to her if she could be just purely and simply angry. It seems as if anger can be expressed only when each is drunk. Her distance and manner provide him license to continue doing what he is doing. They need to learn to express anger to each other without feeling that expressing it will totally disorganize them.*]

DR. Yeah, we'll see what it's all about. But it's okay for me to use this videotape?

> [*I reiterate my desire to use the tape. I want to make sure she doesn't forget she has given permission.*]

CINDY. Oh, sure.

DR. Well, at least I'll get some kind of reaction. Okay?

CINDY. Yeah. You're really putting me to the test, to show that movie and then put me on the subway.

> [*She's joking, but it's an interesting remark. She im-*

plies that it'll be my responsibility if she gets in trouble.]

DR. Well, we'll see now what kind of control you've got.

*[I fend this off, indicating that the kind of controls she
should have are dependent upon herself.*]

CINDY. Thank you.

DR. Take care.

CINDY. Good-by.

DR. 'By.

> . . . you've lost touch with the person
> You thought you were . . .
> (Edward: "To what does this lead?")
> To finding out
> What you really are. What you really feel.
> What you really are among other people.
> Most of the time we take ourselves for granted,
> As we have to, and live on a little knowledge
> About ourselves as we were. Who are you now?
> You don't know anymore than I do,
> But rather less. You are nothing but a set
> Of obsolete responses . . .*
>   —UNIDENTIFIED GUEST

* *The Cocktail Party,* by T. S. Eliot, pp. 29–31.

Van's Search

MR. HOOPES enters the office and hands Dr. Paul his blank cassette
    tape.

DR. Did you hear Cindy's?

VAN. No, I didn't.

    [I wonder how much sharing they do.]

DR. Okay. Well, she has an option of letting you hear it, if she
    wanted to. It's not obligatory. This is the third of October,
    1972. Got an agenda?

VAN. No, not really. No. Um . . . I sort of thought I had but I'm
    not sure I do at this point, so . . .

DR. Well, what sort of things did you have in mind?

VAN. I was thinking about what sorts of things I would talk about.

DR. Yeah?

VAN. And ended up reviewing a bunch of stuff that was involved in
    your article. And, the stuff in the, the GAP thing.

DR. Um-hm?

VAN. Uh, so I guess I was thinking about where I was going to
    place myself in adolescence, or where the issues I thought
    might be coming from.

DR. Did Cindy say anything to you about her being here?

    *[I change the subject quite abruptly. I'm not interested
    in getting involved in an extensive, intellectualized com-
    mentary on the material. I ask about Cindy's reaction
    to the last session because, in general, it's much easier
    to review the other person's reaction than one's own.
    Van is unclear as to what he wants to talk about. He
    appears to operate in large substance in reaction to what*

> *the other person has in mind; at least, this is how he reacts to Cindy.*]

VAN. Yeah, she did . . .

DR. What'd she say?

VAN. Basically she said, uh, she talked about the film, first of all . . .

DR. Yeah.

VAN. She said that that was a kind of troublesome thing for her, in that uh, she felt as she watched that it was very arousing to her, and she felt like when she came back, why it would only be more frustrating, in that she didn't feel that I was ready for that, that kind of intimacy at this point.

DR. Yeah?

VAN. Sort of, freedom to respond to her that way. And we talked a lot about that. And the other thing she mentioned was what she said about me, I guess . . . she didn't say exactly what, but she did say, "If you see the pictures of me [she refers to the videotaped segment of Session II], you might be disturbed by that." And I didn't press for what . . .

DR. Uh-huh.

VAN. . . . she was really referring to.

> [*He is able to talk about Cindy quite easily.*]

DR. She gave me permission to show you a videotape of her last time.

VAN. Yeah.

DR. That's what she's referring to.

VAN. Yeah, yeah.

DR. How do you feel about her . . . ? Do you want out, or you want out of the marriage, or what do you want . . . or . . . ?

> [*This is a question that is best asked alone.*]

VAN. I'm in the midst of a terrific muddled mess, which isn't clear to me at all. My head is not together at any point. Most of the time I'm working on a lot of grief work, in that I feel that the relationship with Jennifer is dead, and that uh . . .

DR. What do you mean dead?

VAN. Well, that . . . I'm not sure that that's a possible alternative; I'm not even sure that if my relationship with Cindy doesn't work that I would want to get involved in that rela-

tionship in any kind of committed way; I'm not even sure that
Jennifer would be interested. I haven't talked to her. I think
the way in which she functions is that she sort of is able to
say, uh, "You take care of that stuff and I'll take care of my
stuff and if it ever should happen that things work out, then
. . . then, maybe things will work out." Up to that point I
think she's in the process of kind of trying to readjust her life,
and . . .

> [*It becomes clear that Van has never felt committed to a
> permanent relationship to Jennifer.*
>
> *Van's blandness seems unusual. Because of his
> prior reference to doing "grief work," I begin to think
> about the relevance of unresolved grief in his life, prin-
> cipally grief for his father. Now I begin to develop in my
> mind a strategy for getting involved with his parents,
> particularly his reaction to his father's death. Part of this
> strategy will be to have him hear a tape of a man going
> through an abortive grief reaction. I wonder at what
> time in this session it will be appropriate to do this.*]

DR. When did you break up with her?

VAN. Oh . . . (sighs) . . . I think the chronology involves starting with the week that Cindy and I had up in Maine,
when the information was put on the table. And from that
point on, uh, I think Jennifer was feeling that . . . I think
she sort of expected that the way in which I would respond,
would be to move out. When I didn't do that I think she assumed that I wasn't going to, and then consequently we started
talking about well, what . . . where do we go from there,
what happens?

DR. Um-hm.

VAN. And I think the way, at least the way I think she's dealing
with the things right now is to assume that I've said good-by.
And she communicated the last time we talked that in her
dealing with things and looking at all the possibilities she felt
I had no other alternative.

DR. What do you mean? You could split from Cindy and marry
her? . . . I don't understand that.

VAN. Well, her, her feeling was that when you weigh all the things on the scale which involved the commitments that I have, both to the family and to Cindy . . .

DR. People have done it . . . split, remarried, things like that.

VAN. True.

DR. ▶ ▶ ▶ Neither of your parents were married more than one time.

> [*I abruptly change the subject, because I wish to explore whether by chance Van has been living out the pattern of one or the other parent who may have gotten a divorce and then remarried. I wish to get the attention off of him and onto his original family members.*
>
> *The theme itself has not changed, yet the focus of the theme has switched back one generation.*]

VAN. That's true (uncomfortable, sullen, remote manner).

DR. That you know of . . .

VAN. That's correct. I know absolutely nothing about my father's family.

DR. Is there anybody around that you could sort of . . . ?

VAN. No.

DR. Did he have any brothers or sisters?

VAN. As far as I know he had one sister, who lived in Chicago at some point, but she was married, so she had another name. And he never contacted her, as near as I know. Even my mother didn't know much background about his family. That's all a blank.

DR. Now, what about Dorothy? Does she know anything about this sister?

VAN. No.

DR. Did you ever ask her?

VAN. Yeah. Oh, we've talked about it a lot, Dot and I.

DR. Your father came from where?

VAN. Amsterdam, Holland. Amsterdam.

DR. And are there any people there who know them?

VAN. I don't really know. I've never tried to make any contact. I have a fantasy that when I go on my trip in January, I'll try to look somebody up, and maybe call a bunch of people who have the same name and see what's . . .

> [*He begins to perk up.*]

DR. He came from Amsterdam to where?

VAN. To New York, about 1920, I guess. Right after the First World War.

DR. Okay. So he had to have a passport or a visa to get into this country.

VAN. I don't think so. I think this was before then, but . . .

DR. No, they had to . . .

VAN. (More interested) I think he was on a, on a . . . not a troop ship, he was on a, a . . . working on a ship or something, and I can vaguely remember the story that he left the ship and never went back, or something like this. I don't even know if he . . .

DR. Was he a naturalized citizen?

VAN. You know, I don't even know.

DR. Did he ever vote?

VAN. I'm sure he must have, but I don't remember.

DR. Do you have a death certificate anywhere? Could you get your hands on it? 'Cause that would contain certain pieces of uh . . .

VAN. (Smiles), Gee, that's an interesting thought.

> [*His bland manner changes abruptly in response to the possibility that there might be information available about his father.*]

DR. . . . Vital statistics (finishing his sentence).

VAN. (Continuing) I don't even know where that could possibly be.

DR. Would your sister know?

VAN. I could check it out. But it's a complete dead end. I can remember my mother talking long hours into the night, we talked, uh, after Dad had died, about the fact that she didn't know anything about Dad.

DR. Now, your mother's brother. Where does he live?

VAN. In Arizona, uh, Phoenix.

> [*He looks directly at me for the first time. Begins to be more interested in being here.*]

DR. Did you ever have any contact with him?

VAN. Yes.

DR. Why don't you . . . he might know things about your father. Did you ever ask him?

[*A picture gradually emerges of Van's almost total feeling of discontinuity from his father's generation. Usually in this type of situation I feel hard put to figure out how to engage such a person on an emotional level.*]

VAN. Yeah. He was, uh, he was not around when my mother and father met. I think, uh . . .

DR. Or better still, his wife. Women have a way of getting that kind of information where their husbands don't.

VAN. Um. His wife is from Santa Rosa, Honduras. She doesn't speak very well, doesn't speak English very well, so . . .

DR. Is she Spanish?

VAN. Yes. So she has no contact. I think she only met my mother once. And that was after my father had already died.

DR. Well, there's a story there. The question is where can you find out the people who have information about it.

VAN. Yes. I've always wanted to know. I know . . . I know a little bit about that. I do know that supposedly he was an orphan, that, uh, he was at a very early . . . he was born in 1902, supposedly, so that, uh, when the Germans marched into Holland, he was handed a rifle and told to go out and shoot people, and uh, he ended up being wounded, left for dead; he often tells that story. Somebody heard him moaning, and they picked him up and brought him back from the battlefields. He had a scar on his lip which he said came from that kind of, uh . . .

DR. No other papers of his that anybody has? Does your sister know his sister's name at all in Chicago?

VAN. No. We . . . we talked about that after my mother died, and, uh, there's just nothing. See, that was a complete mess too. Because my mother remarried, married a man who, uh, uh . . . After she died there was a great big huge blowup. So, uh . . .

DR. About what? ◄ ◄ ◄

VAN. Well, just the regular sort of run-of-the-mill thing about the fact that Mother had some things that Dot wanted, Bob felt like that was unacceptable . . .

DR. Bob is alive?

VAN. Yes.

DR. What's his full name?

VAN. Robert Cubell. C.U.B.E.L.L. I'm assuming he's still alive.

DR. How do you get along with him?

VAN. I never knew the man, really. I was, uh, I'd been married for about, uh, four-five years, I guess, before they remarried, and he was a, he was an ass. Uh, to answer your question, we didn't get along very well. I couldn't tolerate him.

DR. Uh-huh . . . Now here's where you can get information: the hospital where your father was hospitalized. They've got records.

VAN. Yeah. That was somewhere in Michigan, it seems to me.

DR. You know where in Michigan?

VAN. I bet I could poke around and find out, maybe.

DR. 'Cause you have a legal right to it.

VAN. Mmmm.

DR. They would have some information which I think would be useful to you. And if you can't get it, I can write for you, if you want me to.

VAN. Okay. It seems to me there were Catholic nuns. So it was a Catholic hospital. See, for one whole summer my mother took my father to this place. I was only a sophomore in high school, I guess, at the time, and Dot and I lived at home for that one whole summer when they were away. And I can remember him telling stories about the Catholic nuns who used to come around. Holy mackerel, what was it? . . . it seems like it was in Michigan, Detroit, Michigan, somewhere. A private hospital. Why they went there I don't know.

DR. From where did they go?

VAN. Mobile. That's where we lived.

DR. To Detroit, Michigan.

VAN. Yeah. Sounds funny. I don't know why. There was some talk at the time a lobotomy, but I know one was not performed, and this was an alternative to that.

> [*I can imagine how frightening it is for an adolescent boy to have a father hospitalized in a mental institution, where there is talk about the father having a lobotomy.*]

DR. Oh, man . . .

VAN. Just a big, big maze of . . .

DR. That's the way your head is about the past. A big . . .

VAN. About him.

DR. Yeah.

VAN. And uh . . . for anything about his growing-up years.

> [*Getting information about Van's father leads to a complete dead end, so I decide to show him the videotape of Cindy from the previous session, feeling that I will get at least some kind of emotional reaction, which will in turn give me some sense of Van's emotional responsiveness.*]

DR. I want you to see this, because Cindy gets involved with things that have been going on. I want to know your version of it.

VAN. Yeah.

DR. Did she say anything else about being here?

VAN. Uh, let's see. Basically those were the two major things that she mentioned.

DR. Did she feel I gave her too hard a time?

> [*I'm always interested in feedback as to whether an individual feels that I've been too direct; feedback is essential to a therapist for continual reassessment of his methods.*]

VAN. She felt like you made some assumptions about her that bothered her, and that I might agree with those assumptions.

DR. Like what?

VAN. She didn't say. She didn't say what that might be. Uh, she has a feeling that, uh . . . Our last conversation today was, early this morning, she had the feeling that I would come, and in talking about the way in which my relationship with Jennifer works and the way in which my relationship with her has always been, it would uh, sort of make me see something I'd been denying for ten years, and that is that she's not the kind of woman that I need. So she had . . .

> [*Van and Cindy's communication seems sparse, and we have a suggestion of some kind of teasing.*
> *Maybe Van isn't the kind of guy that Cindy wants. This is a good example of projection.*]

DR. Who is not the kind of woman . . . ?

VAN. Cindy is not the kind of woman that, that I basically need or want. There's a tremendous amount of insecurity and feelings of uh, fear, about what might happen today, with some added feelings that I would try to get in touch with Jennifer again (sighs). It's a, it's a crazy business, because most of the time, I really think most of the time, I kind of have said, "Well, damn it all, I've got to do this, I've got to square things away between Cindy and I, and really see what's there."

DR. Yeah?

VAN. But we've never had a chance to do it. But there are times when I really grieve terribly for . . .

DR. For what?

> [*I wonder who Van is really grieving for.*]

VAN. For Jennifer. And I look depressed, and I act depressed, and I *am* depressed. Because I miss her; I think about the experience that we had together, uh, I, I try not to make comparisons between Cindy and Jennifer; some of them are inevitable.

DR. In 1955 your father was how old?

> [*I shift attention back to Van's father, focusing specifically on 1955, when his father was hospitalized.*]

VAN. Fifty-three.

DR. Fifty-three.

VAN. I'm guessing at that, but, uh, I think it was somewhere around that.

DR. Okay, I'm gonna have you see this, and I'll be interested in your reactions. Some of this might upset you. I don't know what you're going to be upset about, and what you're going to react to. She said it was okay [to see this] (referring to Cindy's tape).

> [*I am thinking about the relationship between Van's father's hospitalization for a mental disorder, Van's anxiety about sex, and the videotape wherein Cindy describes her own sexual experiences.*]

(Dr. Paul plays videotape of Cindy talking about sex. When she describes their honeymoon night at the motel, Van says, "Oh, shit!" The tape ends.)

> [*Material on videotape is on pages 96–101 and 104–111.*]

VAN. Fantastic. Mmmm.

> [*I have the feeling that he sees Cindy for the first time, and likes her.*]

DR. Fantastic? In what sense?

VAN. As I watched Cindy on the film, my response is, she's a lusty, gutsy woman, and . . . (full of enthusiasm, and some admiration)

DR. Too much for you?

> [*His face becomes animated. He describes very clearly throughout that Cindy's style of expressing her emotions is indeed too much for him. The essence of the monologue Van unfolds is to indicate the various ways in which Cindy is too much for him: her emotional demands on him, coupled with his feeling that she wants him to be a kind of person that it is impossible for him to be, and his sense that she has betrayed him by her encounter with his brother-in-law. Underlying all this is the sense that Van betrays of feeling that if she gets too close to him, he will be sucked up and will disappear. (This is an interesting image, given his aversion to oral sex.)*
>
> *This state of affairs, where a spouse feels he or she has to be the kind of person the other one wants one to be, seems to begin usually at the time of the emotional marriage. This is defined as that point in time when a couple decide together that they're going to get married. At this point there seems to be a reciprocal abdicating of one's sense of self in order to be pleasing to the other. It seems that this false state of oneness, wherein each feels that one is part of the other, helps the couple avoid their anxieties about this human undertaking, their marriage. This state of oneness begins to evaporate shortly after the legal marriage, and there are various comments that couples make to one another or to themselves, at that time, saying in effect that the other person has "changed." What one is usually unaware of is that oneself has changed. This perception often leads to a chronic*

*battle, wherein each tries to get the other to change to
the premarital self, as a means of recapturing what
some people describe as "that delicious state of engagement." This "delicious state," under the best of circumstances, is a delusional state that nature has contrived
in order to get a couple to the point of marriage. There
were always two people, each of whom was a distinct
entity, who, because of the anxieties attendant to the
prospect of marriage, seemed to blend themselves together into a state of oneness. This dilemma is described by Van when he states that it is impossible for
him to be the kind of person Cindy wants him to be,
which suggests that at one time he believed he could be.
It was, of course, impossible all along.*

*Van is typical of an intelligent, alert man whose
exterior of aloofness and distance masks his inner feelings of anxiety and sense of fragility, when confronted
by even minor expressions of pure emotional states.
This anxiety is then translated into a need to distance
the source of the emotionality, namely Cindy. As Cindy
wants more of a sense of acceptance of herself by Van,
he distances her more, galvanizing a state of panic in
her.]*

VAN. ▶ ▶ ▶ A lot of it is, she overdoes things, to the extent that
I want to say, "For God's sake, get it right" . . . or, "You
know." I think that's always been a criticism that I've never
tried to say to Cindy, but which I think she's felt in many
ways and I suppose in many ways I have said it to her. I
used to joke with her about her being a hysteric.

DR. Yeah.

VAN. You know, like her reconstructions of reality were always
overplayed, as though she were playing to a stage. Uh, there
are times when she comes on like gangbusters, and lately I
can't respond to that. It's just virtually impossible for me to
be the kind of person she wants me to be. I can't, uh, there
are times when I don't want to be close to her. There are
times when she doesn't turn me on sexually. It doesn't mean
I don't care about her. But there are times when she comes

on, and I feel . . . we talked about this too, in fact, we talked about everything she said there [on TV], so it wasn't a surprise . . . but there are times when I feel she will . . . (making a sucking noise) . . . and I have to sort of say, "God damn it, now don't do that." Like she clutches at me and I really feel emotionally like I want to say, "Great Scott, hold it there, stop, don't do it!" And that only makes her clutch harder. And we . . . we talked about that and struggled with it. The more I move away the more she grabs. And I, I know I confuse her, and she ends up saying well how do you want me to be, and I can't tell her how I want her to be . . . It was interesting to hear what she had to say about, uh, her mother's response about her feelings about her early sexual experience and all, and her version of the way some of that operated. Like my . . . I don't know the word she used, somehow, but it had to do with my going bananas Saturday night, kind of thing . . . uh . . . In spite of, I have a different perspective because I was looking through my eyes at it. It was interesting to see how she responded to that and what she picked up. Uh, yeah, I was angry; I was angry at Scott. Just as we drove home, Scott and I in the car, we were talking about . . . see, he's separated from my sister. And that there are a lot of feelings I have about that which we were trying to deal with. At the same time I was saying, "Scott, I know what you're going through, 'cause I'm in a similar position." Scott knew about Jennifer. So as we talked about these things, I felt like I was kind of saying, you know, "Here's where I am. I don't have anybody I can talk to about this stuff. I think you're the kind of person that could understand this," so we talked about it.

Then, Cindy was very very upset about the fact that Scott and I were going to be together. So she stayed around until about 12:30, so that I felt, and my perception was, that she stayed so Scott and I couldn't talk, so I said, "Oh, the hell with it." So I went to bed. And a couple of hours later, I woke up and I hear all kinds of things coming from the kitchen. So I felt sold out. And, I sort of said to Scott, "I think you" . . . I didn't mean to say "shit-face," I said "I think you're a shit. And I, I feel sold out, betrayed; here I spill my guts to you and you try to seduce my wife. After you, you, you've *shat* all over my sister, then you come into my house and try to take advantage of a situation that I told you was there." So I was really pissed off at him something incredible. I couldn't deal with the anger, I couldn't talk about it, I left. There wasn't any way that I could . . . I could struggle with it. Just . . . it was a rage. I haven't felt that kind of rage in I don't know when. It was the kind of rage that was absolutely overpowering. Just unbelievable rage. In fact . . . before, I talked about this to Cindy and saying I was going to get back into therapy. And I had a fantasy that, that getting back into therapy, the first thing, what I saw, what I imagined, this was late at night, and we had just gone to bed and I was talking to Cindy about this . . . I said, my fantasy is I'm standing in the window, the therapist is sitting behind the desk, and I'm standing in the window and sort of like this . . . just *screaming* . . . just screaming my guts out! And it was not fear, it was just rage. And I associated that to, to feeling like hell . . . I'm eleven months apart from my sister and I wonder how often I stood in my crib and screamed and nobody came. It was that kind of helpless, God damn it! You know, this just incredible rage. Uh, I've never been in touch with that in my entire life before. And I don't know why now; and maybe the crisis is provoking it. Uh, I got in touch with it again Saturday night, and I . . . I with the help of alcohol . . . my mesomorphy sort of came through, and I felt, uh, the same kind of feeling . . . not directed to Cindy at all, ◄ ◄ ◄ but it was just directed to objects around the room, and I just sort of made a shambles of my office, just . . . the, I don't know if she told you about the fact that I went jogging, but, uh, I also find when I drink too much if I lay down, my head goes around and around, and the only way that goes away is if I exercise. So I just jog, went off and ran around the block for about twenty minutes, which she interpreted as my going bananas, and I'm sure it seemed like that to her.

[*It is obvious from Van's account that Cindy knows or*

recognizes very little of his need to exercise after he's been drinking.]

DR. Well, I think your rage probably scared the shit out of her.

VAN. Oh, yeah, I know. She's never seen me like that . . . I'm always the sort of controlled, uh, intellectual, uh, snob kind of person that uh . . . she has that image of me from the very first time we met. Although, to some extent that's altered, but I think some of it is characterological; it'll be around for a long time.

DR. What I want to know . . . I don't know how long it'll be around . . . but . . . I was thinking of having you, while you were here today, hear a tape. She didn't hear this tape. This is a . . . you say you heard me somewhere? A presentation somewhere?

VAN. Yeah, I heard *of* you.

DR. Oh, you never heard me present.

VAN. No.

DR. Okay. This is a tape of a couple. This is a tape that I do not have a release for you to record on your tape, but you can record up until the time this thing goes on.

> [*I had this tape set up before Van arrived, and planned to use this as a means of testing out whether an abortive grief reaction was in any way related to some of his problems of the moment. His prior reference, in Session I, to "dealing with losses," coupled with my hypothesis that he lacked a viable relationship with his father, led me to consider testing out the hypothesis with this tape, that is designed to immerse the listener with emotions of grief. A listener can then tune in to such emotions, if he has experienced similar feelings in the past. In other words, I want to know what kinds of feelings other than his own "rage" he has just referred to were too much for him. Van has already mentioned that Cindy is "too much" for him and that his parents' emotional outbursts and "falling apart" seemed too much for him also. (See Session I, page 60.)*]

VAN. Okay.

DR. The story is, we have here a couple who have been married about twenty years, and they have four kids. And the guy's involved with another gal named Charlotte. The guy drinks, but to excess; he has some kind of depression-potency problem with his wife, a not uncommon kind of thing. Uh, they have a girl eighteen, a girl seven, and two boys in the middle. And what I like to do is to have the client try to relate premarital experiences to what's going on in the marriage. The guy's on a business trip, and he goes to the other side of the country, he comes back the night before this meeting, he's been away for about ten days, and he calls his lawyer to initiate a legal separation preparatory to a divorce, because he's made a decision: He wants to marry this chick who is half his age. And he comes in and he announces that this is our last meeting, because "I made a decision." So I immediately get involved with his, uh, premarital sexual history, and he talked about his masturbatory practices, and some of his fantasies, and his wife is here and her reaction was to suggest that this is old hat. She then says they discussed this and that about some homosexual episodes in his adolescence and concerns, and that's old hat too. And then we get involved with the fact that his parents were not married when he was born. He persuaded his father to marry his mother when he was about twelve, something which his father never forgave him for.

VAN. Jeez.

DR. The kind of scene we can expect to see maybe in the next twenty years with all these kids coming out of the communes and so forth. Uh, she came from a family where both her parents committed suicide, her mother when she was about sixteen took a self-administered dose of morphine, and five years before this her father blew his brains out. Uh, and they'd been haggling for a long time. So he comes in, and we get into the sex history bit, and then I ask . . . I try to get involved with his, uh, feelings about himself being a bastard. And he remembered very graphically being eight, nine, ten with the other kids in his gang, being very envious of them because he believed that they weren't bastards. And whether they were or not I don't know, I'm not too sure how *he* knew, but he believed this. It was his fantasy of it. And as it shook out after this, one of the things that threw his marriage into limbo was the first son coming on the scene, because it reactivated his feelings of envy. But he split his feelings, he got pissed off at his wife for giving him a son of whom he was envious. And that's one of the things that helped escalate this to the mess that popped in here. Now, I'm gonna have you hear two pieces of this tape. Because he gets involved with himself as he was as a kid. And I want to make a distinction between the feelings that he sort of discovered, so to speak, and the issue that he's talking about, because the feelings are feelings that every kid has somewhere in time. Uh, that's the first piece. The second piece is his wife's reaction to this. What I'm interested in from what you hear, what do you tune into, and what do you distance. Okay?

VAN. Yeah.

DR. And then we can review its relevance to you. This begins on the question that was erased on the transcription of this, the question being "How often did you ask your father to marry your mother?"

(He plays Lewis tape.)

─────────── **Transcript of the Lewis Tape** ───────────

DR. PAUL. How often did you ask your father to marry your mother?

MR. LEWIS. Oh, quite often.

DR. Beginning at what age?

MR. Oh, probably when I was about nine.

DR. And how would he greet you?

MR. He would be very indulgent. He would be . . . we, we, my father and I, when we get along very well, we can have very friendly pleasant relationships. I mean, at times.

DR. Again I draw the parallel between you and your wife; when you get along, you have pleasant relationships. Go ahead.

MR. But, I mean, for example, I'd say, I've usually, in fact, I think this has been one of the reasons I was successful in my own work is that I've always had to persuade, I mean, I was a kid, my parents were older. They were, they were foreigners in this country. They couldn't speak English. I was sort of the educator, the critic, and the persuader.

DR. You were assuming leadership in some ways in the home?

MR. Oh . . .

MRS. LEWIS. Oh, yes.

MR. I led that family from the time I was probably five years old, and uh, in many, many ways, in many ways. I really martialed the family's direction in many ways. And they appreciated it. They were very proud of me for this, I mean they . . . But I would say to my father sometimes when we were alone, I would say, "Pop, you know it would be very nice if you married Mom. After all, she is a woman, and she, she'd feel better if she were married." Incidentally, my mother would sometimes mention this to me.

DR. That she'd like to be married?

MR. Yes. I mean she would mention it. See, I don't know how I ever got the impression that I was illegitimate, because no one ever said it to me. It's a funny thing. Now, speaking of hearing things. No one ever told me that.

DR. Did you ever see any documents?

MR. No. There's a funny thing. It's a funny thing. I just knew. I don't know.

DR. Do you believe in the supernatural?

MR. No. But something must have told me.

DR. The vapor in the air, sort of . . .

MR. No, no, but I think maybe my mother must have said . . . I remember, I know what, I was with my mother and aunt and one of the things I think has influenced me a lot, my Aunt Mary was a most wonderful person. Oh, she was . . .

DR. Her sister?

MR. Yeah, my mother's sister.

DR. Older?

MR. Younger, and we were, we would go on vacation, not vacation but we'd go to visit my Aunt Mary in North Carolina, and I would be in bed with the two women as a boy.

MRS. Yes, you told me that you used to overhear the women talking.

MR. And they were talking. They wouldn't see each other for a year and they talked for all night.

DR. You'd sleep what, on the end or in between . . .

MR. I'd sleep on the end, and they'd be in the other . . .

DR. What age?

MR. Oh, I must have been eight, seven. And they would talk all night about men, and all night they'd be, the sisters, having a real personal and intimate relationship, and . . .

DR. What?

MR. A personal and intimate relationship, discussing men and discussing life with men and the problems of men and every so often, I'd just get, just wake up and hear . . . men are so and so, men are so and so.

DR. Did that make you feel sort of positive about growing up to be a man?

MR. Make me feel positive? Well, I don't know about that.

DR. What do you think?

MR. I don't know. My mother would always criticize my father. You know, she'd, she'd always be very critical at some times. Then she'd be nice at other times. My Aunt Mary was wonderful, though. There was a remarkable woman. She died when she was a young woman. She was a remarkable person.

DR. When did she die?

MR. She was thirty-five.

DR. And you were how old?

MR. I was about, oh, ten or eleven. She was a remarkable, nice person.

DR. And how did you feel when she died?

MR. Oh, I feel sadder about my Aunt Mary's death than anybody.

DR. How sad?

MR. Miserable, miserable.

DR. How miserable?

MR. Terrible.

DR. What do you remember? Huh?

MR. (Weeping) I feel terrible.

DR. Do you feel that you still miss her?

MR. Oh, yes, I do. She was so nice (weeping). She was so nice.

MRS. She had, she did all the things, you know, for him, you know, when he was a little boy that little kids need that he didn't get at home. You know, she had animals around the house and things, you know, his parents never understood things like that.

MR. She's really the woman I've been looking for, really. She was so nice. She was a beautiful woman. She was so kind.

DR. She was single?

MR. No, she was married. She had a family. She had her children, and, uh, but she was always understanding.

DR. Do you ever see her family?

MR. No. Never had any really close relationship with her family.

DR. Since she died?

MR. Since she died. She was a remarkable, kind person.

DR. Do you know where she's buried?

MR. Yes, Charlotte, North Carolina. I've never been to her grave.

DR. Never?

MR. No. You see, I don't know why I've never been to her grave, but I haven't been to anybody's grave. She's the only person I ever, the only close person that's ever died in our family, you know.

DR. Do you feel that, uh, she's the only one that you really loved that way?

(Mr. Lewis weeping, then silence.)

MR. I've always loved her. She was very kind to me.

DR. She loved you?

MR. Yes, she did (sobbing). I don't know what I'm crying about.

DR. You know what you're crying about.

MR. I don't know.

DR. You don't? You still miss her.

MR. She was so nice. It wasn't anything she did, especially, it was just . . . she was always so nice (sobbing). She always, she was always so sweet and so kind, and there was never a mean or a bad word (sobbing loudly) coming from her lips. She always liked me. There was never anything phony, she was always accepting me as I am. Being with her was like peace, just peace, just absolute peace.

DR. So, in many ways you have been looking for her over the years.

MR. Yeah. I think I've found her. I think I have.

(Later)

DR. (To Mrs. Lewis) What do you think? How do you feel?

MRS. Well, I feel very sorrowful about the rough times he has had, and I understand a lot of things that I've never been able to understand as long as we've been married, things I have struggled with over and over and kept thinking if I could just do better, his attitude was going to be different.

DR. You see, if you could have been his aunt . . .

MRS. Yeah, this is what I realize, this is what I was struggling against all that time, and I didn't even know what I was struggling against.

MR. It's just like a murder mystery. Who's to know it's your aunt? You know, if you listed all the causes?

MRS. In other words . . .

MR. For years . . .

MRS. I always felt, in order to accomplish anything in this situation, I had to do more than anybody else. I had to be saintly. I didn't, you know, insofar as I was in any way personally able to be. But I never was able to really feel free to be, you know, to be well, relaxed or natural. I always had this feeling, I would try, and I would try, and I would try, and it would not result in what I would think it would.

DR. What it sounds like is, this is just one aspect, but it seems that in some ways he wanted you to be his aunt.

MRS. Yes, of course.

DR. And he was furious at you that you weren't.

MRS. Yes, and I never could understand why he got furious at me. I never could understand this. It's puzzled me as long as we've been married. Why you would get so furious at me, when I was trying so hard, and when I really cared so much.

MR. You really think, I mean, are you sure you're . . .

DR. Go to the cemetery in Charlottesville, and you'll find out.

MR. Charlotte.

DR. . . . ville.

MRS. It's just Charlotte [where aunt is buried].

DR. Oh, it's Charlotte [name of other woman], too?

MR. Sure, what else? You guys are so delighted when you find some sort of little nugget. You know, what the hell? Uh . . .

DR. How do you feel toward me now?

MR. Bemused.

DR. Huh? What else? Annoyed?

MR. Oh, no, no.

DR. No?

MR. I have felt annoyed toward you at the last one. I don't feel annoyed. I feel, you know, I think, I think you're a very good man. I think you know your business and you really are good at what you do. I think you're tops, but I have a certain skepticism about these little nuggets.

DR. Oh, yeah.

MR. Although I will say, I will say that, looking back, she has three names I could have called her. No one else ever called her Charlotte.

DR. Oh, really?

MR. Yes. So why do I call her Charlotte?

DR. So you accuse me of those nuggets that you're . . .

MR. Nuggetism.

DR. Nuggetism. But you sort of picked out the one of three nuggets yourself.

MR. So, I mean maybe there's something to it. But there's all a good reason.

DR. There's always good reason.

MR. See, for example, I didn't call her by her first name because she didn't like that. I didn't call her by Teddy because that's the aggressive, dynamic part of her. So I called her by Charlotte which is the name that stood for me for, I guess, my aunt.

MRS. Oh, there's an aggressive, dynamic part of her?

DR. If you want to find out what your aunt still means to you, you go to the cemetery in Charlotte yourself, and you'll find out for yourself.

MR. I'll probably crack up.

DR. You won't crack up. You'll just sort of catch up with yourself.

MR. Okay. I'll do that. I've never gone to cemeteries or anybody's grave. She's the only one that really matters. You know, Doc, you're a pretty good unraveler. That's funny. You know, it's a funny thing because until today I never even mentioned what this girl's name was . . . to my wife or anybody else, so maybe that has something to do with it, too. I don't know. People get so messed up. I feel peaceful now, relieved, like having been through constipation or something.

DR. What? Through what?

MR. Through constipation.

DR. Our time is just about up now.

MR. Okay.

DR. Do you want to come back?

MR. Not really.

DR. I can appreciate that. Would you come back?

MR. Yeah.

DR. I think you've got to do a lot of hard thinking about what happened in the past.

MR. I have been.

DR. No, about your aunt. She's with you. And all you have to do is go down to Charlotte, and you'll find out. I'm not saying you should, but if you want to test this out for yourself where it counts for you.

MR. How did people survive before you guys discovered these little gems?

DR. Oh, they didn't survive. They just kept on fighting.

MR. Well, what happens when you're at complete rest?

DR. You're never really at complete rest.

MR. In other words, you're going to make me so peaceful that I'm no longer sick enough to try for, you know . . .

DR. You never get really complete rest. You're just sort of aware of, that someone that you loved is not here anymore. You still miss them. At least you can put it in some perspective.

MR. That's the funniest thing, the names. Do you mean that because this girl's name was Charlotte was why this happened, because it's never happened before to me on a trip. She has the same color eyes. She has the same color hair.

DR. The next thing you'll say is she's your aunt. I mean the way you're sort of tallying this up.

MR. I'm trying, you know, trying to help you.

DR. Help me? Help you. We're not here to help me. Do you want to come back?

MRS. Yes, I do.

MR. Why does she have to come back? I'm the guy who's . . .

MRS. (Sobbing) No, because this is helping me so much to understand things that have puzzled me for so long, and I never could cope with, and I didn't know what to do about. That's good enough for me.

DR. Maybe get a chance to know your husband a little bit better.

MRS. You said it.

DR. And get to know himself, too.

MRS. You said it. I agree with you one hundred per cent, 'cause if anybody told me this is what would happen today, I would never have believed it in a million years.

MR. Well, these things are completely unrehearsed.

MRS. I want to understand them.

MR. I'm so confused I don't know what day it is.

DR. Monday.

VAN. (Subdued) It's a powerful experience. I'm trying to keep in mind all the things I want to comment on.

DR. There's a lot of stuff there.

VAN. Yup. The first thing I felt like saying was, Norman Paul, you bastard . . .

> [*Van's anger seems related to his anticipation of my "zeroing in" on him.*]

DR. Why?

VAN. (Tearful) Zeroing in like that. And then the other part of me says, Oh, hell. I think I resonate to the man's grief and sadness and found myself crying.

DR. About what?

VAN. I couldn't . . . I tried to figure out what. I was thinking of all the people in my life where that . . . what am I grieving about? And damn it, as far back as I can remember I've been grieving. And I can't think of any person. Uh, Friday night we had friends up, and we went out for dinner, and I had a sort of ah-hah experience then.

DR. Yeah?

VAN. I don't know how we got talking about it, but . . . I remember when I was about ten, I think it was even preadolescent, or early adolescence, I can remember being in
love with Mrs. . . . I was saying this at the dinner table, in
a sort of a . . . I had felt these things before, but they
jelled. But I can remember being in love with Jennifer Jones,
and this talk about the names I think was triggering this. By
the way, I also want to mention that I very much felt for his
wife, who said, for so long I've been trying to live up to
ghosts, and not being able to know why I was not succeeding.
   [*Van makes a connection between grief and being in
   love.*]

DR. ▶ ▶ ▶ Who is Cindy in your life?

VAN. I don't know . . . but let me go back to this other thing.
Uh, I can remember one of my first crushes, fantasy-crushes,
as a very young kid, preadolescent, I'm sure, was, I was, I
was thoroughly over, head over heels in love with Jennifer
Jones. I had, had her picture on my wall, I can see it today!
I used to masturbate thinking about Jennifer Jones; who in
the hell do I have an affair with . . . ? Somebody named
Jennifer! And, I also, also was in love with . . . uh, I had all
kind of fantasy romances and always a sort of unrequited
love, never to be gotten, never to be possessed, always uh,
uh . . . one of the movies I remember had Debra Paget
in it, who is much more a look-alike for Cindy, except she
had blue eyes. Debra Paget was in this movie, *Bird of
Paradise,* and I can remember crying my eyes out when I
saw that movie when Debra Paget jumped into the volcano.
It's incredible . . . !

DR. What?

VAN. (Silence; crying quietly) . . . Shit!

DR. Shit what?

VAN. I still get in touch with some of that sadness too, when I
think about it. I . . . I . . . (his voice breaking) . . .
you name it, in the movies, I identified with the loser. I identified with the guy who never got the gal, who sailed away
and sort of lived the rest of his life . . .

DR. What?

VAN. (Bitterly) . . . Bemoaning his fate.

DR. But who are you looking for?

VAN: I don't know! I swear to God, I thought and thought as he was talking, Who the hell? Who is it? Is it mother? Is it my mother? Is it my grandmother?

DR. (Interjects) No.

VAN. Is it the woman I never knew but always wish I had?

DR. (Quietly) It's your father.

> [*Van made it very clear in the first session that he never had very much of a father. (See page 71.)*]

VAN. Jesus Christ.

DR. That's what you missed as a kid.

VAN. Well, that's true (tearfully). As much as he tried, he could never be there (tearful).

> [*He corroborates that the person he has been seeking to replace is his father.*]

DR. But he wasn't there. (Pause) You know that in your heart, don't you?

VAN. I don't think he knew how (tearful).

DR. Can you ever forgive him?

VAN. I tried to understand him.

DR. You didn't answer my question. Did you ever forgive him?

VAN. (Tearful) I guess not.

DR. Where's he buried?

VAN. He's in Mobile (crying).

DR. (Tearing) When was the last time you were at his grave?

VAN. The day he was buried. [March 7, 1959.]

DR. You haven't been there since?

VAN. I haven't been there since and I haven't been to my mother's grave either. It was a long time ago.

DR. In your heart it's almost like yesterday.

VAN. You know, I thought about the fact too that he left me . . . you know, he fell apart in my life when I needed him to be strong. When I was a young kid trying to cope with the problems of adolescence, I had to be strong for him.

DR. You had to be his parent?

VAN. Yep.

DR. His dad?

VAN. Yep.

DR. You're named after him, aren't you?

VAN. Yep.

DR. It's sort of loaded, isn't it?

VAN. (Crying) Yep.

DR. What?

VAN. Oh, it just puts me back in touch with all those feelings, and . . . of watching him collapse slowly before my eyes, and not understanding. Watching him walk around with rubber bands. (Crying)

> [*Agitated people occasionally wear rubber bands on their hands which they will twist nervously and continuously.*]

DR. Did he scare the shit out of you?

VAN. Twisting them . . . Yes.

DR. Do you remember the fear? What's going on?

VAN. I remember his rage, and I can remember the arguments that he and Mom would have; I remember his "paranoid thinking"; he accused my mother of hanging the clothes on the line a certain way because she was signaling the neighbor next door, and all this kind of crap. (Bitterly angry) Ah, hell, there's a lot of stuff in there.

DR. It sounds as if Cindy's a stand-in for him? She's sort of concerned about who's being signaled to you?

VAN. (Surprised, smiling) Well, son of a bitch.

> [*Van's response makes it possible for me to use a split-screen videotape that I had just prepared.* (*See page 144.*)]

DR. Huh, isn't that so?

VAN. They were both dark-haired and black-eyed. My mother was blonde and blue-eyed. And Jennifer is blonde and blue-eyed (sighs).

DR. Did you ever love him as a little kid?

VAN. My father?

DR. Yeah.

VAN. Yeah, I remember him coming home from work and running to greet him.

DR. Remember how good it felt?

VAN. Yeah. Felt damn good.

DR. It's a long time, isn't it? A long time to keep all this stuff hidden from yourself.

VAN. I kind of spent two years working on it.

DR. Did you get into this at all?

VAN. Yeah . . . but a lot of it is still there.

DR. Did you get that deeply in terms of the feelings then?

VAN. I think only on occasion. I never stayed with it. ◄ ◄ ◄

(Dr. Paul turns on video equipment.)

DR. What? Too heavy?

VAN. No, just, just . . . so much . . . so much that I associate
to, so much to sort out, that it, uh, all kind of things going on.

DR. I'll tell you what I did, it's gonna seem maybe a little spooky
to you. I did a split screen of you and Cindy. So whatever you
think is sort of a little weird there [superimposed heads] is
really true. Okay?

> [*What I did was to superimpose Van's head over
> Cindy's, in order to provide a visual image that would
> validate what appeared to be essentially the problem
> (see page 143) that each has, in a sense, the other's
> head inside his own head, as almost a foreign body
> against which one has to react adversely.*]

VAN. Okay.

DR. See, part of the problem is being a professional. Being a professional means on the one hand, you can intellectualize a lot
of this stuff.

VAN. Yeah. I know. I try not to. Jesus, it's hard.

DR. That's right. And then on the other hand, you can bullshit
yourself beautifully.

VAN. Plus the fact that I'm a pastoral counselor, which means I'm
the world's greatest at that. (Bitterly) I think that's a problem clergymen have more than anyone else.

DR. Well, they have their brand. Lawyers have their brand. How
do you feel being in here today?

VAN. It's good to be here. I know this stuff is there, and I struggled with it so damn long, that I . . . it was debatable
whether to get into couple therapy or individual, and I kept

saying to Cindy, I got so much shit I gotta sort out in my own head that I want individual. But I think it was good that we both came. I still am very desirous of maybe, analysis; I don't know what, but, uh, really sitting with this stuff and working on it because it's been there too damn long.

DR. Well, you see, I don't think analysis works.

VAN. Well, I'm not sure it does either. It might make you a better intellectualizer.

DR. Yeah, but it makes you then more isolated to yourself, in your guts. It makes you more comfortable in an isolated position, that's what it does.

VAN. I can see that.

DR. I think what is really needed if you want to have a viable kind of marriage—not just a marriage—is to be able to feel you are kin to others who have similar kinds of things in their guts.

Analysis treats an individual as if his feeling system is unique to him, without really getting involved with the sharing of experiences. If you want to pursue this, I think I can help you work out a strategy to make contact with those people who would fill you in, in terms of what's been going on . . . as an example, a lot that you have experienced, let's say grief, you call it grief from a little kid on, I would postulate is your father's grief about his own parents. Question mark.

VAN. Oh, Jesus, he used to hold me on his lap, and sing a song—Sonny Boy—to me. Or, no, what was it? Yeh, Sonny Boy. And he used to sing a very morbid song about being a lonely child. He sang it in Dutch. And my mother used to hate it. But I can remember the tender times when he was with me, he was depressed. The tender times he held me on his lap, and he was depressed . . .

DR. Thinking of back home?

VAN. And he was thinking of his own childhood, I'm sure.

DR. Yeh. I told you about Eliot's play, didn't I? T. S. Eliot's play?

VAN. I don't think so.

DR. Well, you ought to read it. *The Family Reunion.*

VAN. Okay.

DR. And you will find a piece of Harry in yourself. Harry is the leading character. It's very beautiful. A lyrical depiction of what I like to think of what I'm trying to be about.

VAN. I'm not sure I got that.

DR. It is a dramatic representation of what I think of this operation.

VAN. Okay.

(Playback of videotape segment from Session I of Van regarding his father's background. During this Dr. Paul says, "You look like you're being interrogated by the FBI. Look.")

        [Material on videotape is on pages 70–74.]

(Next segment of tape is from Session III, Van talking about Cindy (beginning "For God's sake, get it right . . .", followed by Van's reactions to the Lewis tape, Debra Paget, et al.)

        [Material on videotape is on pages 128–130 and 141– 144.]

DR. What'd you think of that? What'd you think of this guy? What? You shake your head.

VAN. Yeah. A whole bag of stuff.

DR. Huh?

VAN. A whole bag of stuff. I don't, I don't even know where to begin. I think . . .

DR. Do you like him?

VAN. Part of me feels sorry for him. Part of me says, you bastard . . .

DR. That isn't feeling sorry for him.

VAN. (With contempt) Bemoaning your fate.

DR. That's telling him to pull himself together.

VAN. Yeh.

DR. Cut the shit!

VAN. Yeah. Like, uh, look what you've got, instead of look what you haven't got.

DR. Yeah.

VAN. I can't put together Cindy and my Dad yet.

DR. Well, we'll work on it.

VAN. And how those . . . that fits.

DR. I'll tell you how it fits. We're gonna have to wind up in just a minute, but I'll tell you how it fits. It's very interesting. One

of the things I got involved with about a couple of years back
is the relationship between the hidden homosexual fantasy
and mate selection.

VAN. Hmm.

DR. This is what we're talking about. And, I've been testing this
out for about four years, and it fits right in there.

VAN. Mmm. Let me try and hear it. The homosexual fantasy?

DR. The homosexual fantasy of the kid vis-à-vis the old man,
which becomes intensified where there is no relationship to
speak of.

VAN. Hmm.

DR. I'll tell you how I got involved with this; it's an interesting
saga. About four years ago I was seeing a couple and the gal
was very much wrapped up with her daughter. Not in a
homosexual thing, but in a very curious way. And the kid was
running around with hoodlike guys.

VAN. What kind of eyes?

DR. Hoodlike *guys.*

VAN. Oh, hoodlike guys. (Laughs)

DR. Right. And the daughter in question was Sally, and she was
sixteen. And what happened was that one day Sally came in,
she had wrenched her elbow playing tennis, and she said to
her mother, because she couldn't internally rotate her arm,
she asked her mother to snap her bra. And the mother got
enraged at her. And the mother and father were here one day,
and mother said, "I can't stand this kid!" And I said, "Why
can't you stand this kid?" "Because she's got bigger breasts."
"Bigger than yours?" "No." She just locked right on to that.
And, uh, I couldn't make any sense out of this. So she just
couldn't stand this kid; it was just a rotten kid. So I remember shortly after that, I went down to Florida to a psychiatric convention, and I was trying to figure out what
this bigger breast business was about. So I got a hold of
Portnoy's Complaint, and I read in a way that if something's
bugging me, I sort of project it into the material and try and
get some resolution. And *Portnoy's Complaint* basically is a
story about a guy and his mother and how they have a co-
conspiracy to avoid a love-making fantasy. And the thing that

garnered the public's interest is how he acts out the fantasy.
And in an oversimplified way, the way people generally
handle this fantasy, is they'll either fight, mother and son, or
the kid becomes an extension of the mother. In which event
there's no need to fight, because it's like almost a physical
extension of a body, one is part of a body.

VAN. Mmmmmm.

DR. It's a fusion kind of thing, which is what you sensed from
Cindy. You said she (repeats sucking noise Van used earlier) . . . does this kind of thing. Well. So I'm reading the
book, and I was thinking about the bigger breasts, and uhm,
about Portnoy's sister, who's a minor character in the book,
and I thought well, if there is a heterosexual fantasy system
between the mother and Alexander Portnoy, what the hell's
going on between the mother and the daughter?

VAN. Mmm.

DR. And I then postulated it must be a homosexual fantasy system
between the mother and the daughter, handled in a similar
manner as the heterosexual fantasy. So I came back, and I
tried to figure out how do you test this out? Because if you
can't make anything operational, to me it's just worthless. I
mean, it has academic interest, uh . . . so what I did was I
got some of these pornographic homosexual flicks. And I
showed one to Sally's parents the day they came in. I told
them I'd been thinking about this problem that you've got
with Sally, referring to the mother, and I said, "I want you to
see this flick, and I want to make it very clear that in no way,
shape, or form in this to be construed as evidence that you're
homosexual, or have lesbian tendencies, or are a lesbian or
to do anything like this. All I want to find out is what you
feel and what do you think seeing this. Period." So I leave
the room, and later when I came back in, I'm greeted by a
tremendous outpour of venom from the mother. "Why are
you showing me these dirty filthy pictures? Blah blah blah
blah." And she found that the movie was repulsive. The word
she used to describe Sally's breasts. And then, after she
cooled down, she then described when she was about twelve
years old . . . this goes back thirty years . . . she and a

first cousin girl had a mutual fondling episode which turned her on greatly, but rendered her so shameridden afterward that every time she saw this gal in an unpredictable setting, I mean apart from, uh, Christmas or Easter Sunday dinner, you know, when she'd see her, and catch her in her line of vision, she'd dart down an alley, or she'd dart down a side street or into a store. The thing that was fascinating about it, and this was a mild, uh, it was a female homosexual foreplay, that's all.

VAN. Um.

DR. The thing that was fascinating about her recollection was that she had forgotten the event that triggered this behavior some thirty years before. The behavior had had its own automatic quality. And she had only been reminded of it when she saw this flick.

And then she remembered how about sixteen years before, uh, when she and her husband had attempted oral intercourse, it was like a bolt of an experience coming out of her temporal lobe. She remembered that in the dark as his head was moving down toward her genitalia, it occurred to her that his head could be a woman's head. She froze, and that was the end of that. We batted around a couple of other things and a couple of weeks later they came back, the husband in advance of his wife. He commented that he didn't know what the hell was going on at home, but Sally had come to him a couple of nights before, and was a little scared because, as she put it, for the first time in her life she felt her mother really loved her, and she was afraid to tell her mother this. Now, to my knowledge she had no idea, no knowledge about what was going on, but the negative vibes in the mother to the kid apparently turned off . . . some of them, I don't know what was going on. Nonverbal stuff is hard to assess. Uh, and from that point on . . . this was about four years ago . . . I've been testing this out, and in going through literature it seemed to me that there were many references to male, father-son homosexual fantasies and few references to the female. And then I thought, Well, obviously, the male thing has been worked out and the female thing hadn't been worked out. The female thing was all written by females, and there are not many gals who are in the field. Testing this out, to me, is the most important thing; I have found out that the problem is equal in the male as in the female. The less of a positive relationship a guy has with his father, the more prone he is to be afraid of a homosexual fantasy.

VAN. Hmm.

DR. The same with the mother and daughter. In brief, that's what it's about. And so what you don't have growing up to help shore up your gender identification, you're gonna try to get the spouse to do it for you as a replacement. And this is where the homosexual fantasy, as far as I'm concerned, has a lot to do with mate selection, screw-ups in sexual behavior, and a variety of different things.

VAN. Hmm.

DR. So this is a little brief account of it.

VAN. I'm trying to apply it to me, and run it through my systems.

DR. We're going to have to wind up . . . How do you feel being here now?

VAN. It's gonna be good to sort of sit back and sort out some of this stuff I have. It's been good.

DR. Now, do you want to come back by yourself, or do you want to come back with Cindy? I'll leave it up to you . . . next time.

VAN. I'd like to pursue some of this, but I don't want to rule out dealing with Cindy.

DR. Well, I don't see this as being mutually exclusive. I see this as sort of a pacing of both. I'm thinking what I would have in mind is to have the two of you in together; and let her see this, and see if you have a different reaction by her presence in here. This business about your father and her might be better clarified by her being here.

VAN. Yeh.

DR. That's what I would think.

VAN. I think part of what you're saying is I picked sort of a strong phallic woman.

DR. Right. To make up for the absence of a father.

VAN. But then I . . . then I . . .

DR. Rebelled against it.

VAN. Yeh. I have rebelled against it only in the last five years. It seems to me I began to change, and before I was very dependent on Cindy, and following my first two years of therapy, I kind of came out of the shell, more of the shell anyway, and uh, began to respond differently to her.

DR. And I would . . .

VAN. Which sent her into a panic.

DR. Well, I would say that, uh, what triggered it off . . . just as a hunch . . . was your becoming a father, and the panic that you had in moving into a slot . . . role . . . which you weren't prepared for by not having your own father.

VAN. Um-hm. It certainly was around the time . . .

DR. How about two weeks from today at, let's see, maybe let's see, two weeks from tomorrow. Is a morning better than an afternoon for you?

VAN. Oh, Wednesdays are impossible.

DR. Okay.

VAN. This is really the only slot that's available in the whole week, and I have to cancel . . .

DR. Okay, Tuesday at 3:00?

VAN. Yeh. Two weeks . . .

DR. From today, at 3:00.

VAN. Okay. And, uh, both of us?

DR. Yeah. I think it would be good. See, the thing that happens in analysis is that there's a tendency to splinter the couple apart, and the inference is, well, the other guy isn't really right for you. Well, no one's really right for one when one gets married. It's a matter of sorting out what happened in the past, in your original family scene. It gets displaced and projected onto the other person.

VAN. Yeah. That's the kind of stuff I want to pursue. And there's all the stuff in my relationship with Jennifer which has worked differently too . . .

DR. Because she didn't have your children.

> [*This is a clue to why affairs work out differently than marriages.*]

VAN. I gotta think about that.

DR. Okay.

We have everything—everything it takes to make people happy. . . .
We could become the great shining example of the world; we could
radiate peace, joy, power, benevolence. But there are ghosts all about,
ghosts whom we can't seem to lay hands on.*

* *The Air-Conditioned Nightmare,* by Henry Miller (New York: New Di-
rections Publishing Corp., 1945), p. 39.

Showdown

Men live by forgetting—
women live on memories.*
—Mrs. Carghill

DR. PAUL. Got a tape?

CINDY. Uh-huh.

VAN. I have to leave right at four.

DR. Okay. You'll get out of here right at four.

CINDY. (Inaudible)

DR. Did you exchange tapes at all?

VAN. No. We didn't.

> [*I wonder why they didn't exchange tapes. I am thinking that I will have to confront them with their resistance to the whole operation, even to the point of suggesting that we consider this to be the last session.*]

DR. Okay. This is the seventeenth of October, 1972. Now what's been going on with you two?

VAN. Lot of talking, lot of, uh, struggling witih understanding where our heads are and what's going on. And more of a settling down into a kind of routine, I think.

> [*In contrast to prior interviews, Van is taking the initiative.*]

CINDY. Yeah.

VAN. More than anything else. In the fact that things were so hassling and hassled for such a long time, at least for . . . at

---

* *The Elder Statesman,* by T. S. Eliot, p. 66.

least a month. We were up to every hour of the morning, but we kind of settled down more to stable . . . home and family interaction. That's been helpful. Getting a little more sleep, anyway.

DR. Um-hm. Did you tell Cindy anything at all about our last meeting?

VAN. Um-hm. But not too much of it. We talked about, uh . . .

> [*Van seems to be reluctant to share what of substance transpired in the last session. Such sharing would have affirmed its reality for him. It would also help explain his behavior to Cindy. He is still running from his guilt-laden past.*]

CINDY. You never can remember.

VAN. No, I can't.

CINDY. To me that's what you say. (Laughs and then clears throat)

VAN. That's how it is. I'm always amazed at Cindy's uh, ability to be a videotape, an audiotape recorder. And I guess I fit into that category of many men who sit in my office and say, "Did I say that?" or "I don't remember that." I find the same thing happens to me. I don't . . .

> [*Van is playing dumb like a Watergate plumber; he remembers nothing.*]

DR. Did you listen to your tape?

VAN. No.

DR. You didn't.

VAN. No.

DR. Well, how come you didn't?

VAN. I don't know; too busy, I guess. I feel that's a bad excuse. I didn't really think about it.

DR. That's a good excuse; it's worthless.

CINDY. (Chuckles)

VAN. Yeah. I thought about what had, what had gone on; I discussed that part with Cindy about my father.

DR. Yeah?

VAN. And the depression associated with that. But I didn't play the tape.

DR. Well, what is your joint sense as to coming here and what you

want to do and what you don't want to do? I just want to
get a rundown from you two people.

> [*They have given me clues of their resistance to ex-
> changing tapes as well as listening to the tapes, which
> constituted their homework. This brings me naturally
> to the issue of whether they want to continue here.*]

VAN. Well, we were talking about that on the way in. Uh, and we
have very different feelings about it. I think I was saying that
there are some . . . I don't have extremely strong feelings
about this, but I have some feelings that there are some issues
and problems that I want to deal with that involve my past
history and my family of origin . . .

DR. Yeah.

VAN. . . . That I wasn't able to get to earlier, and that I feel I'd
like to get to at this point. Um, and I guess I picture that as
doing it by myself. Cindy feels differently.

CINDY. I feel it's just another step, like in our whole marriage,
where he has gone his separate way.

DR. Uh-huh.

CINDY. And not really coming into me and our marriage, but going
his own way and just, you know, doing his own thing. And at
this point in my life I'm really feeling he needs to turn toward me and work with me. He's still saying "I'm going to do
my own thing my own way." That's what I hear in his wanting
his own therapy instead of marriage therapy.

DR. Well, are you trying to say in effect you want to wind this up
today, or . . .

VAN. Well, I think that decision uh, may have to be reached just
in terms of financial problems. We're ah . . . with going to
Cardiff in January, I think the fee is prohibitive. Both of us
feel like we'd like to continue, but we may have to make a
decision on that basis. And that's, that's where it is. I kind of
feel that uh, I don't like to make the decision on that basis,
but I think that's the way we'll have to do it.

> [*It seems that Van is taking the initiative principally to
> figure out how to abort the treatment process. One
> factor that may be related to this is Cindy's reference
> [above] to her almost acquisitive desire to have Van*]

become an appendage of hers. This could be one of the reasons that he is reacting so strongly. The fee issue generally is a distraction from the work involved in trying to sort out the various factors involved in marital incompatibility.]

DR. So this'll really be our last meeting. That's what you're saying in effect.

VAN. I had the feeling that's . . . well, what we decided was we'd make that one of the topics for the agenda today, in discussing where we wanted to go and how we wanted to do that. I've thought of other possibilities of uh, I don't know if you do any stuff with groups, I didn't think so but, uh, what about the possibility of working together in a group while doing something individually, or postponing doing something individually until after Cardiff, because if I got started I really wouldn't be able to do much in two months, November and December.

DR. Well, I . . . uh, let me be, uh, let me tell you how I read this whole thing. Uh, see, there's a difference between what people say and what they think and what they feel and what they do. Usually it's desirable to have some kind of harmony between all these items, so there's some kind of consistency. But it's in the nature of the human being that, uh, especially those who I guess have gone to school beyond high school, that they become good word merchants. Uh, now. See, I'm not too sure if you were to go and do things on your own, your own thing, with an individual therapist, for let's say seven or eight years, that you'd get anywhere.

VAN. Yeah. Well, I wasn't thinking of that long.

DR. Well, sort of thinking of that long, let's say, let's figure that you really wanted to go and give it a real hard shake.

VAN. Hmm.

DR. I don't think you'd get anywhere. And, there's some question as to whether you'd get anywhere here.

VAN. Hmm.

DR. And I'll tell you why. Uh, see, I don't know the notions you have in your head about what you're going to accomplish in some individual setting other than maybe become a more comfortable isolate. But, you see, the tapes, as far as I'm concerned, are very important. And if you're too busy to go and review the tape; it's your tape, it ain't mine. Then it really calls into question the whole validity of the operation. The tape is a means of, sort of, uh, broadening upon your re-flecting capability as to what's gone on. Well, there are a lot of things involved in it.

VAN. I understand you.

DR. I don't know. What do you think, Cindy, about all of this?

CINDY. I'm just really tired of standing back and when he's saying "I still want to do something by myself," I'm really tired of allowing it.

> [*Cindy sounds like a possessive mother.*]

DR. Yeah? Well, it isn't, see, in the first place, it isn't a matter of he doing it with you, it's a matter of he doing it with himself with you. That's a different emphasis. Because the way you put it . . . he's doing it with you . . . I can see from his point of view that you're gonna own him. Do you under-stand the distinction?

CINDY. Yes, I do. Yes.

VAN. This is what I said to Cindy earlier, when we were driving in, was that my feelings about that, my resistance to what I think grows out of some counterdependency, and it grows out of some unwillingness to be, I think perhaps, maybe, to be open about some things, with Cindy here. Or whether or not I could get to some things with her, uh . . .

> [*Van distances both Cindy and myself by becoming a word merchant.*]

DR. Well, let's take that as an example. Would you be adverse to having Cindy see the videotape of last time?

> [*Van is getting too wordy, and I decide to refresh his memory of what he seems inclined to forget.*]

VAN. No. That's fine.

DR. I think it's an interesting document, and it's interesting that a lot was revealed, and came out, which was important.

VAN. Umm.

DR. And it's interesting to me: (1) you [Van] didn't hear it; (2) that in some ways there's a certain suggestion of your wish to distance it, by getting into something more intellectual, maybe. I'm just telling you my reaction to you.

VAN. Okay, I'm trying to hear that.

[*Van seems to be struggling to control everything.*]

DR. You say that you're interested in getting involved with feelings, as long as they're under control. As long as they're programmed.

VAN. Um. That certainly is my theme, my life's theme, my uh . . .

[*Van suggests a sense that his life has been predetermined and is basically unchangeable.*]

CINDY. Uh-huh.

VAN. That's my script.

DR. Yeah, and if that's what you got in your head, I wouldn't see anybody. If Cindy can't stand living with you, she ought to get herself a divorce, and find some other guy. I don't think she ought to be around for the rest of your life to see if you're going to own up to yourself. Unless she wants to . . . I don't see the necessity for it. You know, without big noises.

[*I put the options right on the line.*]

VAN, CINDY. Mmm.

DR. You follow?

VAN. Sure.

DR. I mean, each person is capable of doing what he or she can. I don't feel there's any point in sort of beating somebody on the head because they don't do this or they won't do that, if they can't do it. Take a reading, and then take the appropriate course of action, for oneself. Don't do anybody any favors, because you can get hit right in the head.

Yesterday I had this kid in, who I saw a couple times, a heroin addict, and his folks came up from the South. And they wanted to go to Europe for three weeks, and they wanted me to see him, while they're over there. I said to them, "I don't want to see him. He's *your* kid. If he jumps off a bridge, it's tough." A real flaked-out boy. Looks like Jesus going to the cross. "Well, why don't you see him for three weeks, while we're away?" "No. You've got to make some other disposition."

Wouldn't I do them a favor, because they're referred through some colleague of mine? Nope, no favors. No favors.

It's a one-way street. Everybody's accountable for whatever level of bullshit they're dishing out.

> [*There are many nonverbal implications to doing somebody a favor. The grantor of a favor often will feel a degree of annoyance, if not anger, that he let himself be prevailed upon. On the other hand, the recipient of a favor very often will feel guilty because a favor is something done above and beyond the grantor's basic wishes. This guilt can often generate anger. This sequence of behaviors is very often observed in parents dealing with children.*
>
> *Parents of kids on heroin very often desire to be bailed out without their active participation.*]

VAN. I'm not sure what you're saying to me.

DR. I'm just sort of saying, in a sense, I'm not too sure. See, if you go into some kind of long-term treatment, it's going through some kind of motions, either for your benefit, for her benefit, or for somebody's benefit; so you think. So I just wonder how much of your life you spend going through motions. I guess in many ways it's safer . . . What do you think, Cindy? Am I mean, and cruel, and . . . ?

CINDY. You are saying exactly the same thing I said to him.

DR. When?

CINDY. The other night he started crying. He was really crying . . .

DR. About what?

CINDY. I think he was crying about Jennifer, because he's lost her. And I said, "You know, it feels good to see you having a normal reaction to cry . . ." And then he immediately . . .

DR. How do you know that was what the problem was?

CINDY. Well, that's what he said.

DR. Is that what you said?

CINDY. He said, "All my life I have been dealing with loss . . ." See, this makes me mad, because the videotape is recording, but quote unquote, he said, "All my life I have been dealing with losses. And this is a loss right now, and it's very difficult for me to deal with, and you've got to allow me to cry and feel . . ."

> [*Cindy answers for Van.*]

DR. Yeah?

CINDY. And I said, "It feels good to see you finally crying and feeling. You never do show your feelings."

DR. So what did he say about that?

CINDY. He said, uh, I don't know, it's uh . . . It doesn't feel good.

DR. (Repeats) It does not feel good? What do you mean, it feels what?

CINDY. I don't know, that's just what he said. And I said, "Well, cry if you want to cry."

VAN. Are you talking about the time you went outside?

> [*He's amazed that she remembers this incident, because he's probably been trying to forget it.*]

CINDY. Yeah. It started to rain.

VAN. Jeepers creepers, that's a month ago.

CINDY. Yeah. No, I don't know how long ago it was. Two weeks ago, three weeks ago?

VAN. No, the context of that . . .

DR. What?

VAN. . . . Is, that's the first time I had a chance to deal with some of my feelings, because I felt like most of the time I was putting you back together again, or trying to be . . . that's our old pattern. You fall apart, and I try to put you back together again. And it was the first time that I had allowed myself to get in touch with some of my feelings about everything that had been going on.

> [*Here we see the discrepancy between Van's and Cindy's recollection of the same event. It had a different meaning for each of them. Cindy is relieved that Van can cry at last. Van sees it as a change from Cindy's crying, which prevented him from confronting his own emotions.*]

(At this point Dr. Paul plays back videotape of the three segments from the October 3, 1972 session [III]: Van talking about his family and father; Cindy and Scott.)

> [*Material on videotape is on the following pages: segment 1, pages 121–123; segment 2, pages 128–130; segment 3, pages 141–144.*]

DR. (When tape is over) I think it's pretty well laid out, isn't it?

VAN. What did you see?

CINDY. Well, I just went through about ten different kinds of emotional responses and different levels of feelings . . . I started out by really feeling sorry for you [Van], because you sounded like an orphan your whole life. And I felt how sorry I was for you that you never, as a child, even questioned about grandparents, or your parents' life, or, you know, you never had any of that. And then I got into my own . . . when we got off . . . and I thought about our children, that they've been deprived of grandparents on your side, and your past history, and they have a rich, full experience on my side, but nothing on your side, and there's a real void in that. Then, when we got into the Scott thing, I got so damned angry at you, because again you've been lying to me. And then I got really mad at you. And then, I started hearing . . . hearing you talk about you never get the woman and sail off on the ship . . . and I thought, damn it, what have I been? I think I'm a winner! I think you got a real good bargain when you got me, and I think you got a good life with three kids, and you can't see that I'm the movie star, and you're sailing off on a ship with me? You have to cry because you're the loser? And I saw that pretty woman who has been giving you so much love, and has lived her whole life for you, and you're saying "I'm the loser. I can't love her, and I don't want her to . . . I can't respond to her love; she turns me off . . ." And uh, "I don't ever get the star I want. I don't get Jennifer. I have to settle with what I've got."

> [*It sounds as if Van had lived out his father's sense of having been orphaned.*
>
> *Cindy gets angry at Van at the point where he describes himself as a loser; it seems as if she can't stand to see her feelings of being a loser mirrored by him.*]

VAN. (Overwhelmed) I'm saying that . . .

CINDY. And I know . . . I see me as the father!

VAN. Yeah.

CINDY. You're having . . . if you make love to me, it's a homosexual thing, huh? I mean making love to Daddy, instead of a passionate thing of making love to . . .

DR. This is today . . .

> [*At this point I am showing them a split-screen video-tape, showing on one side, the videotape of the last session, and on the other side, the Hoopeses today watching this videotape. I made this second part of the film previously (see page 160), when I replayed the last session's videotape. The split-screen image is played back without sound, and is what I refer to on page 164, when I ask Van what he sees in himself.*]

CINDY. . . . In other words, when I'm a hot-blooded woman you can't really be turned on to me, because I'm a dad, huh?

VAN. I'm not sure I said that.

CINDY. No, but . . . (sighs) . . . I wonder . . .

VAN. No, I don't think what you heard was . . (sighs) . . . the other side of what I was saying too, and that is the insanity of all that . . .

CINDY. Oh, I heard . . .

VAN. . . . That I always felt the loser.

CINDY. Yeah.

VAN. As I've said to you before, that's crazy.

CINDY. And I said that to you before, "How in the world can you ever see yourself as a loser?" First of all, you have me, second of all, you have three degrees; you went . . . You didn't have parents to support you but you came out ahead with three degrees . . . I mean you've got a life that, if you had fantasized about, you would've wanted it, I would assume.

VAN. Why the hell do you think I'm here, and not off in an apartment somewhere?

CINDY. Okay.

DR. What does that mean?

VAN. It means that I understand what she's saying, and that, that a lot of me responds to that, of course! But when I get some of that depressive shit out of the way, I do understand and see what I have. And how important that is. And, and the fact that in spite of all that stuff . . .

DR. Well, you really don't deserve it so . . .

> [*I am expressing what I sense of Van's feelings which he has been struggling to deny, i.e., that he doesn't deserve any sense of well being in the marriage.*]

VAN. Now that's part of the dynamics, too, I'm sure, that I don't feel like I deserve that, so I have to sabotage the good things when they happen. I think there's a lot in that, too.

DR. Well, what do you people want to do?

(Pause)

VAN. That, that is an open end, rather than coming to a conclusion. I . . . I very strongly feel that there's a hell of a lot of stuff that, that I've got to deal with.

DR. Just a second, I want to interrupt you. You don't gotta do anything.

VAN. Yes, I do.

CINDY. Yes.

VAN. I gotta do it for me.

DR. What?

CINDY. He's not sleeping, he's not eating. We're falling apart.

VAN. (Simultaneously with Cindy) I got to do it for Cindy.

CINDY. He's got to do something.

DR. You don't have to do anything for her.

> [*This is an attempt to separate their respective identities, an attempt to get each one to be able to think and feel for himself and not need to make decisions for the other.*]

CINDY. No . . .

VAN. I would . . . okay, if you want to use different words, I feel very much an imperative at this point to get some of that stuff out of the way, if it has encumbered me for so long, I want to get this stuff shelved, finally, with a nice cover around it, maybe, although that's . . .

DR. As long as it isn't too much of a bother.

VAN. I don't know why you're goading me, but I feel you are . . .

DR. It isn't a matter of goading, I'm just reading you, I'm just telling you back what I read.

VAN. I don't feel that here. Maybe . . . that's the way it's coming through.

(Both are almost shouting)

DR. Well, what do you think about you seeing yourself there? When you were there, on the other side of the screen? What did you see in yourself? The stem of the pipe held tightly in your mouth, like breath-holding to get through this . . . then . . .

VAN. I . . . I don't know what to say, except that, that internally those feelings aren't there. As near as I can put my finger on things, I feel like I'm trying as best I can to be open and receptive and to deal with things and to feel what I feel, and to talk about it as best I can. If it comes through controlled or as if I'm playing a role, I don't know what to do differently.

DR. Yeah?

VAN. It's the same kind of issue that Cindy talks about sometimes, when I deal with feelings and she says, "You're not dealing with feelings." I think I'm uptight there because Cindy got angry, she says, "You're lying to me again" stuff . . . well hell, there's a whole . . .

CINDY. You were!

VAN. There's a whole summer of lies, of course! And that was still part of it! What the hell do you want me to do, sit back . . . I suppose if I hadn't cared about, about you, I would have said, "Go out and screw Scott . . . that's fine."

CINDY. Don't use that expression, "care." You did not care about me at that point. You were only feeling yourself. You were not caring about me. It was yourself you were feeling . . . ! If you cared about me you would've said, "I've been having an affair, and let Scott . . . enjoy Scott. I know how it is to have another person relate to you." I said to you, "Van, for the first time in a year . . ."

VAN. That certainly is . . .

CINDY. "Scott has just said something comforting to me, and you have shitted on it." And I said, "I have said I have . . . I've felt for a long time you've been having an affair," and I said, "Damn it, level with me. If you've been having an affair, tell me right now so I can enjoy the feeling that I just had and I . . ." Ohhhhhh! (Her voice a mixture of frustration and righteous anger)

VAN. You didn't . . . you wanted me to give you permission to go down and screw Scott. I'm sorry I couldn't do it.

CINDY. And that's . . . yeah, right! You're on the pot, but you're not gonna let me get on it!

DR. You don't have to ask him for permission. He didn't ask you for permission, did he?

> [*This is another attempt to untangle them.*]

CINDY. No, but damn it, that's the way I've been doing my whole marriage, is always asking permission to see how he feels . . .

DR. Well, isn't that what you've been doing your whole life, before you were married?

> [*I dilute the intensity of the exchange by focusing Cindy's attention on her need for permission from her parents, which antedated the marriage.*]

CINDY. Yes. I had to get everybody's approval before I did anything to make sure everybody would think it was all right.

DR. That's not the greatest.

CINDY. It sure isn't.

DR. So don't blame him, because you were sensitized before he came along, to asking people for permission.

CINDY. That's true too. I was very much sensitized to be a perfect being, and to get everybody's approval for everything I did, and . . . (sighs) And I have always given to everybody else. I have lived ten years with you, loving you and trying to make you feel good, and then in return asking to be loved back. That's the only thing I asked from you is to be loved. And the way I ask you, it turns you off.

VAN. You never felt loved from me?

CINDY. Nope, not from you. I did before we got married, when you wanted to . . .

VAN. Oh, damn it.

CINDY. If it's on your terms, I felt loved. But if it was when I had the needs and I wanted to be loved, then you closed the door on me. It had to always be your terms. You know, that's the part about your affair that bothers me, because I know that with you and Jennifer, you would have taken the initiative to say, "Hey, meet me at Copley Square tonight for dinner." With me you've never done that. Tonight I said, "Can we go out for dinner after your class?" You know, I felt I took the

initiative. And you had to turn back and without any enthusiasm and not act like you care. And I know with Jennifer you
were always able to meet the motel rendezvous and meet at
the restaurants, and set up times with her, and in our marriage
it has always had to be me who comes up with any romantic
ideas.

DR. I want to ask you about that. Why are you throwing this back
at him?

CINDY. Well, because the only way I feel loved is when I set myself, I mean I set settings. He never initiates them.

DR. Yeah, but I mean what are you complaining about? I don't
understand. You've gone through this rigamarole before
with him, what do you want him to do? He can only do what
he can do.

CINDY. (Wistfully) So he can't love me? I'm hearing you say you
can't love me.

VAN. I didn't think that's what I was saying.

CINDY. No, okay (voice falls).

DR. You got yourselves a blooming mess.

(Pause)

VAN. I think maybe you picked me because I wasn't the volatile,
controlling person that your father was, in part.

> [*Van spontaneously picks up the theme of the relevance
> of Cindy's parents in their present marital squabble.*]

CINDY. Right.

VAN. Okay.

CINDY. Okay.

VAN. Now you're punishing me because I'm not.

CINDY. I'm punishing you? I thought I was the one who got punished. I thought I was giving you the rewards.

> [*They start to squabble again about who's right and
> who's wrong. The usual outcome is for both parties to
> come away hurt and resentful. Squabbling represents a
> co-conspiracy to avoid sorting out the relevance of those
> destructive behaviors derived from the original family.
> Neglect of such focus leads each party to re-experience
> the hurt state lived through before marriage.*]

DR. Which rewards? Who's getting any rewards out of this?

CINDY. I thought he was.

DR. (Yawning) Nah! You people are just too involved with one another.

CINDY. I know I'm too involved with him . . . He's not involved with me.

DR. He's involved with running away from you.

CINDY. Right.

DR. That's being involved . . .

CINDY. And this minute is exactly an example of our whole life. There's a man waiting for him right now, and I don't feel I have another minute that I can use for my own time.

DR. There's a man waiting for you where?

VAN. Ohh.

DR. Where's the man waiting for you?

CINDY. He has a patient right now.

VAN. (Speaking at the same time) I have an appointment at 4:30. Uh, in Boston.

CINDY. Everytime I have an emotional need or something when I finally get to you, there's somebody that gets to you more quickly, who's more important than me. You have never really . . .

DR. Well, the options are, you can live the way you have been, you can get a separation, you can go and get individual counseling, where the odds are that you will probably get a separation and divorce, as I see the two of you, uh, and I don't know what else . . . What do you think of yourself there, Van? Today? You got her head in your head, and she's got your head in her head.

> [*At times, the only way you can get people to start thinking about what they're doing is to rock them a bit, and this is done by confronting them with the reality of the existing options.*
>
> *At this point I play back a brief excerpt of the prior session of Van alone. I'm playing this back without sound, so that he and Cindy can more readily see the few superimposed images, which lead to my reference to his having her head in his head, and vice versa. See page 144 for description; material on videotape is*

                    on pages 104–111 and 121–123.

VAN. I don't know . . .

DR. What?

VAN. I draw a blank, I really do.

DR. Nothing?

VAN (Sighs) When I was listening to the stuff that I said last time,
I . . . it's difficult for me to, to look objectively as though
I'm seeing somebody else. But as I listen to that again, I
again see the sadness, the depression, the little lost boy sort
of stuff that I think has been around for a hell of a long time.
Everything else comes out of how I'm feeling, not what I'm
seeing in the picture, it comes out of . . .

DR. Well, what do you *see?*

VAN. Well, I see somebody who's sitting and listening, thought-
fully pondering things. I don't see somebody who's explosive,
I don't see somebody who is uh, overly reactive and . . .

> [*Van describes himself almost entirely in terms of the*
> absence *of emotion-related qualities. This parallels the*
> *neglect of overt feeling in his life.*]

DR. Pretty well controlled.

VAN. Hell, yes, it's controlled, but it's . . . it's not . . . *I* don't
see somebody who is rigid and you know . . . I have been
that way, and if you think that's a picture of somebody who's
controlled . . . maybe ten years ago, you would have really
gotten a picture of somebody who's controlled . . . and
frightened. I don't see this guy as *frightened* and controlled,
as though he's going to go out of control, or that the world is
gonna fall apart.

DR. I would bet that if Cindy decided that she was going to get
herself a lawyer and get a divorce, you'd get frightened and
get out of control. As long as you've got her on a yoyo, things
are pretty well in tow.

> [*I challenge his self-image of imperturbability. He is*
> *an expert at self-deception.*]

VAN. Oh, I'm certain that uh, I've said this all along too, when
I've felt like she had the trumps. If she was going to play
them, it would really be devastating. And there wouldn't be
anything I could do, except respond to it by doing what I
could . . .

CINDY. (To Dr, plaintive) Why did you . . . did I hear you correctly when you said the odds are we will separate and get a divorce? You see us that far gone?

VAN. That wasn't what I heard, but maybe you would want him to answer.

CINDY. Yes.

DR. If you got individual counseling, I said.

VAN. That's what I heard.

CINDY. Oh. You see I'm glad I asked you to say it, because I just immediately panicked, I thought Oh my God, do you really see us that far gone.

DR. (In a resigned, detached manner) Well, you people are pretty far gone.

CINDY. I'm surprised you say that, because I just . . . I got volatile just now, but, for the first time in ten years, it seems like I am just now starting to have a marriage, as far as really wanting to work and build on one.

DR. Well, see, let me back up just a bit. You can't have a marriage unless you have a self.

CINDY. Yes. I can see that.

DR. And you [to Cindy] haven't got much of a self.

CINDY. Right.

DR. And you're like a lot of people who try to get a sense of self by leaping into a marriage.

CINDY. Right.

DR. And it doesn't work. Not only it doesn't work, it can't work. And if it looks as if it can work, it certainly doesn't work for the kids.

CINDY. Um-hm.

DR. That's one place it doesn't work.

CINDY. Um-hm. Then maybe that's why I'm just now starting to get excited, because I'm just now starting to feel some things, on a different level. I'm getting excited recently about some of the feelings that I'm starting to have.

DR. Like what?

CINDY. Well, I've been reading, uh, I read the books *Open Marriage* and *Transactional Analysis* in the last few weeks . . .

DR. Yeah?

VAN. I think that's part of why you clung to me so tightly, as

we've talked about that before. You said that in many other
ways too. About the way our relationship works, part of
it . . . (sighs)

> [*Van seems to be trying to confuse everybody so as to
> avoid owning up to his own role in the marriage, and
> to distract Cindy from her sense of improvement.*]

DR. See, the problem in a different way is whether you're going to
recognize that what you have had to date was a bust, and then
you're going to try and develop something different. But then,
I get the sense with Cindy that there's a certain kind of
clutching, trying to recapture what you feel was there in the
past, though whether it was there in the past or not is beside
the point.

CINDY. Uh-huh.

DR. I don't think it was.

CINDY. Uh-huh.

DR. Because if one of two people in the marriage feel that something's missing, it . . .

CINDY. Uh-huh.

DR. . . . Calls into question the integrity of the whole marriage.

CINDY. Uh-huh.

DR. You might be making all the volatile noises that he suppresses,
you see.

CINDY. Uh-huh.

VAN. It certainly was true of our early marriage.

CINDY. Yes.

VAN. It's one of the things that attracted me to Cindy, I'm sure.
She could act out my impulses when I couldn't. When things
altered was when I first got into therapy, as I began to change.

CINDY. Uh-huh.

VAN. I didn't need that . . .

CINDY. Uh-huh.

VAN. . . . And we did a switch.

DR. See, the reason why I would caution you about individual
therapy, is that the negative transference in individual therapy
is never that well handled. And the spouse is the one that
catches that.

CINDY. Uh-huh.

VAN. Yeah.

DR. It's generated in the context of the therapy or the analysis, and the other one catches it. And they don't know what the hell it's about. And it leads to increased distancing.

> [*In the course of any kind of one-to-one psychotherapy or psychoanalysis, there are generated both positive and negative feelings on the part of the patient toward the therapist. These feelings occur in the setting of increasing patient dependency on the therapist. In any setting where such a heightened dependency relationship develops, negative feelings will be generated. Often these feelings are expressed by the patient toward the therapist in the treatment setting. It is common, however, for these feelings to recurrently spill over outside the therapy room onto the other people in the patient's life. Such feelings, for example, can target in on a spouse who will be taken by surprise. Over time, this can cause increasing distance and misunderstanding between the patient and his spouse.*
>
> *Though the intent on the part of the therapist or analyst is to be helpful to his patient, the chain reaction of emotional responses from the analyst through the patient to the spouse is such that no analyst can ever be aware of all the consequences set in motion by the individual-oriented therapy. Indirectly, unwittingly, the analyst may imply that there is something wrong with the spouse, relying principally on biased perceptions provided by his patient. It is possible that the analyst might say that the spouse was the wrong person for the patient to have married. This is a monumental judgment to make without having the individual present to explain his or her position.*]

VAN. Yeah. I think you're right. (Pause) Well, I think one of the things that attracted me to Jennifer was the fact that I said it as "I'm okay—you're okay" kind of stuff . . .

CINDY. Uh-huh.

VAN. . . . That the way in which she had put things together for herself came out . . . came out so that my relationship [with Jennifer] was different than my relationship [with Cindy] had ever been.

CINDY. Right. You were parallel maybe in your . . . feelings and transactions where you and I have always been . . . you're the parent and I'm the child, I'm the . . . yeah, maybe you two were right together and I . . .

DR. There's no shadow of death in your relationship with Jennifer, as there is with the two of you.

VAN. Um . . . no   shadow   of   death? . . . my   father's death . . . ?

DR. No, but in a marriage, until death do us part.

VAN. Hmm . . . Oh yeah, hell, walking along lonely beaches is far different from living in an intimate relationship. You don't have the same pressures and the same uh . . . Yeah. You don't have the same commitment. That's certainly true.

DR. See, when you said before, you don't look scared, I think you're scared to find out how much you hated your father.

VAN. I never have gotten into that stuff, and I really want to.

DR. Too scary . . . Too heavy.

VAN. Why don't I feel it then? Why don't I feel frightened?

DR. You won't feel frightened, because you know you're going to run before you get there. And then you can keep on saying, "Well, I know I ought to get into that, or I want to get into that . . ."

VAN. Okay. I don't think my decisions are based on running from therapy. I think that's, that's got to be done. I feel an imperative . . .

DR. You see, you can feel it as an imperative . . . a lot of people feel imperatives all their lives . . . you know, I oughta do this or I oughta do that and never do it.

VAN. Okay. That's, well . . .

DR. You're a procrastinator.

VAN. True. True. About a lot of things.

DR. Yeah.

VAN. I haven't felt that's been the motivation for my decisions.

DR. To do what? What decisions?

VAN. For instance, the decision I mentioned about coming here and the . . .

DR. Well, see, I don't think you had expected that things would move as fast as they did here.

VAN. (Sighs) Hmmm. I tried to consider that. And I didn't come up with that.

DR. Well, I was telling you my reading of it all.

VAN. Yeah. Okay, well, I need to listen to that. Now, I think my statements were . . . I don't know whether I said it to you or not, but . . . I was glad that it's been moving as fast as it has. It got to things that I hadn't gotten to in two years in my other therapy. But anyway.

DR. See, in some ways, Cindy, you take on the shadow of his father, and in some symbolic level the reason that he couldn't get too involved with you is like you're the symbol of death. He's got to run. Follow?

CINDY. Uh-huh.

DR. How were you at track?

VAN. At track I ran the 100 in 12 seconds; I was pretty good.

CINDY. Real fast.

VAN. Pretty good.

DR. Pretty good runner.

(No one laughs)

DR. Well, I could only tell you what I think . . . I'm going to tell you what I think. And so I don't know what you want to do. Other than run.

VAN. (Haltingly and very low, barely audible) Let's schedule an appointment for next week . . . well . . . hell, I can't. I have to look at my schedule and see . . .

> [*Van's request for an appointment in some ways indicates that he is aware of the validity of all that had been said about himself before.*]

CINDY. Please put yourself as a priority before the . . .

DR. He can't because his father didn't.

CINDY. This is what bothers me. If only . . .

DR. This is where his father is very much involved in his head.

CINDY. Everybody gets priorities before you.

DR. Before what?

CINDY. He does himself.

DR. Well, he's not worth it. It wasn't worth it that much to his father.

VAN. Now you're giving me opposite messages that he gave me

before when I was allowed to put myself first, but today
you're . . .

CINDY. Well, you do in some respects.

VAN. At any rate I do have to (sighs) . . . oh, shoot . . .

CINDY. What's next week's schedule that's pressing so much?

VAN. I have a staff meeting every Tuesday at 3:00.

CINDY. Yeah, I know, but I mean, certainly . . . maybe we can
can find another time.

DR. Well, I can't make it next Tuesday at 3:00.

CINDY. Before you rule it out, find out the possibilities of
times . . .

DR. Let me see. (Goes to get appointment book.)

CINDY. (To Van) Can you have your secretary hold down for ten
minutes?

VAN. What times do you have available?

DR. Next week? Next week is the twenty-third . . . Friday morning?

VAN. What time?

DR. 10:30.

VAN. No. I have an 11:00 class. My week is a bitch. You name
the times and I'll see. Monday, Wednesday, and Friday is,
uh, 8:30 or 9:00 . . .

DR. In the morning?

VAN. 8:30, I guess. At a quarter to nine we could make it.

DR. Thursday mornings you can't make it?

VAN. Thursday morninnnnnnnggg . . .

DR. Here's what I'll do. I'll have to sort of check; I could call you
tonight. Will you be home tonight?

VAN. Yeah.

DR. What time are you gonna get back?

VAN. I'll be back about 8:30, 9:00.

DR. Why don't I call you after then, and I'll see what I can finesse.

VAN. Okay. Yeah, I'll see what I can switch around. Thursday
morning I have to go to Newport. I consult at Newport.

DR. Okay.

VAN. Every other Thursday, so . . . this Thursday I won't be,
but the next Thursday.

DR. I'll tell you one thing, if you want to get . . . Two things that count in this operation, here . . . one, is listening to the tapes, and two, is getting other family members in, in terms of increasing the odds for a positive payoff.

VAN. That may be difficult, they're all out in South Dakota.

> [*Van answers for Cindy, as it is her parents who live in South Dakota.*]

DR. Well, I'm just telling you, you know, over time.

VAN. Yeah. Okay.

DR. And then you'll save the tapes, and when it's all over you can listen to them, and see what kind of a zoological paradise you came from. Okay? I'll give you a call then.

VAN. Okay.

CINDY. You need to call . . .

VAN. Yeah, I need to call, uh . . . What did we do with the case [for the tape]?

DR. Here . . . The reason I had to get tough, is because I find you tough.

VAN. I resent the fact that I had to . . . [on phone] . . . Hi, could you tell, uh, well this is Dr. Hoopes anyway, but could you tell my client who's coming at 4:30 that I'll be just a little bit late. But I will be there. Okay, thanks.

DR. You resent what fact?

VAN. That I have to see about six people to pay for this one hour! I do resent that, and I try not to resent it.

DR. Well, while you're resenting it, the thing is, if you'll listen to the tapes you'll get out of here quicker.

VAN. Fair enough. Message duly noted and recorded.

(All laugh).

DR. Okay. 'By.

. . . This is where you start from. If you find out now . . . things about yourself that you don't like to face: well, just remember that some men have to learn much worse things about themselves, and learn them later when it's harder to recover, and make a new beginning.*

—EDWARD

* *The Cocktail Party,* by T. S. Eliot, pp. 178–179.

Turning Point

I've spent my life in trying to forget myself,
In trying to identify myself with the part
I had chosen to play. And the longer we pretend
The harder it becomes to drop the pretence,
Walk off the stage, change into our own clothes
And speak as ourselves . . .*

—LORD CLAVERTON

VAN. Ohhh, I haven't stopped moving.

DR. Pardon?

VAN. I haven't stopped moving . . .

DR. Since when?

VAN. From the train.

DR. Which train?

VAN. Uh, the express coming in from Providence. It rattles you around.

DR. You got a tape?

VAN. Yes.

DR. Okay . . . One November 1972. Who wants to begin today? (Mumbled) Who wants to begin today?

CINDY. Oh. Begin today. Uh . . .

VAN. Now, I have to gather my thoughts a bit . . . Uh. Uh. Well, we listened to the tape . . .

    [*Breakthrough.*]

DR. Yeah? Get anything out of it?

VAN. (Voice less clipped) A lot of, uh, reinforcement about the, uh, comments you were making. You know, I begin to hear

* *The Elder Statesman,* by T. S. Eliot, p. 102.

myself over and over again sounding the same way. I come
on like a, like a stodgy professor.

DR. Yeah?

VAN. The sound on the tape is incredible in that respect. Uh, I
begin to see how people respond . . . I begin to see how
Cindy responds to me as being that controlled and, uh, uptight about things. I did some, some head stuff, I don't know
how much I got into feelings, but I did a head stuff over the
time, too, using some of uh, Cohen's understanding of transactions and relationships and his description of uh, boundaries . . . space, time and energy boundaries. And I think it
was sort of very clear to me that one of the things that oper-
ates in our relationship is that Cindy's energy boundaries, and
her ways of dealing with energy are much different from
mine. And it's the old issue of control again; I have to make
sure that everything is just right, and I take in bits of information slowly, and if it comes too quick I have to say, "Wait
a minute," you know, "slow it down, and I'll take it in," so
that, so that I can get . . .

> [*Van seems to require an intellectualized explanation
> for coping with his feelings, as usual.*
>   *"Bits of information" is a computer analogy.*]

DR. Or blot it out.

VAN. Or blot it out. Yeah. Right. And I could . . . it made me
think of, I went from that to thinking about things like, uh,
sex, that, uh, Cindy when she orgasms, uh, she doesn't freak
out, but you know, she really, really enjoys it, sort of uh, goes
bananas sometimes.

> [*"When she orgasms"—another mechanistic phrase.
> Orgasm is a noun, not a verb. The effect of this bad
> English is to distance the reality. Van says "orgasms"
> as a verb instead of "comes" or "goes off" because an
> expression like "go off" has reverberations of "going
> crazy," going "round the bend," "off the track," or
> whatever, and is too close to what he fears.*]

CINDY. (Giggles)

VAN. That uh, in times past has sometimes turned me off. And I
was trying . . . I've been trying to figure out why that's

true, and what is there about our sexual relationship that,
that uh, that made it happen that way.

DR. Made what happen?

VAN. Well, that made it difficult for me to respond to her in the
way in which she felt she wanted to be responded to, and
could make me more comfortable about our sexual relationship. And I think it's part of the same thing. I express feelings,
I express things physically in a much more controlled, uh,
much more heady, much more, uh, Cindy always calls it
sophisticated; I don't think it's that as much as it's . . . it is
a control issue. I guess what I'm saying is that in a variety of
areas of our relationship I begin to see how the control issue
pervades everything I do.

> [*As Van talks about their sexual relationship, it seems
> as if he begins to relive certain features of it, and the
> anxiety attendant to focusing on his own role in their
> sexual relationship makes him sound confused.*]

DR. Yeah.

VAN. And gets in the way of, uh, some of the things that we have
to do. I don't know what I'm talking about . . . and I don't
know what I'm saying.

DR. Now let me tell you or react to what you just were talking
about . . .

VAN. Yeah.

DR. About her orgasm.

VAN. Yeah.

DR. Uh, it's controlled, but the fear is the loss of control.

VAN. Ummm.

DR. And what can happen to people who lose control. And . . .
just pushing this further . . . it's as if, when she has an
orgasm, she loses control, and I think the signal back to you
is that she might go bananas. You said bananas . . .

VAN. Uh-huh.

DR. And cannot come back.

VAN. Umm.

DR. Freak out permanently.

VAN. Umm.

DR. And then the whole issue in my mind there is . . . what is

the relationship between sex and insanity? You know, if you
go back to a fundamentalist upbringing.

CINDY. Uh-huh.

VAN. Yeah, touch it and you'll go blind stuff.

DR. That's right. Or you'll go crazy.

VAN. Yeah.

CINDY. Uh-huh.

DR. So that it would then follow that withholding sex would be a
way of protecting her from going insane.

VAN. Hmmmm. (Sighs) Yeah. I'm trying to think of the messages
that I got about sex. And I come up with a blank. The messages I got from my parents were that they didn't have sex.
I remember one occasion which was particularly guilt-pro-
ducing for me. I don't think I've ever said this before, but uh,
my father had a lot of financial difficulties at one point, and
this was right after, I guess, he went into business, maybe it
was right before, I can't remember. I think it was right after.
But we lived in a very small place, and uh, there were only
two bedrooms. I slept in the same bedroom with my mother
and father.

DR. At what age?

VAN. Oh, this is when I was a sophomore, freshman in high school.

DR. And what was the bed arrangement?

VAN. Ummmmmmmm. I'm trying to . . . I'm sure this is true.
part of my memory says no, that isn't true; I slept down on
the couch. But uh . . .

CINDY. Uh-uh [meaning no].

DR. You were there?

VAN. No, you weren't there.

CINDY. No, but I know what . . . I remember your mother was
telling me about her feelings about that arrangement.

DR. What'd she say?

CINDY. She said she's . . . this goes to a lot of stuff about Van's
sister who is eleven months younger than Van, and how Dorothy always got everything and his mother said, one time, "I
always feel so bad that poor Vanny had to sleep in the same
room with Daddy and me."

DR. For how long?

CINDY. ▶ ▶ ▶ I don't know, but she says, "We felt it was important that Dorothy have her own room, and poor Vanny was
just left to have to do the best he could." And she said, "It
always bothered me that he had to sleep with his mom and
dad."

VAN. I have foggy memories of it. I can remember when my sister
went away to school, then I took over her bedroom. So I
had a bedroom of my own when I was a senior. But it must
have been in the sophomore and junior years of high school
that I either slept on the couch in sort of living room-kitchen
combined. Hell, there were only three rooms in the whole
stupid place. But I . . . whew, boy, that's a . . . thinking
about that sometimes, I don't think about it because of sort
of a horrible situation it was. But at any rate, I do remember
walking . . . this was my senior year at high school, because
I remember walking from my bedroom through the bathroom
into my parents' bedroom . . .

DR. Yeah.

VAN. . . . And they were making love.

DR. So they did make love.

VAN. Well, that was the only time I ever saw it. But . . . when I
walked into the room, I can remember my father rolled off
of my mother and he was on top.

DR. Yeah.

VAN. And I remember he rolled over and sort of rolled over to
his side of the bed with his face away from my mother, and
she was absolutely bullshit at me.

CINDY. Oh.

VAN. She . . . she said later, I think it was either that evening or
it was the next day, she said, "That's the first time your father has ever treated me as a woman in a long time," and to
the effect, "You ruined it."

> [*Van's mother really shouldn't be sharing her sexual
> problems with her son. This has the effect of strength-
> ening the incest fantasy in him, along with guilt about
> the fantasy and about "ruining it." His mother seems
> offhandedly seductive.*]

CINDY. Oh.

VAN. And I can remember feeling horrible. Just absolutely horrible, because I had walked in on them without announcing myself. Or anything like that.

DR. Why would you do that?

VAN. I went to get a drink of water in the kitchen.

DR. Well, you know, it's just a matter of courtesy to knock on the door.

VAN. Oh, but maybe you don't understand the arrangement of the, the . . . it was sort of . . . it wasn't done, it wasn't anything unusual for me to walk through that bedroom.

DR. No, but it gets involved with what you're talking about when you first came in . . . space. It was as if that was part of . . .

VAN. Their boundaries.

DR. Their boundaries, and your boundaries were interchangeable. Their space and your space were the same.

VAN. Yeah. Well, it certainly was true for at least a couple of years. I can't really . . .

DR. Did you see them when you were in their bedroom changing dress, or . . .

VAN. No, I don't remember.

DR. You don't remember. That sounds like a very loaded scene.

VAN. It is. Oh, it was. Very powerful.

> [*Van's confusion suggests that as he relives the scene, he speaks of the scene as if "it is" still happening.*]

DR. You know, you had an option of requesting that you could've gotten a sleeping bag, and slept in the kitchen, if it's that tight. You know, kids have options, whether they think about them or not.

VAN. That's why I say it's fuzzy to me, because there are times I remember sleeping on the couch in the living room. But there are other times that I remember sleeping in that bedroom.

DR. Did you ever think of screwing your mother?

VAN. Well . . .

DR. That would follow, I mean, in terms of what you're describing.

VAN. I remember very negative feelings, negative feelings about any eroticism toward her. And it must . . . I'm sure it has something to do with defending against some feelings. Because I remember my . . . it was almost a reaction formation.

DR. Uh-huh.

VAN. That is, my mother was very heavy, and I never . . .

DR. What color hair did she have?

CINDY. Blonde. She was blonde and had blue eyes. But I can remember that her weight was offensive to me. I never saw her as an attractive woman. I saw her as heavy. Her legs were very large. I can remember . . .

DR. She was always heavy?

VAN. No, earlier when I was a little kid . . .

DR. Yeah.

VAN. She . . . earlier when I was a little kid, she probably weighed between 130 and 140.

DR. What height about?

VAN. She was about 5′6″. But through most of my preadolescence she was about 230. So she was very obese.

DR. Maybe she put on weight so she wouldn't attract you.

VAN. No, she had lots of weight long before that. I think she put on weight for other reasons earlier as a little kid. She had no relationship whatsoever to her father and mother. Shoved around, lived with an aunt here and there, and her father was off searching for rainbows, and . . .

CINDY. Pictures of her show her as a real fat little kid.

VAN. She was a fat little chubby kid too. Well, I'm trying to hear what you're saying too. I would have said that she had difficulty with that in terms of other relationships outside of the marriage, and after my father died. That her weight protected her from her femininity. Or protected her from having to deal with that.

> [*Van goes into lengthy defensive gyrations in avoiding a direct answer to my question about an incest fantasy.*]

DR. What was your relationship with her?

VAN. Ahhh. (Sighs)

DR. How loaded was that?

VAN. I get bits and pieces of things that come to mind, I get pictures of being a momma's boy. Terrible time. I had school phobia, more or less, in the first grade. I screamed and yelled when she left. I was very, very attached to her. I spent most of my early childhood being very dependent on her.

> [*Recent studies about school phobia indicate very clearly that the principal source of a child's overdependency on the mother is the mother's dependency on the child. The child then acts out the mother's generally unrecognized aversion to having the child leave her.**]

DR. You didn't have much of your father, so there was a relational imbalance there.

VAN. No, that's true. I rarely remember doing anything with my father by himself. In fact, I don't remember anything, except I remember one time when they fought, my father took my sister and I for a car ride, and we were panicked. I was panicked at least. Both my sister and I were crying because we thought he was leaving mother. She threw her rings in the sink in a big scene, and he took us off in the car and rode around for a couple of hours. Not a word was said; he never said a word the whole time. So it *was* loaded. I was very close to her.

DR. He was gonna kidnap you from Momma.

VAN. Yeah. I think that's the fear that didn't get verbalized, but I think it's the fear that we had.

DR. I don't know what she had . . . Did she ever tell you about how she felt about those scenes?

VAN. On that occasion, I think . . . on that occasion it seems to me she spent some time talking to my sister and I, maybe the next day, about the fact that she was angry at Dad.

DR. I mean have you talked to your sister about these things?

VAN. Oh, my sister was uh . . . she dealt with the home situation much different than I did. She dealt with it by being angry, by exiting . . . any chance or opportunity, she went, zip!

> [*His sister, Dorothy, apparently is a different kind of runner; a faster runner than Van.*]

DR. Your sister?

---

* Johnson, A. M.; Falstein, E. I.; Szurek, S. A.; and Svendsen, M., "School Phobia," *American Orthopsychiatry 11* (1941): 702–711.

VAN. Yeah.

DR. But I mean, you still talk to her about what she experienced?

VAN. Yeah. So her experience was anger at all that stuff. My experience was feeling sorry for my parents, as best as I can recall it. I felt badly about it . . . I felt guilty for it, maybe at some level I felt responsible for whatever troubles they might be having. Where she was always kind of out of the door, never really involved.

DR. Involved but not letting it appear.

VAN. Yeah, I became my mother's confidant. She would tell me about all the problems and troubles. In many ways I sort of was a substitute for a nonverbal, noncommunicative father or husband, who . . . jeepers, most of his life he just sat around on the couch and watched TV and read . . . and worked. He spent his whole life working.

DR. Is that what you've been doing?

VA N. I used to, a hell of a lot more than I do now. You can report better than I can about that. I sure used to.

DR. Miss your mother?

VAN. Hmmm?

DR. Do you miss your mother?

VAN. I can't get in touch with that. There are times when I do.

> [*He denies that he does; then says he does.*]

DR. Cause she was your lifeline as a kid.

VAN. Yeah. (Sighs, pauses) I miss both my parents. Yes. And on some occasions I run from those feelings. There are times when Cindy says, "I know you must be thinking about your mother now."

> [*This is projection on Cindy's part. She later says she's very sensitive on Mother's Day herself.* (*See page 186.*) *She can't know when he's thinking about his parents, but she can sense that* she's *worrying about hers.*]

DR. Um-hm.

VAN. Or, "You must be thinking about your parents because it's a holiday," and so on, and I'll generally say "Yes," but . . . or, I'm not sure; I do run from those feelings.

> [*Van validates some of the statements I made in Session IV about his being a runner.* (*See pages 154 and 173.*)]

DR. Cindy, how do you feel things are going between the two of you, within yourself?

CINDY. Really great. I really feel I've had a turn-on experience lately, with uh, with my husband and with my marriage.

DR. In what sense?

CINDY. And with myself. Well, it just . . . we're just relating differently, we're . . . I mean, I'm always having good feelings, I'm not having any more tight gut feelings in situations, and I, I'm just feeling things differently, reacting differently, I . . . we've had three kinds of settings where the old Cindy would have gotten a tight, gutty-reaction feeling, and I'm on top of those feelings. And I really see Van coming on. We're doing some uh . . . I don't know, I can't describe it, but I'm feeling it's . . . we're having some new behavior modifications (laughing) or something . . . we're really in an ex . . . kind of, I guess, in experimental stages, but I can really see that . . .

DR. We are all the time, experimental.

CINDY. I'm really feeling that we're trying to practice what some of our insights are.

DR. What do you feel about the tapes; do you feel they're useful?

CINDY. Oh, yes. In fact . . .

VAN. It's amazing how much you forget.

DR. Yeah.

CINDY. And the way I sound when I'm talking to you . . . when I think I'm just talking . . . ◄ ◄ ◄

VAN. We decided that Cindy comes on, as a castrating bitch or shrew, and I come on as little professor, uh . . .

> [*A quantum leap for the Hoopeses: Each is able to see with a sense of humor how each looks to the other. This level of insight has been achieved primarily through the use of audiotape playback at home. The Hoopes's ability to see their roles so fast is unusual, however. I think in large substance it has to do with Van's recognition of his hidden grief about his father, and Cindy's ability to understand that Van is not a computer and has feelings of his own. This, in turn, lets her feel that she is not alone.*]

CINDY. Yeah.

DR. Milquetoast.

VAN. Yeah. Oh, sure! (All laugh) Ecch! It's terrible.

CINDY. Caspar.

VAN. Oh, God, Yeah, it's been uh . . . I find that there's less threat about things when we talk about things, that I can raise issues or try to talk about things and Cindy can respond to them without personalizing them to the point that I feel like she's being destroyed if I say them.

DR. Uh-huh.

CINDY. Yeah. Well, for the first time my gut doesn't react that way, and I don't know why. But it's not my gut that's sending messages any more.

VAN. Yeah, and I don't know either. But it's a hell of a lot more comfortable feeling than the tension that was around our relationship before.

CINDY. Well, one thing for sure, I've been able to see that the way Van has always dealt with me, it was nothing I ever did . . . well, I'm assuming this, but anyway . . . nothing I ever did or would say to Van would ever threaten him. He would just be able to take the information and deal with it and stay cool, calm, and collected. And then he would . . .

VAN. On the surface anyway.

CINDY. Well, see this is it. But . . .

DR. He was like a computer processing it, a data processor.

VAN. Yeah.

CINDY. But just hearing just now, with him talking, I realize how emotional I am and how unemotional he is, because I'm very sensitive on Mother's Day, when I really get to missing my mother . . . I immediately feel his loss, for his mother. And I want to deal . . . and I say, "Gee, I'm feeling depressed for you today for your missing your mother," and . . .

VAN. I've always had to protect myself from that.

CINDY. And I just realize . . .

VAN. My whole life I've spent holding everybody else together. My father I had to hold together, my *mother* I had to support because my father was falling apart, my sister I had to, to uh . . . I became the mediator, the savior, the therapist, the shrink in the family . . .

CINDY. Yeah.

VAN. . . . The negotiator . . . all those roles were mine.

CINDY. Yeah.

VAN. And I . . . so I guess I run from those feelings. I don't deal with them because they were always something I didn't have the luxury of dealing with.

CINDY. Yeah. I know.

VAN. I couldn't get sad, my mother was . . . my . . . or, *and* my father were so damned sad all the time.

CINDY. And then you got this wife who overreacts . . .

VAN. Why in the hell do you think I picked you, I guess? Because you could do things I couldn't. Maybe in my unconscious I knew that kind of spontaneity was . . . could help *me* grow.

CINDY. Yeah. And I . . .

VAN. And you needed my control.

CINDY. Yeah.

VAN. I think, anyway . . .

CINDY. I know, like, Van said the other day . . . I mean I'm not exactly sure how he worded it, but the other day he said . . . this makes you angry, when I try to recall . . . anyway, in dealing about Jennifer, he said, "I was hoping," or something, "that when I told you about it, that you would've been able to say, 'We have a crisis, now what are we gonna do about it?' instead of falling apart." You know, I went berserk . . . And I thought, just now, he has always dealt calm, cool, collected; "Let's talk." And I have always overreacted; I do want to cry and scream and throw things and that's how I've always reacted. And he was disappointed in me that I didn't take this news and channel it and then make the best of it instead of falling apart.

> [*They have started to sort things out, to differentiate themselves: "That was me, and this was you." They own up to their respective pasts. Gradually, they will be able to put their behavior into perspective.*]

DR. Like what? What did you expect she would do?

VAN. I don't know, I had, somehow I had the expectation that when it finally . . . things were at a point where they were

just . . . you know, it was crazy to go on the way it was.
It was desperate.

DR. Yeah.

VAN. Things were . . . So I guess I had a feeling that I . . . as
I said things to her that I was gonna say, "Look, we are at a
point where nothing makes sense, we're beating each other
to death, we gotta do something about it; we're at the point
where we gotta do something. Here's some more information
which further reinforces the fact that things are a bust. What
the hell are we going to do about it?" So I got about that
far . . .

CINDY. (Laughs quietly)

VAN. . . . And the shit hit the fan.

CINDY. Uh-huh.

VAN. And I . . . after I said that, after I said I had expected that
you'd be able to deal with things differently, then I thought,
Well, that's a hell of a lot to expect from anybody.

CINDY. Of course it is, especially when you say that there was a
possibility you came close to divorcing me and marrying another woman, and I'm supposed to take on that crisis and
say, "Oh!" Like the first time we were, he presented Jennifer
to me . . . the very first time, we were in bed, and he said,
"I have met this person I'm very strongly attracted to. I don't
know where it's going, but I want to pursue it. She's a turn on
for me." And I'm laying there, and I'm hearing him, and I'm
thinking, "Oh, okay, great." The next morning I wake up, and
I'm vomiting and so forth, and I run to the campus and find
her. He wants to bring her home so she can babysit, and he
wants . . .

DR. What? So the three of you can be in bed together, I don't
know.

CINDY. That's just it, and he wanted to make a happy threesome.
So I go on the campus to . . .

VAN. I haven't tried that yet, it might be worth it.
    [*Van says this good-humoredly*.]

CINDY. (Laughs) I tried to meet her and be her friend for my
husband's sake, because he's for the first time leveling with
me. But I can't do it.

[*Cindy has an interesting pattern of being very accommodating to her husband. She has done this before, when Van was attracted to another student (Melissa). See Session II, page 89.*]

DR. You should have tried harder.

CINDY. And I reacted as jealous, and I told her, you know, "Hey kid, I know you're after my husband, hands off, he's mine," and she promised she'd never see him and he promised that . . . but anyway, he was asking me to deal with this . . .

VAN. Okay, but . . .

CINDY. . . . Without emotion.

VAN. Okay, but there's another historical piece of information that I don't think I've talked about . . .

CINDY. Uh-huh.

VAN. . . . Which further exemplifies the federal casing syndrome.
[*Federal casing refers to making a big federal case, including arraignment, grand jury evidence, indictment, etc.*]

CINDY. That's true, too.

VAN. . . . That I struggled with.

CINDY. Yes.

VAN. My first experience in comparative anatomy . . .

Dr. Yeah.

VAN. My first course in comparative anatomy, I must have been four, three or four, with Sophie, a little girl next door. And I can remember . . . it was a really exciting kind of experience, we were doing little kiddie things, and I'll show you mine and you'll show me yours, and all this stuff. Well, my sister found us and she told my mother. My mother called me into the house, and she said, uh, "You have two options."

DR. Just like that?

VAN. Just like that. And I can almost . . . she was both . . . she gave me what TA people call a "gallows transaction."
[*TA means Transactional Analysis. Gallows Transaction: any inappropriate smiling or laughing reaction to a person's misfortune.*]

DR. Yeah.

VAN. ▶ ▶ ▶ She told me, "This is terribly serious," but she said it in a smiling way, like she was chuckling, because I was a little kid, playing with my penis. So I got . . . I can remember those two messages. But she said, "You got two options. You can get a spanking and go around the house all day long without clothes on, because if that's what you want to do then I'll let you do it. Or you can run around the block nude for your punishment."

> [*His mother seems to have as the ultimate end of this punishment to shame Van and not allow him any dignity, even the small dignity a child is entitled to. She lets him choose how he's going to make an ass of himself. She's got a fine instinct for degradation.*]

DR. So what'd you do?

VAN. I took the spanking and sat around the house.

CINDY. Oh!

VAN. Crying all day long, covering myself with . . .

CINDY. (Shocked) Oh.

VAN. . . . Anything I could find.

DR. Did you ever see her in the nude?

VAN. My mother? Yeah. I have more recollections of walking in on her when she was sitting on the john. Sitting on her lap.

CINDY. (Laughs)

DR. In the john?

CINDY. (Laughs)

VAN. Yeah. In fact, I can remember I walked in on my grandmother once.

CINDY. Oh, Jesus!

VAN. And she nearly . . . she nearly collapsed, you know. (Gleefully)

CINDY. You crawled up on her lap, too?

VAN. Oh, my God.

DR. It sounds like a new version of the Madonna scene.

VAN. Well, it was . . . she was on the throne. That was a sort of, uh, it wasn't an uncomfortable thing at all. I remember that very readily. ◄ ◄ ◄

CINDY. Gee, Brian wanted to do that the other day, to me.

VAN. Well, hell, we're open about that kind of stuff, too. If the kids walk in we don't say, "Oh! Oh! get out, get out!"

CINDY. No.

DR. But you got to figure out how to have generational boundaries between yourselves and the kids.

[*In any family which includes parents and children, one thing that parents often overlook is the need to work out a way of life which will convey to the children that there are two generations of human beings present, parents and children. Many parents feel that, in order to assist their children in feeling more comfortable about their bodies, it is desirable to casually walk around in the nude. Or in other kinds of families, parents feel that it is natural to have children sleep in bed with them, and on occasion observe the parents making love. However well intentioned such parents are, the children in such settings will often have difficulty with aspects of life outside the home, for example with studying, because they are chronically stimulated sexually. This distracting stimulation can become very intense in adolescence, where a developing young boy, for instance, might begin to masturbate while thinking about mother's body. For this reason, it is important that the parents' bedroom be off limits to children, especially when the parents are dressing or making love. I find that one of the cheapest items that can lead to security for a child is a hook and eye placed inside the parents' bedroom door. This item, available at any hardware store, costs 12¢. Not allowing a child in his parents' bedroom can contribute to his sense of security and ability to cope with being alone in his bed at night. The child knows he is not entirely shut out, for if he needs the parent he can knock on the door.*

In any event, if there are changes to be made, parents should inform children that the door will be locked at night, and they've decided that they want to have their privacy; if the child wants in, he can knock. The same can be done for bathrooms. This tactic can begin at the age of one year.

If there is a limited amount of bed space available,

> *rather than having a child sleep in the bedroom with the
> parents, he can have a sleeping bag in a living room or
> parlor.*]

CINDY. I agree.

VAN. Yeah.

DR. Otherwise you're gonna fuck their heads over.

CINDY. Oh, yeah.

VAN. Yup. But I think, well, what the issue I was getting to was,
the kind of federal case stuff that . . .

DR. You were sensitized to.

VAN. Yeah. . . . Oh, I can remember feeling guilty . . . my
God, I felt guilty. I was very sensitive as a child, anyway, and
very, very much needed to please. There's a lot of that stuff
that still exists in me. I need to please. It's difficult for me to
confront authority figures; it's difficult to get angry, difficult
to say what I want to say around Big Daddies or Big Mom-
mas, even, or to be angry and confronting and limit-setting,
you know.

> *[Every child is sensitive.]*

DR. ▶ ▶ ▶ You must have been a bit pissed off at me last time.

VAN. Oh, yes, I was. The closest I got to it was saying that you
were goading me. I really do . . . I really didn't tell you
how angry I was.

DR. How angry did you feel inside?

VAN. Pretty damn angry. And, but, it's a mixed feeling. I felt angry
and helpless. And I can remember saying to Cindy after the
session, when you . . . I felt that *you* had dumped on me, I
felt that Cindy had dumped on me, and I was sitting here
thinking, "God damn it!" . . . and about that time you
said to Cindy, "What are you jumping on him for, what do
you want him to do?"

CINDY. Bitching about him.

VAN. Yeah. And I sort of said, Thank God, you know, that felt
good, that somebody said, "Lay off for a minute," because it
was another one of those boundary things, that people were
dumping so much stuff on me that I couldn't push it away or
deal with it. But then, you see . . .

DR. Now I want to know, what did you feel inside in terms of the anger toward me?

VAN. It gets focused on . . . I think as best I understand it in my head, it has to do with resistance. That's not what you're asking me.

DR. No. You're making a head thing out of a gut thing.
[*Intellectualizing in order to avoid feeling.*]

VAN. I know, I know.

DR. It's as if you're a little bit skittish about telling me what was going on inside.

VAN. I think I'm better able . . . aw hell. I did it the first time by saying, when you came in after you played that tape I listened to, I said, "Norman Paul, you bastard!" I didn't say it in a . . . I said it in a way that I smiled and made a joke out of it . . .
[*Making jokes is a way of diffusing unrecognized anger and anxiety.*]

DR. Like it was a joke.

VAN. But I think I . . . yeah. But I think I'm angry that you zero in on me and get past my defenses. That's heady, too. I don't know what else to say. I think I'm angry that you charge so much money.
[*Defenses are barriers against feelings.*]

DR. Yeah.

VAN. And that I have to pay it. I'm angry that there are times you make me feel I'm a little boy. Maybe that's part of it. That you represent a very powerful figure.

DR. Like your momma.

VAN. Yeah, and I feel taken to task, ◄ ◄ ◄ and that I have to be defensive, or I have to, uh, I have to say things to state the case better, and stuff like that.

DR. Are you angry that things are moving, too?

VAN. I tried to think about that, when you had said it, I listened to it on the tape, about uh, maybe I was saying this was the last session because things were moving so fast. I can't get in touch with that, but it makes sense to me. I would say here that I want to move fast, I really do . . . here . . . but it makes sense to me that maybe moving fast also fits into that same old pattern of it's got to be my decision.

DR. It's got to be your pacing.

VAN. My pacing, my control. So it certainly makes sense to me, that part of what I'm angry at is that you're pushing me faster than I want to go.

DR. Which I would interpret meaning that the way you want to go is to think that you want to go somewhere, but go nowhere.

VAN. Yeah, it's probably right. I'm sure I'd be good at that.

CINDY. He thinks you and I . . . am I interrupting . . . ? I mean, I'm sorry I'm saying what you [Dr.] think, but I have a feeling that he thinks he wants to deal with Jennifer and he wants to deal with what that stuff is all about, and he thinks that you and I are preventing this. That he can't really deal with it with me here . . . Don't you [Van] think what I'm saying is right?

VAN. But you have to say that in the past tense, because that certainly was how I felt a month ago.

CINDY. Okay.

VAN. I'm not sure that I still feel that way.

CINDY. That's important. I just felt like, we left one session and he kept saying, "I really have to deal with that, and I really want to deal with that . . ."

VAN. I was still hurting . . . depressed.

CINDY. And I thought . . . think . . . that we're allowing it, (the issue of Jennifer to be dropped), that you two are allowing it. I wonder if that's what's some of this pacing was about. He's been feeling good. The whole family's felt his feeling good.

DR. Can you stand it?

VAN. Me?

DR. Yeah.

VAN. Jesus Christ, I hope I don't sabotage it.

CINDY. Well, you almost did this morning but you caught yourself. That's why I asked you.

VAN. Well, that's the first time I've been cranky in a while.

> [*Does Cindy feel people who are feeling good can never get angry, or depressed, or cranky?*]

DR. How do you feel coming in here today?

VAN. Well, I went through another episode that Cindy talked about when I got up. It was fine, I was ready to go, and interested to see what we were going to talk about . . .

> [*He acts as though he will have no control over what will happen.*]

DR. Yeah.

VAN. And Cindy was upset because the kids wouldn't get ready quick enough.

DR. Yeah.

VAN. And as we got through all of the complications of getting the kids squared away and getting on the train and all, I felt myself going into what I told Cindy was a blue funk, which is sort of like, uh, you sit around and gnash your teeth and feel bad.

DR. Yeah.

VAN. And it just . . . I felt it kind of just as if, yuahh [a noise], I was sinking into a black hole.

> [*If this is the sound I'm thinking of, the comic books used to spell it: YAAAAAAHHHHHHH! or EEE-YYYAAAHHH!*]

DR. Is that the way you felt around your momma?

> [*Bringing it back to the past again.*]

VAN. I don't know. I don't know.

DR. Sinking into her black hole . . .

VAN. God, the symbolism is incredible. I'm sure that a lot of it I'm associating to something else. I'm sure that, that a lot of the stuff that went on in my adolescence and even now, involves her. I'm sure that, at least I'm more certain that things like I always from a distance wanted to be with . . . to date blondes, but I always went with brunettes. That there was something untouchable . . .

> [*Referring back to pages 181–182, regarding Van's negative feelings about any eroticism toward his mother, I was trying to turn his attention back into the setting when he was an adolescent,* when he was struggling to distance himself from any kind of erotic fantasies about his mother, and at the same time relating*]

---

* See *Normal Adolescence.*

*some of his blue funk and depression of the moment
back to that era.*]

DR. What color hair has your sister got?

VAN. She's blonde.

DR. Blonde too.

VAN. I can think of a number of occasions where I always sort of
fantasized about dating gals that were . . . gals that I
thought I really would like to be around; never even tried.
Sort of admired them from a distance. It was always brunettes that I dated. I'm sure it has something to do with the
heavy Oedipal loadings . . . or whatever you want to call it
. . . toward my mother, that blonde people were, were taboo. It was too threatening, too frightening, uh, too much
like screwing mother or something.

DR. You were overly stimulated by momma?

VAN. I think so.

DR. And the only way you could handle it, when you were talking
about the way inputs hit you now, if it's too much you gotta
take it in pieces or you blot it out. I think this is the way you
handled your adolescent years.

VAN. Yeah. (Pause, thoughtful, reflecting) 'Course, that was the
time when my father was falling apart, too. I ended up being
a nice guy, fair-haired boy . . . sort of approach to the
world. Take care of me, I'll be a nice guy. I was voted the
best-dressed . . . ah, oh shit! (laughs) . . . the best-dressed
and *neatest* boy in the sixth grade. What a shitty thing! When
you think about it. God damn it, a little kid, a little boy,
ought to be able to get dirty. You oughta be able to run
around and look like a ragamuffin.

DR. But if you did you'd cross your mother.

VAN. Yeah.

CINDY. Can I tell you something else about yourself that I just
remembered? When you were a junior in college my mother
came to the campus to meet Van, and his mother was there.
And we were in a big cafeteria, so there were a whole lot of
people. We got ready to leave, and Van kissed his mother on
the mouth. And my mother said . . . Later, she said, "I
knew, Cindy, that he'd make you a good husband, because

the way he was treating his mother . . ."

VAN. Devoted to my mother.

CINDY. Devoted. And after we left, his mother said goodby to my mother, "You know, Vanny has always kissed me goodby, and he's still not too big to kiss me goodby." Do you remember that?

VAN. I don't remember that at all.

> [*If a mother kisses a son on the mouth it suggests that they view themselves as lovers. The mother helps to stimulate quite intense erotic fantasies in the son, which can't help but lead to a variety of guilt-laden experiences. It is interesting here that Van has forgotten this incident totally, which suggests the intensity of the guilt he experienced.*
>
> *I wonder, too, apropos of the mouth-kissing, how much Van's mother took out her resentment of his father in seductive behavior toward their son.*]

CINDY. That really sold my mother on you. (Laughs)

DR. You didn't French-kiss her?

VAN. No, but we . . .

CINDY. But hey!

VAN. There's something that we, I or me, just put together too. Cindy's always complained that I never like to kiss her, and I've always said, I don't know, I said something on one occasion which comes up again and again, which I don't really remember.

CINDY. (Laughs)

VAN. It had something to do with, uh, the way in which Cindy and I kiss. And I was lying in bed, and suddenly became aware of the fact, that I can remember as a little kid resenting and feeling repulsed when my mother would kiss me. Because she would open her mouth, and when she kissed me, she would sort of go, you know, like, I felt like she was (slurp) that kind of stuff. And my lips would always be wet when she kissed me. I remember even as a little kid going, God, that kind of stuff. And part of it was very reminiscent of uh, the things that at least I had complained about before.

CINDY. Right! We'd make . . . when we were having intercourse he'd put his face down in the pillow. He didn't want to have any kind of mouth contact.

DR. To protect his head.

CINDY. I don't know . . . But I commented I thought it was the kissing aspect, and that's when he said, well, something, I don't know, but anyway he commented on my kissing.

VAN. Yeah.

DR. Well, through the eyes of a little kid of three and four, if your mother's kissing you that way, let's just take that as an example, a little kid wonders whether he or she's gonna disappear into mommy's mouth. So you got two dark holes. One on the mouth and one down below.

VAN. I'm sure that that feeling of being clutched at is very old.

CINDY. Uh-huh.

VAN. But I felt it very young, at a very young age.

CINDY. You've never liked for me to clutch you. You know, we'll be watching TV or go to the drive-in or something, and I try to clutch, feel, and . . . well, used to, not now . . . but you used to quite often push me off. And then I of course read all this as rejection to me that he didn't . . . he was turned off with me.

> [*Van was turned off by that image of his mother which he had placed upon Cindy.*]

VAN. My sister said something to me as well. She said, "Every time I hug you, Van, you're . . . you're stiff," I said, "Yeah, I know, Dot, I can't . . ." It's not true with . . . it *is* true with a lot of women, I guess . . . friends. But certainly it's true with her; it's very difficult for me to be relaxed. I notice it particularly with Dorothy. That, that's too threatening too. I can remember feeling erotic feelings about Dorothy. There was one summer that Dot and I spent alone together, that's when my mother took my father up to, uh, Michigan.

DR. That was when you were . . .

VAN. I was about a sophomore, I guess.

DR. In high school?

VAN. In high school. My sister would have been a freshman.

DR. Did you sleep together?

VAN. No, but I thought about it.

DR. Did you pet?

VAN. No, I thought about that too. I had all kinds of erotic fantasies about that. I can remember thinking about sleeping in the nude and maybe leaving my blanket off or something so she'd walk in and see me.

CINDY. (Clears throat)

VAN. No, I never . . . never acted the fantasies out. I had a lot of fantasies about her. I had a very rich fantasy life as an adolescent. More fantasy and masturbation than anything else.

DR. No, uh, when you went into training therapy in 1965, what was the time sequence between starting that and your mother's death?

VAN. It was after that . . . February, whenever it was. Yes, I had gone down to be ordained after Christmas, that's right.

CINDY. We had also lost a baby . . .

VAN. Cindy had a miscarriage earlier that fall.

DR. What month?

VAN. I don't think I got into therapy until the September of that '65. So within four, five, six months after my mother's death. I can remember one of the words in the letter that Thornton (his previous therapist) used, when he sent it to John Mayhew who made the referral. He [John Mayhew] showed me the letter. One of the things he put was "latent depressive." And one of the things we talked about was I had a whole series of losses which I never got in touch with. I never allowed myself to really feel or work through. I really felt that I had.

DR. You mean during those two years?

VAN. Yeah. I was pretty much depressed, off and on for . . . I've been pretty much depressed off and on, for a lot of my life.

DR. So this business of Jennifer is really an attempt to retrieve mother, in some ways.

[*Jennifer was blonde and blue-eyed, too.*]

VAN. I sure kicked those thoughts around, for a long time. I don't understand what Jennifer is. That's a possibility. Uh . . . it may be that I'm . . .

DR. Or Dorothy.

VAN. Yeah, or that . . . I've gotten to the point where things are going really good, I finished my dissertation, you know, I'm on top of the world, and I have to sabotage it. By doing something stupid.

> [*Van's reaction to finally completing his education is not an uncommon one; namely, upon the completion of an important task, there is a letdown, coupled with the need to undo the sense of joy in success. This is very often related to latent guilt about achievement.*]

DR. The need for grief.

VAN. Yeah, to mourn . . . I need to be in mourning. If I'm not, then I find a way to do it.

DR. Then it sort of sounds like what you put on Cindy is your problem: you know, if she has excessive pleasure, let's say orgasm, orgasm equals pleasure . . .

VAN. Yeah.

DR. . . . That she'll go bananas. It's as if *you* might go bananas if you haven't got grief.

VAN. Hmmm.

DR. And that *you* might end up in that sanitarium in Michigan.

VAN. I know there's a hell of a lot of fear that I've never gotten in touch with about that.

DR. Are you making any stabs at tracking that down?

VAN. Yeah, I talked to my sister on the phone. . . . And we have a physician's name. She thinks she can get an address, so we're . . .

CINDY. Oh good.

VAN. We're gonna try; she wants to know as much as I do. We know the doctor's name now, she remembered it, Fleming.

CINDY. Why don't you try Melvin Frye? He would be a source for some of that stuff.

VAN. Yeah, he would.

CINDY. I would think your mother can find . . .

VAN. No, it was Alfred Eliot, the Baptist Church in Alabama.

DR. If you get me the information, I'll send away for the records of whatever is available.

VAN. Dorothy thought the hospital was called Fleming Sanatorium.

DR. Do you know where in Michigan it was?

VAN. Detroit is the best we could figure out.

DR. I hope it isn't closed.

VAN. I don't know. I think it was a private . . . I'm sure it was a private sanatorium. Fleming was the psychiatrist in Alabama; it was his father's outfit. As near as we can remember. Or at least his father was on the staff of this place.

DR. So it may have carried a different name.

VAN. Yes.

DR. Well, let's see if you can get whatever you can get, I'll track it down. I want you people to see the first time you came in, and see what has happened since.

VAN. It sure feels different. It'll be interesting to see.

DR. This is September 22. One thing I want to know, you know exactly the time, it's five weeks ago about. I want to know how much time does it feel like. It may feel different from the actual chronological difference in time.

> [*I want to help them feel an accurate sense of time and understand their progress within it.*]

(Videotape playback of Session I.)

> [*Videotape material is on pages 47–50, 51–60, and 70–74.*]

(Comments during the playback:)

DR. (To Van) You may be better able to see mannerisms of your father and mother before we got involved with them by looking at them now.

VAN. I just got in touch with some feelings that reflect on what's going on here too. You [Dr.] seem very remote to me. I don't know if it's me or you.

DR. Yeah.

VAN. But the way in which you're sort of over there with all that paraphernalia tucked around you . . . kind of sets up the same kind of feelings that I'm not sure I can get to you, I'm not sure I can be close to you. Or that you want that. And maybe that's part of where the anger's coming from. And when you walked out of the room, I feel it again . . . I say, By God, I'm paying this guy money, and he walks out of the room!

DR. It's as if I become a two-button switch depending on your feelings of the moment. At times I'm Big Momma, and then at this point . . .

VAN. It's my father.

DR. Yeah. And you're also projecting onto me your own notions of yourself.

VAN. Hmm. I don't know how much of that's . . . what stirred it up I think was too, I think the talk about being here and what it was like to be a child.

(Videotape ends.)

DR. How long ago does that feel?

VAN. When it first started, it felt like years . . . about . . .

DR. How many years, about?

VAN. I think my response would be six.

DR. Six years.

VAN. Yeah. Part of it's still very current. But part of it seems like a long time ago.

CINDY. It's so interesting you said that; it was exactly what I felt . . . But again, I guess it was because to me it was . . . I haven't felt that way since six years ago when Melissa entered the picture . . .

VAN. Is that six years ago?

CINDY. Yeah.

DR. How do you feel about what you saw there, Cindy?

CINDY. I thought that, well, I was thinking that there was only twice in my life that I've felt that way, and how stupid it really sounded and looked to be feeling that way. That's really, that's really weird that I'd be having that much feeling and that sad, just by what's been going on. I mean I was really . . . I looked like my whole world has ended, and I . . . heard what I was saying, and I thought, "That is so stupid, that I'd be acting so violently."

> [*"Stupid" seems to refer to the genuine experience of painful emotion, which had been derogated and devalued within her original family setting. Cindy treats herself in a similar fashion.*]

DR. What's stupid about it? That's what I don't understand.

CINDY. Well, because it wasn't really . . . I mean, just what she's saying, it doesn't sound like it was worth allowing yourself to get in such a worse depression, in such a worse state that you just couldn't cope. And I wasn't coping.

[*Cindy has great difficulty recognizing that it was she who was so desperately depressed.*]

DR. Six years ago Brian came on the scene.

CINDY. Yes.

VAN. So it must have been . . .

CINDY. Wait, we had a terrible summer before we got Brian.

VAN. Holy smoke.

CINDY. In May he came home again, and told me he was gonna have lunch with this nice person who was my very good friend.

VAN. Was that before Brian?

CINDY. Yeah. It was the summer before we got Brian.

DR. May of 1965?

CINDY. And he was gonna meet her in Providence for lunch and uh, I fell apart. And reacted exactly the same way. He got back and said they picked up sandwiches and they walked, and sat and talked about books, and she was another blue-eyed, sophisticated, highly intelligent person, and he wanted my permission to do this kind of stuff. And she called him that night to talk to him, and I went berserk and had the exact same reaction, same feeling. I remember going in to the baby's room . . . I had had the bedroom set up for like four months before we got Brian, because we didn't know at what point . . . and I remember going in there and kind of throwing myself across the baby . . . the crib, and screaming, and having a terrible tantrum. Have you forgotten that?

VAN. No, no, no, I'm just amazed that that was six years ago, and that the same stuff was going on.

CINDY. Exactly. And I went into therapy then, and uh . . .

[*Obviously there was something wrong with Cindy that she got so upset about Van's involvement with another woman.*]

VAN. That's when you first started seeing . . . oh, that's right. You started to see Ladd then.

CINDY. Yeh.

DR. Hmm! This is today. See what changes have occurred.

(Videotape playback of Van regarding sharing bedroom with parents)

[*The material on videotape is on pages 180–185. The concept of change under the best of circumstances is difficult to nail down. Change in human behavior can be assessed only by comparing the actual data at two different points in time. The actual data here, the videotapes of September 22 and of today, present the evidence of the way these two people were behaving at two different times. By presenting the videotapes to Cindy and Van, they can make a determination themselves as to what changed. Without such comparison they can only have hazy, vague notions.*]

DR. What do you think of these people?

CINDY. I like them.

VAN. Hell of a lot different from the first one. Yeah. Hell of a lot different.

DR. Can you stand it? That's the real problem.

VAN. Huh! (Laughs) Yeah, I sure think so. I hope so. God, if I can't . . . it's bad news. Yeah, there are a lot of positive things happening right now. I think we're much more capable of giving each other some stroking.

[*Stroking: any act that says "I know you're there."*]

DR. Uh-huh.

VAN. I feel more capable of meeting Cindy's needs, without feeling drained.

CINDY. And I'm not communicating that I have so many needs any more.

VAN. Yeah, I see you becoming more of a person.

CINDY. I went out drinking last night with the girls. My new liberation . . . I couldn't wait to get home.

DR. (To Van) Did you see the sixth-grade kid who's the neatest in the class?

VAN. Yeah, still. (Laughs) Still.

DR. He's got his tie rumpled.

VAN. Yeah.

DR. (Joking) Rumpled . . . it's bad . . . bad (humorously).

VAN. I was aware of doing that, feeling more comfortable about it.

DR. Uh-huh.

VAN. And it felt comfortable. But I still get dumped on, from time to time, by my friends for being a clotheshorse. Some of my students took bets one time about how many closets I must have. It's a dirty thing to do.

CINDY. (Laughs)

VAN. I'm getting better about that stuff.

CINDY. I don't see that as a problem.

VAN. Well, it fits the whole thing though. It symbolizes the issue.

CINDY. Well . . .

VAN. I feel in a lot of different ways I'm able to give myself permission to do some things that I never have before.

CINDY. Uh-huh.

VAN. I see it as reflected in my teaching, I see it reflected in relationships, with friends, and in our relationship, and with the kids. I certainly feel like I can be with them much more.

DR. Yeah.

VAN. The whole summer is a kind of a . . . bad scene. I really wasn't there when I was there.

DR. Yeah. See, the hypothesis in all this is, which I think is valid, is that as soon as you became a father the implicit fear would be that you'd end up in a sanatorium, somewhere in time.

VAN. Umm.

DR. And that's why it's important to get the facts about that.

VAN. Mmm. Son of a gun. Pshew! What about adolescence, Great Scott! When they get to be adolescents.

DR. Yeah. That's why you ought to save these tapes and periodically review them . . . there's part of your life on those tapes.

VAN. Mmm.

DR. After we wind down, and out, so you don't forget.

VAN. Yeah. I teach adolescent development in case work. Holy cow. I'm writing a book on adolescent development. I wonder if there's some stuff going on in that too. I'm still working through some things.

DR. Trying to prevent adolescents from going bananas.

VAN. Yeah. Maybe . . .

DR. See, the inference is that by coming in on your father and mother . . . that scene . . . that you could really give her an orgasm, mother, and who would go bananas in that setting?

VAN. Yeah.

DR. And right in the midst of all this, somewhere in there, your father goes to the sanatorium.

VAN. Yeah.

DR. When you said that you felt Cindy's becoming more of a person, there's a very subtle kind of projection. It's as if you're becoming more of a person; you're gonna sort of give her the vibes to be herself.

CINDY. Uh-huh.

DR. It's a reciprocating kind of thing.

VAN. Yeah, I think that's true. That's certainly true.

DR. But the main fear I would put in terms of being a father and of moving into his footsteps.

VAN. Mmm. Yeah, all kinds of things come to mind I associate with . . . feelings about fears of being successful, being so damned depressed after I got my Ph.D.; being a success means right around the corner you're going to collapse.

DR. Or you can get momma. She wants you to be a success.

VAN. Yeah . . . Wow.

DR. She could then have your baby.

VAN. Hmm.

> [*I wonder if in Van's case the achievement of success and its excitement is viewed on a fantasy level as equivalent to the excitement of consumating an incestuous love-making episode with his mother. The ultimate of that fantasy would be orgasm for Van with his mother, leading to conception of their baby. This is obviously a hidden fantasy.*]

DR. We're gonna have to wind up in a couple minutes, let me just alert you to a couple of things. Uh, one. As you're feeling better, the inference would be, how much further do we have to go in here, and then the implicit issue there is how you'd feel losing me. And that will sort of bring up a whole host of other kinds of loss experiences again.

VAN. Yeah.

DR. Which then is a way of . . . the way to counter that would be to get involved with somebody for a long-term relationship.

VAN. Hmm.

DR. Where maybe nothing much would be accomplished, but you would be able to finesse or avoid the winding down, leaving process, as that's where you're most vulnerable.

CINDY. Uh-huh.

VAN. Yeah, I never said goodby to Thornton.

DR. You didn't?

VAN. I never really terminated with him; I stopped going. I never talked it through. I've been aware of that for a long time; that I couldn't say goodby.

DR. Did you say goodby to your folks when they died?

VAN. I'm not sure I know how. Knew how. If you mean did I really grieve for them, and work through that grief . . .

> [*The first step in grief is the conscious recognition that somebody you cared about or loved or were very much attached to, is dead. The conscious recognition that someone actually is dead is to be able to be aware of the saying of goodby to that person forever. There cannot be any grief without the recognition of the death and final goodby. There are people who go through a number of years appearing to grieve for somebody without ever having confronted the fact that the person is dead. This behavior can be called pseudo grief, because it takes the form of crying or wailing in the service of denying the reality of death, and is an expression of anger at even the thought that the person might be dead.*]

DR. Or you can say goodby to them. There are different ways of doing it. Uh, let me tell you what I think. I think that one, you ought to get that . . . get to me that information about Michigan, and I'll move on that. Secondly, I think before you go to Cardiff or wherever you're going on the Continent . . . I do think it would be valuable for you to make a trip to your parents' grave . . .

CINDY. Oh (surprised).

DR. . . . And see what comes out there, whatever it is. And some people will go and take a little cassette recorder with them so they capture the freshness of their reactions, whatever it might be. And they can review it later. I'm thinking in terms of how to get you people to the point in time where you can, with the vicissitudes you can expect and the uncertainties, you can have a certain sense of expectant mastery in terms of what's coming down the pike.

CINDY. Uh-huh.

VAN. Yeah. The first thought I had when you started mentioning that was, uh, we've . . . I've been feeling a hell of a lot better; I know Cindy has, but I didn't want that to be a flight into health . . .

> [*"Flight into health" is a psychological term to describe some patients' feelings that they are suddenly well. A flight into health is a resistance to delving deeper into one's problems or reviewing past problems. Actually, what happens as a result of decoding one's behavior is not a change in the nature of one's problems, but rather one's perspective on them and the capability to bear one's own feelings and fantasies.*]

DR. Uh-huh.

VAN. . . . An escape. I wanted it to be something that could be a permanent way of dealing with things to come, yeah.

DR. The tapes are key pieces in terms of reinforcing, not a flight into health, but a stability into health.

CINDY. Uh-huh.

DR. In a sense I guess you're both aware that what's most important is what you people are able to do on your own.

VAN. You know, tears are coming into my eyes as I'm thinking about what you said about going to see the graves. It's a goddamned pilgrimage. But I gotta do it, I guess. I should do it. No, I won't say it that way. It's a pilgrimage that may be very helpful.

DR. It's a matter of forgiving them and forgiving yourself. The forgiveness scene is very much loaded in there.

VAN. Yeah. The stuff has been there so goddamned long. Ahh! I really run from it. (Sighs)

DR. It's time to stop running, for yourself . . . Well, what would you say, about three weeks from now?

VAN. Same time?

DR. Can we meet later in the afternoon? Is that possible?

VAN. Yeah, I'll just cancel out a different course.

      [*Van is now able to be more flexible with his schedule.*]

DR. It's the day before Thanksgiving. Is there a recess?

VAN. I think classes get out at noon; that would be good.

DR. How about at 4:00 in the afternoon?

VAN. Sure.

DR. You, Cindy, may at some point be thankful he got involved with Jennifer.

CINDY. I've already told him I have. I think I am . . .

DR. Very strange, isn't it?

(All laugh)

VAN. Shit. `

DR. And then maybe there can be peace.

CINDY. As we eat our macaroni and cheese all week and sing our praises to you. That's what ambivalent is . . .

VAN. Don't say that.

CINDY. Oh, I'm sorry.

VAN. Okay, you may say that. I don't feel that way any more.

CINDY. I do . . . I realize I'm so excited . . . I look at you like a cure for cancer. If we had cancer we'd have to pay the best surgeon to remove it. So I can't look upon therapy as sacrificing our family budget.

VAN. I'm just amazed at how, how fast things developed and how much I do feel attached . . .

DR. Uh-huh.

VAN. And how really much I would feel that loss. That surprises me to no end, because I usually don't feel those feelings, as I've been saying all along.

CINDY. I'm just so excited that I get to be here to see it happen, that's what is exciting to me about marriage therapy. If this had happened privately you couldn't come home and tell me.

VAN. Certainly not the same way. Now, we got to run.

DR. Okay, fine; I'll see you.

CINDY. Goodby.

DR. Goodby.

VAN. I appreciate that.

DR. You're welcome.

If a man has one person, just one in his life,
To whom he is willing to confess everything—
And that includes, mind you, not only things criminal,
Not only turpitude, meanness and cowardice,
But also situations which are simply ridiculous,
When he has played the fool (as who has not?)—
Then he loves that person, and his love will save him.
I'm afraid that I've never loved anyone, really.*

—LORD CLAVERTON

* *The Elder Statesman,* by T. S. Eliot, p. 102.

On Being a Man; On Being a Woman

DR. This is for pre-Christmas. People're going bananas.

> [*A plastic banana has been suspended from the top of the doorjamb, and Cindy and Van ask about it.*]

VAN. Yup.

CINDY. Let me run to the bathroom.

VAN. Do you want me to give this to your secretary?

> [*"This" refers to insurance forms which have to be filled and filed for partial reimbursement of the cost for these sessions.*]

DR. Okay, thank you, I'll put it right over there. Someone knocking on the door?

VAN. Sounds like it.

DR. How're things working out?

VAN. Good.

DR. Really?

VAN. Yes. I feel very positive about things.

DR. This is the twenty-second of November, 1972.

> [*The date is routinely referred to, to identify each tape.*]

CINDY. (re-entering the room) Now I may sit still.

DR. How would you say, what would you say, how are things working out?

CINDY. Just great. I've had a couple of regressions.

DR. Yeah.

CINDY. But basically things are just still a real turn on. Um, I feel like a couple of times we've kind of sabotaged some good feelings, but we've been able to pick it up pretty fast.

[*Cindy suggests that life should be almost continually ecstatic. If this is her expectation, she's obviously headed for disappointment. She seems to believe the myth that everybody has to be happy all the time. It would then follow that any unhappiness either has to be denied, or if acknowledged, someone else has to be blamed for it.*

The other option is to accept the inevitability of some unhappiness as part of human existence. The problem for the individual, then, is to resolve these feelings of unhappiness or live with them as best he can.]

DR. Listen to any tapes?

CINDY. Yup.

VAN. We went over the last one.

CINDY. I listened to mine with you by myself, and then I listened to this last one. I'm not even feeling some of those feelings that I talked to you about on the tape.

DR. Huh.

VAN. Which ones?

CINDY. Wanting to have an affair, wanting to have someone make love to me.

DR. You people making love together?

CINDY. Uh-huhhh (a very neutral sound).

VAN. Yeh. We uh . . . heh, heh (laughs, and Cindy laughs too) . . . It's been good sex.

CINDY. He lets me scream and kick and (laughs). It's been good sex, it really has. It's been very good.

DR. Just a second. I've been having a wild season . . .

CINDY. You ought to change places.

DR. (Laughs, leaves room)

VAN. (Looking at the movie projector) Was that that movie thing you saw; you got a movie . . . ?

CINDY. Yeah.

VAN. I want to see that. I never got to see it.

CINDY. Maybe he'll let you borrow it and you can take it home. (Laughing) I want to do it in our own bedroom now, cause

I want you to see some of the things I want you to do to me. (Laughs)

> [*Cindy sounds a little self-centered here. The phrase "I want you to see some of the things I want you to do to me" is a little unsettling. She appears not too interested in what they might try together. It is important, however, to remember her past experiences during which Van held back from her.*]

VAN. Things like what?

CINDY. Oral sex. You have to see the movie. Van, it's too bad we can't do it in my home.

> [*Cindy has learned to become more self-assertive, because she knows that Van is now able to accept this. Yet she still considers their home "my home." She hasn't let him back in it yet.*]

VAN. That's true.

CINDY. How do you feel about things, Van?

VAN. They're better.

CINDY. I know that you're not getting enough loving. I get the feeling that it's something that you're not doing just because you know I want to now.

VAN. (Laughs)

CINDY. Now what are you laughing at?

VAN. I don't know. (Laughs again) I don't know . . . He [Dr] asked me how things were going, and I said, "Shitty!"

> [*This is an obvious maneuver on Van's part to tease Cindy, as a means of either neutralizing her enthusiasm for this marital therapy operation, or to provoke her to be angry at him.*]

CINDY. Did you really?

VAN. No I didn't. I said, "Good."

DR. (Returns) You know . . . how do you figure things happening so fast? I'm just thinking it's just two months ago.

CINDY. For myself I've been doing too much . . . a lot of homework. For me, just reading the book, *I'm OK—You're OK,* it's just clicked so much of some of my feeling in this crisis setting. I don't know if that has anything to do with it, but basically that just helped to give me kind of an outline of maybe some of my frustrations.

DR. Yeah. (To Van) What do you think? I think it has been very quick. Don't you? I don't know . . .

VAN. Yeah, I'm sitting here thinking like, uh, I hope to God it isn't a flight into health. Because it really feels good.

CINDY. That restaurant experience, you know, I . . . that panicked me in a sense, because I thought . . .

VAN. Which one?

CINDY. My birthday.

VAN. Oh yeah.

CINDY. Because I thought, we'd really been having a turn on, everything's just been too hunky-dory, and then zappy when we got angry at each other, it was really a violent scene.

DR. Yeah.

CINDY. I don't mean violent, I mean we were really angry, and I thought it's all over now; I mean it's not as perfect as I thought it was.

> [*This is a bit of a breakthrough for Cindy: to finally be able to discriminate between expressing anger and becoming violent.*]

DR. Is that what you're looking for, perfection? That's what it sounds like.

CINDY. Probably, because I think that's always been part of my pattern of . . .

VAN. I don't look perfect to you.

CINDY. Yeah.

DR. And then you're gonna be in trouble.

CINDY. Yeah, right.

VAN. Uh, I . . . I suppose, I don't feel this, but my intellect tells me . . .

DR. Yeah.

VAN. . . . though a lot of this stuff may be gut . . . some of the walls come back up, so that I haven't gotten close to some of the pain as much. But I don't think that's necessarily true, because I've . . . well, let's see now. I've got to think about this, because in some ways it still . . . I'm thinking about your uncomfortableness and . . .

DR. In what?

VAN. In my, uh . . . (pause) . . . I guess I, well, let's see, I'll put it this way. I guess what I've been doing is kind of saying, Jennifer is gone, now you can talk about it because that's upsetting.

DR. To whom?

VAN. To Cindy.

DR. Yeah.

VAN. And I wonder if I'm not doing the same thing again. I wonder if I'm blocking out my feelings in order to keep you from responding.

CINDY. Well, you *are* . . . you are making me feel very uncomfortable . . .

VAN. But she is gone . . .

CINDY. Because you turned toward me in making me feel for the first time in a long time that I'm number one in your life, and giving me some reassurance that I'm important to you again.

VAN. Well, we're able to party again.

DR. It's interesting how difficult it is to articulate what the hell's been going on.

VAN. Yeah, it is.

DR. And you see what you say about *I'm OK—You're OK,* I'm not too sure if you read that book a year ago you could have done so much with it.

VAN. True.

DR. I think it just would have been a cognitive input with meager benefit in terms of what you could translate into your own lives.

> [*At times when I become anxious as to where a given situation is going, I am apt to handle my anxiety by intellectualizing. Here the brand is similar to that showed by Van in the beginning session.*]

CINDY. Uh-huh.

DR. That's what I think of it. I'm very often impressed by the difficulty in articulating what happened, when things work out.

VAN AND CINDY. Um-hum.

VAN. Yeah.

DR. See, I think, you know, I'll just tell you the way my head is working. You know, this is the sixth session. This is session number six.

[*Cindy indicates her being important to Van is directly
related to the emergence of a harmonious sexual relationship, and he confirms this in his reference to being
able to "party" again, using "party" in the sense of sex
play. I try to distract them from the issues of partying
and chronic happiness. I wish to emphasize that it is
hard to know what accounts for improvement, and to
learn exclusively from written materials.*

*I'm now beginning to think how and when to in-
troduce a homosexual film. Since Van and Cindy say
there has been improvement in their sexual life and
other aspects of their relationship, I look for residual
problems. One of these might be the issue of gender
identity, which is a core problem for each person. The
sense of maleness or femaleness—gender identity—involves with it the capability of imagining being of the
other gender. This capability is related to the inherent
bisexuality of each human being (a Freudian concept).
The question for the therapist becomes how to help individuals to become more accepting of their hidden
homosexual fantasies. To do this, I use the homosexual
film, which has the effect of sanctioning the fantasy and
reassuring the patient. The theoretical basis for the use
of the film derives from the thinking of Sandor Ferenczi.
(See Ferenczi in References.) In a series of papers,
Ferenczi indicated the desirability of resolving some of
the problems of psychoanalysis. He sought to counter
the analyst's passivity by such activities as (1) preventing or prescribing certain forms of behavior, for example, omitting rituals in obsessional individuals and
actively encouraging phobic patients to have experiences
that activate the phobia; (2) arbitrarily setting a time
limit for the therapy; (3) using "forced fantasies" to
speed the exposure or unrecognized conflicts; (4) adopting a role vis-à-vis the patient which would acceler-
ate the treatment by stimulating the individual's neurotic
transference reactions.*]

VAN. I want to be a little flip and sort of say, well hell, we're integrated people . . .

> [*These after-the-fact assessments represent ways of covering up lack of information as to what accounts for changes. Certainly in Session I, Cindy did not appear too integrated, with the story of a dissociated suicidal attempt the previous night; and Van was quite well disconnected from his own past. This notion of Van's doesn't hold water.*]

DR. Yeah?

VAN. Right.

DR. I don't know what the hell that means.

(Everybody laughs)

VAN. I don't know. I think our relationship . . . I want to say it wasn't that bad for that many years . . .

DR. You want to bring the kids in some day?

> [*I change the subject to the children, as the issue of who's integrated, etc., is leading, I feel, to a dead end. I'm interested in helping the children express whatever feelings—insecurity, guilt, or whatever—they may have about their role in their parents' unhappiness.*
>
> *In extreme situations, children of a dissonant marriage will get involved with self-destructive behaviors, including drug addiction, designed to blot out their sense of guilt and pain. I'm also interested in meeting their children: Cathy, Mary Lee, and Brian. This will enable me to suggest to Van and Cindy alternate ways of coping with them so that each can feel more comfortable in his role as parent.*]

VAN. Why not?

CINDY. Sure.

DR. And see what they are about?

CINDY. I don't feel I'm still a very . . . I mean, that like last night is an incident where I still feel there is some of my old pattern operating, uh . . .

> [*Cindy reverts to the situation of the previous night. This is her way of letting me know that she is not yet ready to get involved with the children; that there are*

certain things about her own being that continue to demand attention.

When Cindy says "my old pattern," she refers to her inclination to become angry when she feels herself distanced by Van. Part of the difficulty when changes occur has to do with Cindy's concern about whether she deserves such improved self-esteem. This seems to be related to the issue of whether one deserves something better than the parent of the same gender. Although intellectually she can rationalize that she deserves happiness, the undercurrent of guilt periodically recurs.]

DR. Yeah.

VAN. There's still stuff going on.

CINDY. Yeah, I think maybe I am . . .

DR. What?

CINDY. Maybe I'm not giving a good picture of our home life, but there are still some ups and downers, but uh . . .

DR. There's always going to be ups and downers.

CINDY. But we come out of it in a different way than before.

DR. Yeah.

CINDY. We're all so easily ticked off.

DR. Still.

CINDY. Yeah. He came . . . You got real mad at me last night when you jumped into bed, and I couldn't figure out why you couldn't allow me to be mad, because it was my place to be mad, and why you got mad instead of letting me be mad.

VAN. Yeah, that was a similar pattern.

CINDY. Yeah.

VAN. That was the same old stuff.

[This seems to be the pattern in which Van is inclined to see Cindy as a father who's not interested in him. Van, therefore, distances her by proxy. In reaction, Cindy tries to get closer to Van, attempting to fuse with him. This kind of situation very often leads to men having affairs with other women.

It's also a question whether Cindy's father resembles Van in having been involved with other women. The obvious inference here is that Cindy was acting out her mother's conflict.]

DR. Are you interested in . . . I mean, do you fantasize about other women as much as you did?

VAN. Let's see. (Pause) ▶ ▶ ▶ I guess I'd respond to that by trying to think about what it was like before, versus what it's like now.

DR. Maybe you don't know how it was like before?

VAN. Well, I'm trying to put that together.

DR. Yeah?

CINDY. Why do you have to think about that question? Why can't you say yes, I do or no I don't?

> [*She is belligerently short with Van in not allowing him to think through the question about these fantasies. Her insistence suggests her continuing inability to accept Van's fantasies about other women. Van's hesitancy suggests that he is concerned about her reaction.*]

DR. He's trying to compare.

CINDY. Oh.

VAN. I'm trying to compare the two. Because before, there was a time . . . it was like I was telling about . . . John . . .

CINDY. Yeah? Okay.

VAN. . . . The time when all I used to think about was, uh, or, or all the conversation with all my friends was about, uh, what would it, what would be the situation uh, what would it be like if you went out and screwed somebody?

DR. Yeah?

VAN. So there's a lot of uh, fantasy about love, preoccupation with, uh, who's got the biggest boobs, and wouldn't she be nice to lay, and walking around RU [Rhode Island University] when I was writing my dissertation and stuff, uh, wow, look at that broad . . . I still appreciate looking at pretty gals, and I still have fantasies, but I don't seem to be preoccupied in the same way. I don't feel as, as . . .

DR. That you're scanning for it?

VAN. Yeah.

DR. As you had before.

> [*It's in the nature of a healthy human being to have fantasies and be sexually attracted to many different*

*people, whether one is married or not. To not have
these fantasies would indicate stagnation (most people
are unaware of how they stagnate). The major problem is in realizing that the fantasies don't have to be
carried out.*]

VAN. I don't think I'm on the make in the same way, yeah . . .
that I was before. Well, a lot of it I attribute to the fact that
our sex is much better. Because I'm able to be with you in a
way that I maybe never was before.

> [*Van makes it very clear to Cindy that he enjoys sex
> with her, and being emotionally intimate with her.*]

CINDY. That's for sure.

DR. Is he different than he ever was before?

VAN. I'm able to be much more active. I'm able to enjoy, I'm able
to enjoy Cindy's activity.

DR. Yeah?

VAN. It really rang true, this business about sex means somebody's
gonna go crazy, or control stuff, and when that rang true I
was able to sort of get on the, on the ride . . . interesting
use of words comes to mind . . .

> [*This is an interesting way for Van to express his new
> ability to accept Cindy's loss of control, and to enjoy
> that in the sexual setting.*]

CINDY. (Giggles)

VAN. . . . Get on the ride and enjoy it.

CINDY. Yeah.

VAN. . . . Sort of go with it rather than . . .

CINDY. Yeah, I can be cooking breakfast or something, and you
want to touch me now.

VAN. Yeah, I'm more conscious that uh, I . . . want physical
contact.

CINDY. You have your own feeling which is how I wanted . . .

(They all talk at once)

DR. Excuse me, Van. You had two years of therapy in '65 through
'67, right?

> [*My switching the subject is related to inquiring about
> the different outcome between what's transpired in the
> sessions to date, versus what had occurred over that*

> *two-year period. I'm trying to indicate to Van that it's questionable whether he needs any further one-to-one therapy, as well as to find out the difference between the outcome here and the outcome in the previous two years of therapy.]*

VAN. Yes.

DR. And did that bring out this order of change?

VAN. It didn't bring about the same kind of changes.

CINDY. That brought out negative changes.

VAN. Well, it brought about . . . a parentectomy.

> *["Parentectomy" presumably refers to the excision of unrecognized inhibiting or guilt-inducing features derived from a parent and from oneself. What happened was that he became freer from his parents' influence. This freedom, however, was also expressed by distancing Cindy whom he unconsciously saw as exhibiting traits of his parents. (He was unaware that he had projected this onto Cindy.)]*

CINDY. Yeah.

VAN. It brought about growth on my part, but it was growth away from you, as I would look at it now. It brought about a strengthening of my own resources so that I became more a person. I don't know if you saw it that way, but I felt that way, that I was less and less dependent upon you, as I was earlier, so that I felt I grew. But I don't think . . . it . . . I was able to grow by integrating that into our relationship as much as I grew away from you.

CINDY. Yeah. And maybe, have I caught up with you right now, where you're at?

VAN. I think that the way our relationship works *now,* is far different from the way it has ever worked . . .

CINDY. Yeah.

VAN . . . (Softly) in our marriage. The way in which we can talk about things. Although I still get spooked by things, and . . .

CINDY. Yeah, and you did a dirty thing . . . he did a real dirty thing to me.

DR. What?

CINDY. Uh, he brought home a, uh . . .

VAN. I didn't see it as a dirty thing.

DR. What?

CINDY. It *is* a dirty thing. Now let Dr. Paul say if *he* thinks it's a dirty thing.

DR. What?

CINDY. He brought home a, a pic . . . a newspaper, student newspaper, and there's a nude woman in it, a centerfold, and he showed it to me, and I just had no reaction, like *Playboy* or anything, and he said something about uh, she's in my class. And I said, "Gee, that's great . . ."

DR. Yeah?

CINDY. And he said, uh, "Yeah," I don't remember the whole context, but she's my, uh, the editor of the paper's fiancée and she's in my class, and I said, "Gee, now you told me the first time that she wasn't on campus, that she was somebody brought in from outside," and you said, I said "why are you telling me the truth now," and you said, "Because I didn't think you could handle knowing she was in my class every day."

VAN. Chuckle, chuckle. I remember saying "Chuckle, chuckle."
◄◄◄

CINDY. Yeah. So for two days I go around the house thinking, "Damn it, he must not still be reading *I'm OK* if he thinks that he still has to lie." So then . . .

> [*The exchange between Cindy and Van is an illustration of a teasing maneuver, aimed at recapturing their past dissonance. Part of this slippage is related to the disbelief that their marriage could be so different, as well as the inability to give up such a long-standing and familiar pattern. The confirmation for all this is Van's "Chuckle, chuckle" as if he gets considerable pleasure in recapturing or in stimulating Cindy's lingering mistrust.*]

DR. Well, then, do you want to move on today into new areas?

> [*I still have in mind the use of the homosexual flicks. The inability to bear one's insecurity about one's own gender very often is expressed in fantasies about other*

partners. Van in talking about this gal in his class reveals not only his own insecurity vis-à-vis Cindy, but also his lingering anxiety about his own gender identity. He distracts himself by provoking Cindy.]

VAN. Sure.

CINDY. Umm.

VAN. I don't know what that means (slightly belligerently).

(All laugh)

VAN. 'Cause what we're talking about you don't want to hear about, or . . .

DR. No . . .

CINDY. He's trying to bring up . . .

DR. What?

CINDY. Are you trying to find another point to cause a crisis?

DR. No. No, I'm trying to figure out how, in anticipating certain fantasies, you can avoid crises. Got it?

> [*This is related to the central issue of this book: In anticipating certain fantasies, one can avoid crisis.*]

VAN AND CINDY. Yeah . . .

DR. Um, and, let me just tell you a couple of things. I don't . . . did we ever get involved with the whole business, we touched on it a little bit, of the role of the homosexual fantasy?

VAN. You mentioned that to me, and I don't know . . . that was in my individual . . .

DR. Right, and did I tell you about the lady that I saw?

VAN. Yes.

DR. And about the flicks, the homosexual flicks? I don't think I did.

VAN. I remember that her fantasy or her difficulty was, as he was going to have oral sex, she wouldn't . . . she wasn't able to do that.

DR. Right. Did you hear his tape on that?

CINDY. He won't . . . I don't think you wanted me to hear it, right?

VAN. Well . . . Where is that tape? I don't know . . .

CINDY. You told me that you had it in your briefcase.

DR. (Laughs and leaves room to answer an emergency phone call.)

VAN. Hang on there!

DR. Goodby.

CINDY. (Laughing)

VAN. I don't think that's what he's trying to say. I think he said we got a lot more work to do. I feel we do.

CINDY. Oh, I know we do.

VAN. I feel I got a lot of work to do.

CINDY. Last night was another incident, and . . .

(Dr. returns)

VAN. Well, certainly I feel I got a lot of work to do.

DR. Well, why don't you want her to hear your tape?

CINDY. Yeah, why don't you? Why don't you hand that over to me?

> [*This is the old reciprocating control issue. If Van hands the tape to Cindy, she will become aware of a piece of him, which he is reluctant to share, fearing this will help to make him more securely her private property. It's interesting that this defensive maneuvering is in anticipation of getting involved in the issue of the homosexual fantasy system and distracts both of them from moving ahead into new areas.*]

DR. Do you think she can't take it?

VAN. It must be the same pattern.

> [*As described above, Van's reluctance to be visible is modeled on his father's invisibility. This reluctance provokes Cindy to be more controlling, in turn justifying Van's distancing of her.*]

DR. Okay, I'm going to go ahead with this thing. If we can get on with it today, it will be easier for her to . . . or for you to think of her getting involved with that [tape of Session III]. I discussed with Van the role of the homosexual fantasy in mate selection. . . . I got involved with how I got involved in the relevance of the homosexual fantasy system . . .

VAN. Jeez, I feel tense. I really am . . . even as you're talking about this.

> [*Van is right in touch with his feelings. He can express them.*]

DR. Ah, I suspect you will. Okay. Uh, in terms of not just mate selection, but the relationship between mother and daughter and father and son. And just briefly, let me tell you how I got onto this about a little over four years ago . . . almost five years ago now. The years just keep on clinking along. I saw a couple, a lawyer and his wife, and they had three kids, adolescents. And one day they came in and the wife said that she couldn't stand Sally—her sixteen year old. And what couldn't she stand about Sally? She found the kid repulsive. And it happened that she [Sally] had wrenched her elbow playing tennis, a couple of weeks before, so she could not internally rotate her arm. So she would ask her mother to snap her bra for her. And it was that activity that she requested her mother to be involved with that drove the mother bananas. You know, she found the kid repulsive, and what was most repulsive was that she had bigger breasts. And I couldn't get her to expand on "bigger breasts." "Bigger than yours?" or somebody else's? "No, I just can't stand this girl." So . . . and I had seen the kids a couple of times before, and just by a gross inspection there wasn't anything inordinate about Sally's bustline. So I went away to some convention, I was trying to figure this whole thing out. What's this all about? So I read *Portnoy's Complaint*. Did you ever read it? (Both nod) And I, I have a funny way of reading things; I read for both the content and then what's not in there. And sort of ruminating about Sally and her mother; what's this all about? *Portnoy's Complaint* ostensibly is about a mother and a son engaged in a co-conspiracy to avoid the recognition of a love-making fantasy between the two of them. And the way it's handled is that the mother and the son regard one another as a unit of one, or, they're fighting all the time. Usually you have combinations of this, mothers and sons, or father and daughters. And the reason the book garnered so much public interest was it documented how Alexander acted out his sexual fantasies with all these gals. So I'm thinking about this, I'm thinking about "bigger breasts," and Sally and her mother, and then it occurred to me that in the book there is a secondary character, and that is Portnoy's sister. And I was thinking that if there was this heterosexual fantasy system going on between the mother and the son, what's going on between the mother and the daughter?

CINDY. Um-hm.

DR. I then concluded that there *must* be a parallel track, a homosexual fantasy system going on between mother and daughter . . . And, handled in a similar way; either they're look-
alikes, fused as a unit, or they're fighting all the time.

> [*The clarification of the reason they are fused or fight-
> ing all the time: The fusion means that they are not
> separate enough to see themselves as two different, dis-
> tinct persons. Fighting all the time serves as a distrac-
> tion from thinking about or having the homosexual
> fantasy.*]

VAN. In every family . . . ?

DR. I think from what I have observed and studied, that this is a
universal parameter, in both a boy's and a girl's life. And it's
different in a girl than in a boy. I've explored this now with
about three hundred families, and it's there, I mean there's
just no question about it. And with the mother giving birth to
a girl it's a different bag altogether, because there's a thrust
to have the kid become a carbon copy of herself. And with a
boy it's already different by virtue of gender. They may try to
mold him, but not as a replica of self. It's different. And
there are a lot of gals who get mixed up in their own heads
between the fantasy of becoming a lesbian when they are
nursing a daughter. And they get some sensual pleasure, and
then they get their fantasy and bingo, they begin to think
"Gee, I'm going queer." It doesn't mean that they're going
queer, it just means they're having a fantasy; that's all.
Which, in a sense, really gets at the heart of what's a problem
in our culture, the confusion between the fantasy and the
reality.

VAN. Yeah.

DR. In effect, there is no harm in imagining anything, as long as
you know that it does not have to be actualized.

> [*In other words: Thinking is not doing.*]

VAN. That's, that's the Jesus condemnation.

DR. What do you mean?

VAN. As a man thinketh in his heart, so is he.

DR. Yes. Right. Right. So you have a marvelous reinforcement from religious doctrine, which helps people get confused, and I think, in part, it contributes to people going bananas.

VAN. Yeah.

DR. I mean like sex making people crazy.

VAN. Yeah.

DR. I mean, uh, you can believe anything, and you can go crazy just believing something. But in any event, I got ahold of some pornographic flicks, uh, mild lesbianlike porno flicks, and I showed it to Sally's parents after I came back. And I said, in effect, uh, that I want to make very clear what the rules are in this operation. I'm gonna show this film, a short flick, uh, and in no way is this to be construed as evidence that you're a lesbian, a homosexual, have lesbian tendencies or homosexual tendencies. All I want to know is what do you think and what do you feel seeing this. So I left, and when I came back, the mother was quite vitriolic. "You're showing me dirty filthy pictures, and they're repulsive, repugnant," the same words she used in reference to her daughter.

And then she gets involved with memories, and a remembrance of when she was about twelve years old, that was thirty years before, where she and a first cousin girl had a mutual fondling episode which turned her on during the episode, and afterward, rendered her so guiltridden—shameridden—that whenever she saw this cousin in an unpredictable setting, she would dart down an alley, or into a store, but she could brace herself to see her at festive occasions like Thanksgiving or Easter or Christmas. But the fascinating thing was that that behavior had assumed an automatic quality. In other words, she'd see this cousin, and she would dart down the street, but she had forgotten for the previous ten years what had triggered it off, until she saw the flick, which reminded her [of what had happened thirty years before]. Then she remembered that one night, and this is what Van's talking about, one night when she was trying oral sex with him [her husband], she remembered that as his head was moving down toward her genitals in the dark, it occurred to her that his head could be a woman's head. It scared the shit out of her. I mean, the power of the fantasy is extraordinary. In any event, a couple of weeks later the guy came in ahead of his wife, and we reviewed some other things, and he said he didn't know what was going on at home, but Sally had come to him a couple of nights before and said she was scared. Scared to tell her mother that for the first time she felt her mother really loved her. Now this is without the kid knowing anything about it.

And, there were no guidelines for using this kind of material. You know, I didn't know what was going to happen. Then, after the first time, that first scene, I explored it in a variety of ways, and I had assumed at that time, about four years ago, after going through the literature, that this was worked out with fathers and sons. I found out that most of the literature is written by men. The meager references to the female homosexual fantasy system were mainly because very few women had written about it. And what it really indicates is that, in order to be able to understand the female homosexual fantasy system from the male's position, you've got to be able to imagine being a female. And vice versa. In effect, in any event, if you're gonna be married and you're gonna try to be able to meet the needs of the other person, you gotta imagine being the other person. Not just in name, you know, but in terms of physiology and gender, which can be very threatening. Uh, especially if you're brought up with a wariness about homosexuality. For a man, with a lot of men I've seen, if they cry, they feel they're becoming homosexual. Bingo. Magically. So, what I was thinking of doing is to show you two kinds of flicks, a male homosexual flick and a female homosexual flick. Uh, the evidence for this is demonstrated in the aversion very often of mothers and daughters touching one another.

> [*The general theme: If you marry and wish to meet the needs of your partner, you have to imagine being that person physically, physiologically, and emotionally.*]

CINDY. Uh-huh.

DR. Usually from the daughter's part . . .

CINDY. Uh-huh.

DR. . . . with mother. Uh, and usually that's all they'll think about, you know, is this touch; some gals will think that mother's making a pass at them. And guys certainly will have that kind of feeling about fathers, at times. And the question is, who's radiating the fantasy? So you really don't know, with the parent and the child. See, I would say, with you, Van, your father's distancing of you in part may well have been that fear in his own head, as related to you.

VAN. Uh-huh.

DR. And for each person, there is I think a heterosexual-homosexual balance . . . fantasy balance.

VAN. My first thought is that my dad distanced himself from most everybody. And that may have . . . that may have been part of what was operating in his relationship with me, but I think he also had sufficient other difficulties in being close with anybody.

DR. Uh-huh.

VAN. That increased that.

DR. Uh-huh. Well, he remains an enigma.

VAN. I'm going to Alabama, by the way, December eighth. I'm gonna go down and visit my parents' graves.

DR. Did you get from your sister the name of the place?

VAN. No, she didn't know it either. But I'm gonna try to find out, when I'm down there in Alabama.

DR. Okay. So, are you game for this?

CINDY AND VAN. Sure. Ah-hah.

VAN. We didn't watch any at that convention we went to, did we?

CINDY. No. We fell asleep and missed it.

VAN. Yeah.

CINDY. That's the only thing we didn't see.

VAN. The AAMC convention in New York, uh, the topic of the convention was on sexuality and fantasy, fear and therapy, fear and . . . something like that. It consisted of a whole series of a semipornographic, supposedly educational, sexual education films. With, uh, starting with masturbation films, male, female, and heterosexual, black, white, group sex . . .

CINDY. Children films; something like that.

VAN. Children . . . I don't remember that one.

CINDY. We didn't see that one, that was what I was so upset about.

DR. Children doing what?

CINDY. Um, a mother and a . . . well . . .

DR. A mother and her daughter?

CINDY. Yeah, and of a . . . husband . . . father and a little boy.

VAN. Really?

CINDY. That's what I was so upset about. I thought it was terrible that they would have, uh, uh, these children act out something like that.

VAN. Really? I remember Harry saying that that was the next logical sequence, but I don't think it was ever . . .

CINDY. Yeah, and they were incensed about it, that they would have these children be the actors.

DR. Where were they done? In . . .

VAN. Seems to me they came from California.

DR. They do everything out there, don't they?

CINDY. Yeah.

VAN. . . . came from California, some sex education center. I, uh, well Tuesday night, since the issue has come up, I had some, uh, brief thoughts about those issues.

CINDY. About Jennifer?

VAN. Yeah.

CINDY. About Jennifer.

VAN. Oh, yeah.

DR. What? (noise of movie projector permeates room) . . . Just a second. You go ahead.

VAN. I had a bunch of students over at the house, senior social work majors, mainly, and their dates.

DR. Yeah.

VAN. Well, one (sighs), one student, guy named Jack, uh, on one previous occasion . . . when there was a sociology club meeting at one of the local pubs, and a bunch of the faculty were there and all of the sociology majors. He got a little bombed on beer, and, uh, was sitting next to me. And I had mentioned about a week before, I said this, the guy is gay . . . the way in which he stares at me in class is incredible, and very uncomfortable.

CINDY. Yeah.

VAN. But usually when women stare at me that way, I can deal with it, but when a guy stares at me that way . . . I was aware that there was something going on there. Well, at this thing, he leaned over to me about halfway thru the evening and he said, "I don't know whether you've noticed this or not, but I've been very attracted to you lately, and wanted to be around you," and all this kind of stuff. And I said, "Well, we'd better talk about that." Well, he never showed up to talk.

(Sound of projector)

DR. Yeah.

VAN. Then at the party, when we were in the kitchen, he and I were in the kitchen alone, and I went out into the other room, the living room, to say goodby to some people. He came out and asked me back into the kitchen. And he said, uh, "I'm in love with you."

DR. This past Tuesday?

CINDY. No, Friday.

VAN. Two weeks ago Friday. At which point I said, "Oh, Jack, that's a bummer. You got to talk about this stuff, so that it gets cleared up." Again, he never showed up. Stopped coming to class. Then uh . . .

CINDY. It shook him up so much he didn't even come back out . . . he stayed out by himself . . . I couldn't figure out what had happened to him.

VAN. Me, or Jack?

CINDY. No, Jack.

VAN. No, I'd never had anybody do that overtly to me. I've had lots of women come up and say, uh, "I've got a nice apartment. Why don't you come over?"

CINDY. You've had one other guy, though, in college, who was fascinated with you.

> [*Cindy seems rather proud of this and quite involved, although this is more apparent from the sound of her voice than in this text.*]

VAN. I also had . . . jeepers creepers, I also had a, a uh . . . I had an experience when I was coming back from Atlanta, on a bus trip, and I must have been . . . I don't know, eight? Coming on a bus trip that a guy had tried to, to uh, unzip my trousers, put his hand on my leg and the guy sitting next to me put his hand on my leg and slowly moved up. Scared me to death, absolutely to death. By the time I got to uh, Mobile, I was sitting like this . . . and he was trying to pull my hands away. I didn't know what to do, what to say . . .

DR. You were eight at that time?

VAN. Yeah, I was about eight, it seems to me. It was my first boy scout . . . see, no, do you have to be twelve to be a boy scout? It was my first . . .

CINDY. I don't know.

DR. She wasn't there.

(Cindy laughs)

VAN. Boy scout summer trip . . . I don't know why I'm asking.

DR. Well, what you're talking about with Jack you can expect to be increasingly common on campuses.

VAN. Yeah, they're . . . I read a lot about it, but never had that experience.

DR. Well, you can expect to have it, because that's . . . the thrust.

VAN. I don't know what to do with that information yet.

DR. Well, seeing this might help you.

VAN. Yes, the other side of . . .

DR. You know, if you can have a fantasy, then you can handle it much more readily when you're confronted by a real situation.

VAN. It doesn't . . . it didn't frighten me or make me uncomfortable. I felt like I could say to him, "I'm not interested," without being punitive.

DR. Yeah.

VAN. And sort of saying, "I'm straight. That's the way it is."

DR. Well, what would have happened if you were to say to him, "How would you like to sort of try something different?"

VAN. I don't know, I've never had fantasies about it.

DR. Well, let's see what you do with this.

VAN. Okay.

DR. Okay? This is called "Big and Little Ralph."

VAN. Ahhh.

CINDY. I wanted you to show him that picture sometime you showed me.

VAN. Which one?

DR. About a gal.

CINDY. Yeah.

(Dr. shows film. Comments during showing of film are by Cindy and Van. Dr. leaves room.)

CINDY. (She tells Van to press buzzer on telephone to alert Dr. to return.)

VAN. God, Cindy . . . I don't know how they do that . . .

ˑˑˑˑˑˑˑˑˑˑˑˑˑˑˑ Description of Film ˑˑˑˑˑˑˑˑˑˑˑˑˑˑ

Two young men, completely naked, are lying on a double bed. One sucks and kisses the other's penis, while being fondled on the back and the neck. Little Ralph lies on his back; Big Ralph then lays on top of him so that their penises are touching. Now they switch positions. They pause to lubricate their penises with a cream. Big Ralph places his penis in Little Ralph's anus. They have anal intercourse, using several positions (i.e., both lying down, then one lying down while the other kneels).

The camera focuses in on Little Ralph masturbating during anal intercourse. Little Ralph then lies on his back masturbating while Big Ralph kneels over him masturbating. They ejaculate together. They both lie back appearing depleted.

The next scene shows them clothed, walking down the stairs together. Big Ralph leaves the house, leaving Little Ralph gazing forlornly into space.

This is a very matter-of-fact movie. Very little affect is shown. There are erections throughout. The film is in color, and runs ten minutes.

ˑˑˑ

(Dr. returns, turns off projector.)

DR. This is a multimedia operation.

VAN. Mmm.

DR. Your tape is still on. Okay. What'd you think of it?

VAN. Let's see. I found the, the uh, the oral part the most erotic. The anal sex, I just sort of felt like My God, how can they . . . how is that possible, not how could they do that, but how is that possible? Uh, but the very first part was erotic . . . arousing. But the other parts weren't. And then, the last scene where he's standing alone, he looks sad to me. He looked lonely and sad. Like . . . forlorn. Empty.

DR. (To Cindy) What'd you feel about it? Any of it turn you on?

CINDY. Yeah, the oral sex . . . just the penis, gee (elatedly) just seeing it, but then I realized it was two men, my skin was kind of crawling, thinking it's sad.

DR. What's sad?

CINDY. To me it was just sad.

DR. Because what?

CINDY. I don't know. I was just feeling sorry for them . . . but that's all.

DR. That's interesting. Why feel sorry for them?

CINDY. I did.

DR. Why?

CINDY. I, I can't tell you why. I just . . .

VAN. It's the same kind of thing that happened in New York.

CINDY. I feel sorry for them!

VAN. My feeling was . . . Well, my feeling more about the woman masturbating in the San Francisco film was, was, what she really needs is a man.

CINDY. Oh, that didn't bother me, because I masturbate and that . . . I didn't ever think about that.

VAN. I don't know, but that was my thought. Now in this situation I also had a kind of fleeting thought . . . like what they needed was a woman. That it would have been even more erotic if there had been two men and a woman in the film, rather than just the two men.

CINDY. Yeah.

VAN. . . . for me.

DR. Did it remind you of anything, or make you think about anything?

VAN. My first response when the guy was on the picture there, I sort of said, That looks like Jack.

CINDY. Yeah.

DR. Oh, really?

VAN. Yeah.

CINDY. I thought that too.

DR. Interesting. Any other reactions? Remind you of any dreams?

VAN. No.

CINDY. Did you ever do that with a boy when you were young?

VAN. Yeah, we had, we had mutual masturbation things, uh, we had, uh, I can remember it was with Jim Skinner, we all went skinny-dipping in a river in Mobile, and masturbated each other.

DR. Did you ever see two boys doing it?

CINDY. Did I? No.

VAN. Nothing else comes to mind.

DR. How do you feel now, after having seen it, compared to what you may have felt before you saw it?

VAN. I don't feel tense about it. Uh, I feel a sense of . . . I feel myself trying to explore my fantasies in that area. Trying to get in touch with whatever feelings are there.

DR. Yeah.

VAN. And that's a bit of a struggle.

DR. Why?

VAN. But I feel that . . .

DR. I want to know how you would think of it.

VAN. Well, I guess . . . yeah. I guess I feel permission to do that. And there are very few situations I think for me in which that's permissible . . . to get in touch with those fantasies.

DR. ▶ ▶ ▶ You mean this provides some kind of a sanction for you to be able . . .

VAN. Yeah.

DR. To explore those fantasies.

VAN. Yeah, I don't know of any other opportunities, times, occasions, when that's true.

DR. So your tension about it when I first broached it . . . just the word, you got tense, remember?

VAN. Yeah, when you started talking about it. When you were explaining it to Cindy.

DR. But that tension doesn't exist in you now?

VAN. I don't feel tense.

> [*The tension that Van experienced before the film was related to his fear of homosexual fantasies. But after being confronted with the film, his fears were dissipated.*]

DR. (To Cindy) Do you feel tense?

CINDY. No.

DR. How do you feel about seeing a female one?

CINDY. I don't really think it . . . could bother me.

DR. Okay.

CINDY. My cousin and I just had such a good experience as an adolescent, and I . . . it doesn't bother me. I don't think.

DR. Okay. Now I want you to imagine this one here, see if you can imagine you and your mother doing it. Okay? ◄ ◄ ◄

CINDY. Me and my mother. Oh! (mournfully) That would take fantasy.

DR. What? I want you to put your mind to work on it.

CINDY. Yessir.

> [*Cindy is just too good to be true.*]

DR. Okay. (Starts film, "Funsville," and leaves room)

CINDY. (During film) Oh, my god. Oh, good heavens.

VAN. She's a pretty girl.

CINDY. Mine's not in color.

VAN. Has she a dildo on?

CINDY. Now *that* bothers me.

~~~~~~~~~~~~~~~~ Description of Film ~~~~~~~~~~~~~~~~

Two young women lying naked on a bed appear to be having intercourse. Their pleasure appears to be intense. One is wearing a dildo. They fondle each other's breasts; their bodies writhe in rhythm. The woman on top wears the dildo. There are many expressions of tenderness. Together they undo the dildo. They fondle and kiss each other's vaginas.

Suddenly the camera shifts, showing one of the women masturbating herself. She appears to enjoy it immensely.

The next shot shifts back to a close-up of a vaginal kiss. The picture ends showing one of the women lying on her stomach as if in a baby picture, smiling a lascivious smile, sliding her tongue along her teeth as if she were licking an ice cream cone.

This film is in black and white, and takes ten minutes.

▄▀

(Film ends; they ring buzzer and Dr. Paul returns)

CINDY. I don't think I could see my mother at all.

DR. How come?

CINDY. Why? I don't know, I just tried to see it as my mother and me. No way!

DR. Don't you think you could force yourself to imagine that?

CINDY. No.

DR. You got a real block on that.

CINDY. I can with my own daughter.

DR. Your daughter, but I'm talking about your mother.

CINDY. Not my mother.

DR. Why not? That's curious.

CINDY. I don't know. I just can't with my mother.

DR. What kind of feeling do you get when you start thinking about your mother?

CINDY. I find a kind of a fat slob that I would be very unattracted to, who would be very unattractive to me ▶ ▶ ▶ She repulses me when she's nude. I look at her fat body and I think, "Gee, why is she so fat and sloppy-looking?"

DR. What if she wanted you?

CINDY. What if she wanted me?

DR. What if she wanted you?

CINDY. It might feel kind of good. I don't know. I don't know what if she wanted me . . .

DR. What do you feel thinking about it?

CINDY. It might feel good, it might be good.

> [*It sounds as if Cindy is alluding in some ways to the experience with her cousin, which was a good experience, where maybe her cousin wanted her. In any event, it does suggest in her own mind/fantasy system, her availability to her mother if her mother took the initiative . . . a quality of interaction that exists between a mother and a compliant four-year-old child.*]

DR. What do you think about all this, Van?

VAN. When you asked her to imagine her mother . . .

DR. Yeah?

VAN. I was trying to see if I could imagine my father. That *is* difficult to do. I can picture it, I can imagine it, but it isn't an erotic fantasy.

> [*I'm impressed with Van's immediate response to work on himself and his ability to imagine a homosexual scene with his father rather than focusing on to Cindy's reaction.*]

DR. Does it fill you with sadness?

CINDY. Sadness?

VAN. Nothing's coming from up here [abdomen] to here (pointing to his head).

DR. What do you feel here [abdomen]?

VAN. I don't get anything.

DR. Feel nothing?

VAN. Yeah.

DR. It is an emptiness there?

VAN. Yeah, it's flat.

CINDY. It is for me too.

VAN. I kind of remember when I was a little kid, wanting to uh, see my father's penis when he was urinating. But he always used to hide it.

DR. What?

VAN. He would hide.

DR. What do you mean he would hide?

VAN. Well, I am thinking now, let's say if he was standing up at a urinal . . .

DR. Yeah.

VAN. . . . He would, uh, he would hide himself, you know, he would move right into the urinal, so that, that, uh, I couldn't see anything. I remember thinking . . . that I wanted to see it. I was a little kid.

DR. See if he had one too?

VAN. No, I had thoughts about how big it was. I knew he had one.

DR. How'd you know?

VAN. I guess I had glimpses of it.

CINDY. (Snickers)

DR. Yeah?

VAN. I didn't get a chance to study it, I guess. When I was a little kid, I was curious. It seemed to me as I think about it, it seemed to me that he was uncomfortable and I felt guilty about wanting to look. That's what goes through my head. That was a no-no, that was taboo, you shouldn't see that.

DR. Cindy, what are you thinking about?

CINDY. I'm thinking about some of the times my mother would, uh, comment about my body, and I can remember in April just being sensitive about my mother commenting about my breasts and saying . . . how was it she said it . . . "How fortunate you are," or something. "I never had a body like yours," or something. And I remember thinking then, "Boy, I'm sure not going to let my body look like your body either." And it kind of bothered me. I wonder if when I get older if I do turn into flab like her.

DR. Did she have a thinner body when she was young?

CINDY. Yeah, well, when she got married she was real tiny.

DR. How'd she get so fat?

CINDY. My Daddy likes her fat . . . ha ha, so she says, every time she goes on a diet . . . but she lost a lot of weight about fifteen years ago. He was always nagging at her. I think it was mainly because she didn't cook him good food. He loves to eat. But all of the women in my family are fat slobs. Every one of the women. And all the men like them fat slobs.

> [*Cindy and her mother are both very accommodating women insofar as Cindy's mother is as fat as her husband wants her to be, and Cindy brings home Van's girl friends.*]

DR. You want Cindy fatter, Van?

VAN. Do I want her fatter? Uh-uh. No way.

CINDY. Yeah.

VAN. No, not that, I don't.

CINDY. And they all tell me, even the men in my family, all my uncles and everybody, when I go home they say, "Boy, you just don't look well. You need to gain weight."

DR. You're sick.

CINDY. Yeah.

DR. You're about to die.

VAN. I can remember your father making comments about your mother being, having fried eggs . . .

CINDY. Yeah.

VAN. . . . And you were awfully big. And he was comparing you and your mother. ◀ ◀ ◀

CINDY. Yeah.

DR. And you were also big, what?

VAN. Breasts. He was talking about Cindy's mother having fried eggs, versus Cindy having big breasts.

DR. What do you think about that, Cindy?

CINDY. Well, I used . . . in high school I had real big breasts, and I was very self-conscious because my mother and daddy were always talking about my breasts. I can, now that I think about it, my daddy was bragging and my mother was jealous, but it . . . the first bra they bought me, I had to model it in front of Daddy.

DR. Nude in front of Daddy?

CINDY. Uh-hm [yes]. It was a Valentine gift, from Mommy and Daddy. "From Mommy and Daddy," the card said, and it was this little lacy bra, and mother said, "Go put it on, and show your Daddy," and Daddy said, "Well, you don't need to go out of the room, just put it on," and he fastened it for me. And they all were so proud of me. (Laughs)

DR. Each take a feel?

CINDY. Excuse me?

DR. Each take a feel?

CINDY. Each take a feel? I don't remember that. (Cindy and Van chuckle) I can remember being so embarrassed how proud they were when I was in my first bra.

DR. You were how old at that time?

CINDY. I think I was about twelve.

DR. Oh, there's nothing like keeping it in the family.

(Everybody laughs)

DR. I saw a gal the other day, who was her father's lover between ten and sixteen. She tried to get married; engaged twice, couldn't hack it.

CINDY. You know, I really am getting . . . when I think about
it now, I'm getting worried about myself, because when Brian
. . . I'm always wanting to pet Brian's little butt, and I'm always wanting to hold his penis when he urinates, and I get
so excited at his erection. I don't mean excited sexually, it
just . . . I look at that little penis and I'm so excited that
I have a little boy penis. That bothers me now; am I going to
have problems with my son?

> [*Cindy's reference to her having a little boy penis sug-
> gests the validity of Freud's thesis that boy babies repre-
> sent a replacement for a woman's fantasy penis, or that
> a son is a potential lover.*]

DR. He may have problems with you.

CINDY. Gee.

DR. What are you so excited about?

CINDY. Because I'm so . . . I wonder if I'm already turning on
my six-year-old son.

DR. You may be; you ought to stop turning him on.

CINDY. I should stop . . .

DR. Turning him on.

CINDY. Yeah.

DR. If you want to turn yourself on, go and masturbate, go ahead
and do that, but leave the kid alone.

CINDY. I know it, and when I think about it, I'll be holding him
and I just . . . I just want to squeeze him and kiss him all
the time. Have you noticed that, how physical I am with
Brian?

VAN. No, it's not out of character, because you're physical with
all, all kinds of kids.

CINDY. Yeah. I . . . I just, I know that, but . . .

VAN. The issue has come up before; we've talked about it before.
In fact you mentioned to me, do I ever remember having
erotic feelings toward Mary Lee, because you felt . . .
that . . . you had erotic feelings about Brian.

CINDY. Yeah.

VAN. I remember I said at the time that uh . . . you know, that
I did (softly).

DR. Well, it sounds as if you're watching his penis grow, like your folks were watching your breasts grow.

CINDY. Right! That's what I was just clicking in on, when I was thinking about that, when I was telling about my daddy being proud when I wore my first bra; I was so excited with Brian's first erection.

> [*It is amazing how family patterns tend to repeat down the generations.*]

VAN. Yeah, I can remember that . . .

CINDY. I went running out in the yard for Van . . .

VAN. Screaming . . .

CINDY. . . . to come see it.

VAN. "Come see it, it's big!" (in falsetto) "It's huge!" I couldn't figure out what she was talking about.

DR. Did you take a picture of it?

CINDY. I wanted to. (Everybody laughs) No.

DR. With a movie camera.

VAN. Oh God.

CINDY. In fact, when I had him, and as he started coming out, I screamed at the doctor, "There it is!" and the doctor said, "What?" and I said, "A penis!"

VAN. When he was being born.

CINDY. Yeah.

VAN. Yeah.

DR. You haven't got it out of your head.

CINDY. I have a fixation on penises, I think, thinking about seeing that movie.

DR. Sounds like it.

CINDY. In fact I'm finding out I have a fixation on sex.

DR. Is that what you think you'd find if you had oral sex with your mother? That she has got a penis in there, somewhere?

CINDY. I really can't even stand the thought of thinking about oral sex with my mother.

DR. Every time you think of Brian's penis getting erect and you're jumping with glee, I want you to think about oral sex with your mother. And finding a big penis coming out of her.

> [*Here my intent is to get Cindy to substitute a fantasy of oral sex with her mother, as a means of distracting her from the intensity of her preoccupation with Brian's*

bigger and better penis.

> *Observations of play and drawings by both boys*
> *and girls provide support for Freud's theory that every-*
> *one fantasies that he/she was born with a penis but,*
> *because girls have been naughty, they lose theirs. Fur-*
> *thermore, if a girl could become "real good," she might*
> *be able to grow a new penis. The theory also includes*
> *the fantasy, shared by both boys and girls, that behind*
> *the pubic hair in the mother lies a hidden penis.* I feel*
> *that Cindy would be well advised to get preoccupied*
> *with this aspect than to continually arouse little Brian.]*

CINDY. Ucchh.

DR. I want you to start doing that . . .

CINDY. *Why?*

DR. What?

CINDY. Why?

DR. Why do I want you to do that?

CINDY. Yeah.

DR. So you can leave the kid alone . . I mean, I can see the kid
growing up, and he's looking at your face, and your eyes are
just glowing, and he's saying, "Gee, I mean, is that going
to be here tomorrow? Are you gonna bite it off?" I'm thinking about him.

> *[This is related to a little boy's perception that he can*
> *lose his penis by having it bitten off, especially if Mom*
> *looks so thrilled. Maybe that thrilled look is equated*
> *with being envious and wanting little Brian's penis.]*

CINDY. Yeah.

VAN. You always did like to bite babies' butts . . . (Cindy and
Van laugh) I remember you saying that.

DR. When are you people going to Wales?

VAN. We're leaving town the twenty-seventh of December to go to
South Dakota. I wish we had time to talk about some of
that stuff. I have some feelings about going out there, and
facing her parents, and her brothers and the whole family and
the whole world sort of who knows that I've been . . . in
their eyes, I've been wayward.

---

* See Freud, *On the Sexual Theories of Children,* in References.

CINDY. What do you mean in their eyes?!

VAN. Okay. Sorry about that.

DR. In their eyes . . . ? Do you people want to come back here before you go to Wales . . . uh, South Dakota, one time, or how do you want to play that?

VAN. Uh, yeah.

CINDY. I'd like to come back.

VAN. Yeah.

DR. And then are you going to Wales for what? Six months?

VAN. Yes.

DR. Something like that . . . You can take your tapes with you, can't you, and listen to them there.

(Pause)

DR. It's interesting. My sense of the two of you is that, by and large, your own relationship has sort of turned a corner and uh, it seems to me you're getting solidified. Sure, there are ups and downs, and if you're looking for perfection you're never going to get it.

CINDY. Yeah.

DR. Maybe in heaven, but not in this world. The reason I say this is because, if you notice, our thoughts are turning toward the kids.

CINDY. Uh-huh.

DR. Uh, and that usually doesn't happen to people struggling with themselves that much.

CINDY. You know, another thing about my children is that little Mary Lee . . . I'm wondering, I'm really wondering, if some of the times when I'm really wanting to shake her to death, is because she's a blue-eyed blonde child, that I think . . . you've made jokes about it all along, in the . . . when we adopted her, he used to say to me, "If you think she's pretty, you ought to see her mother." Now that I think about it . . .

DR. Do you know her mother?

CINDY. No, but he would insinuate that he was the mother . . . the father, and that . . . I just wonder about some of my not being able to really love Mary is that blue-eyed blonde business.

VAN. That's really hostile humor, isn't it?

CINDY. It sure as hell is now, that all this blue-eyed blonde business is coming out too.

DR. Maybe you're hostile at blue-eyed blondes. Male and female.

VAN. Oh. I was thinking hostile to Cindy, by comparing her all the time with blue-eyed blondes.

DR. No, but the net effect is to make that kid be rejected, by your comments.

CINDY. Yeah.

VAN. Uh-huh.

DR. Okay. This is today.

(Videotape playback, segments 1, 2, 3)

> [*Segment 1 captures their relationship prior to the homosexual films; segment 2 captures their reactions after the male homosexual film; and segment 3 captures their reactions after the female homosexual film. Material on videotape is on pages as follows: Segment 1: pages 219–222; Segment 2: pages 235–236; Segment 3: pages 237–240.*]

DR. What are you thinking about, Cindy? You look a little confused.

CINDY. I look confused?

VAN. I was just going to say the same thing. First time I ever saw you . . . seeing you feeling uncertain, looking uncertain.

DR. I think it has to do with the concern that you're going to end up with that big, fat, slobby kind of body. Huh?

CINDY. I agree.

DR. And what I want you to do between now and the next time, which will be the last time, uh, is I want you to work on why you'd want to have a body like hers.

CINDY. Why I would?

DR. How does that sound? Like Momma's.

CINDY. Why I would want a body like my mother's. There's no . . . I wouldn't. I can't think why I would.

> [*Again here I'm attempting to get Cindy to become aware that in part she desires to be like her mother so on some level she can have her father sexually. This is a normal fantasy complex that I'm trying to help her recognize. To be mother and have mother's body would*]

help her avoid recognition of her own homosexual fantasy vis-à-vis mother, because, in effect, she would become her mother. And this, in turn, would make legitimate the consummation of her sexual desires for her father.]

DR. Okay. Can you come on the Monday before you go to South Dakota?

VAN. That's the eighteenth. That may be the last class. What time?

DR. Any time that day.

VAN. Early in the day would probably be better, 'cause I, I think I have an evening class.

DR. 9:00? 10:30? 11:00?

VAN. 10:30 would be easier.

DR. 10:30 okay?

VAN. Yeah. 10:30 the eighteenth.

DR. Okay, fine: Work on some theories as to why you both are working out so quickly, other than you're so well integrated.

VAN. (Laughing) Yeah, I knew that was gonna come back to haunt me.

DR. 'Cause I don't know what the hell that means.

VAN. I don't either. It sounds good.

DR. Yeah, sounds good. It's an after the fact assessment. Okay?

VAN. I don't want to forget anything this time.

CINDY. Yeah, right.

DR. Okay, got everything? I'll see you. 'By.

> He proved that it was mostly vain and wrong
> For human hearts to suffer tides of troubles,
> Inflict anxiety upon themselves;
> And just as children, fearing everything,
> Tremble in darkness, we, in the full light,
> Fear things that really are not one bit more awful
> Than what poor babies shudder at in darkness,
> The horrors they imagine to be coming.
> Our terrors and our darknesses of mind
> Must be dispelled, then, not by sunshine's rays
> But by insight into nature and a scheme
> Of systematic study . . .*
>
> —LUCRETIUS

* *The Way Things Are*, Book VI, translated by Rolfe Humphries (Bloomington, Ind.: Indiana University Press, 1969), p. 203.

As indicated on page 229, Session VI, Van went to Mobile, Alabama, to visit his parents' graves. In addition, he visited with friends of his parents as is described in Session VII. While at his parents' graves, he recorded on a portable cassette tape recorder his experience there. The transcription of this fifteen-minute tape follows.

Van's Visit to Ponte Clare Cemetery, Mobile, Alabama, December 8, 1972

. . . make sure of feelings, both of ambivalence, a bit of sadness, but also—there's a bit of (sighs) feeling that . . . it really hasn't been that long since I've been here before.

I think it's going to take a while for the impact of this setting to kind of get down into me . . . As I sit here and look at the various graves that are around, I guess the thought that comes to my mind more than any other is . . . how incredibly short life is. How incredibly filled with all kinds of complications and problems that . . . sometimes we're able to cope with, sometimes not. The sun is very warm; the air is warm; this is really a lovely place. I wish I had some flowers to put on their graves. In fact, I may go and get some and bring them back. I haven't found them yet, and I think I'll go now and try to locate them.

As I walk among these graves, it seems to me that I should find them close to a tree. But I haven't been able to find them yet.

The gravestones are all flush with the ground. The raised lettering is . . . kind of stares out at me; I have a feeling that I'm sort of looking, but not looking because I'm afraid I'm going to find it.

(Sobbing) I think the full impact . . . only strikes you when you finally reach the place and on seeing the stone.

I sort of want Dad to know that . . . I'm okay. And that it's all right. That he did his damndest to be the kind of father he thought I needed. I didn't realize there would be this kind of grief . . . He had an awfully short life, 1902 to 1959. I think what I remember most about him . . . (sighs) was captured in that song about the hard-working hands. He worked damn hard! The only way he knew how. And I guess I thank God for him. I try to think about forgiving him for not being able to be close. A man can only be what he can be . . . And he gave me life.

It kind of looks deserted here. And I wish, I wish to God I had some flowers. He was so lonely all of his life. I'm sorry he's lonely here. Because Mom is buried somewhere else. In life maybe they weren't together, even in death they still aren't together.

I try to picture the day of the funeral and how he looked . . . but I find that incredibly difficult to do. I think I remember him in a blue suit with a black tie. Because he always wore a black tie . . . And I remember his face looked so drawn. Even in death he didn't look peaceful.

I think the feeling I have more than any other is that . . . I never knew my father. I never really got to know him. We never really had a relationship where we could talk, discuss, deal with things together. I knew him, but I didn't know him. And I don't know if anybody ever did.

(Sobbing) I find that I don't want to leave him here. I have the feeling that when I leave this time it'll be such a long time before I come back and visit again.

It makes me want to reach out to him. Because I guess I never got the chance when he was alive. It's kind of strange the things that you remember. I'm sitting here on the grass and thinking about how my dad used to work so hard in that yard trying to take care of it; spent his whole life, it seemed, worrying about things that he didn't need to worry about.

Another feeling seems to be coming over me now as I sit in the warm sun. It's a feeling that this is a nice place. And it's okay to leave him here. There really isn't any other place for him to be.

It is very difficult for me to leave and go and find Mom . . . I'm not sure why at this moment. Whether it's because I don't want to experience more grief when I find her grave, or whether it's really Dad that I miss. Maybe it's because Mom had some relationships. She had some friends. She had some people who cared about her, and she cared about them, but Dad never had anybody.

I can finally be at peace here. (Sighs) And at rest.

As I think about it more, it seems to me that I was able to put Mom to rest. And I was able to grieve for her, but that I couldn't grieve for Dad. I was so locked up then inside myself I couldn't let myself grieve. That was probably part of it. And the other part was that in many ways, maybe I had buried him a long time ago. Maybe I hadn't said goodby, because I had never really said hello.

There's a part of me which says that I'm to blame for not saying hello. That I can't blame Dad for all of that. But he did his best, he did all he could; I did all I could. So there was a mutual response, or lack of it that we had between us. That was the problem. That my reaching out to him and his reaching out to me failed because maybe both of us shared the same problem. Now I think I'm ready to find Mom.

Right now I have the feeling like I would say, "You're okay, Mom. I loved you. And I felt your love" (voice breaking).

Mom's grave has . . . has a floral bouquet. (Crying) Of Christmas Poinsettias. And Holly. I don't know who put them here. But I'm glad they're here. And even more it makes me want to go and get flowers for Dad's grave.

───────────────────────

Walter Kerr comments about Eugene O'Neill's autobiographical drama, *A Long Day's Journey Into Night:*

I think he [O'Neill] wrote it as an act of forgiveness. Not as a pontifical forgiveness, mind you, not as an absolution for the harm that had been done to *him*. That he was damaged by his family is only a fact now, a piece of truth to be put down out of respect for the whole truth; there is no residual rancor. He seems to be asking forgiveness for his own failure to know his father, mother, and brother well enough at a time when the need for understanding was like an upstairs cry in the night; and to be reassuring their ghosts, wherever they may be, that he knows everything awful they have done, and loves them.*

* New York *Herald Tribune Book Review,* February 19, 1956, p. 12.

Saying Goodby

> . . . there's no end to understanding a person.
> All one can do is to understand them better,
> To keep up with them; so that as the other changes
> You can understand the change as soon as it happens,
> Though you couldn't have predicted it.*
>
> —COLBY

[*Cindy enters office; Van goes to bathroom.*]

DR. Are you ready to sail out of here?

CINDY. No! (Groan) It's gonna be to the last minute.

DR. How are things generally working out?

CINDY. Life's getting pretty panicky and chaotic right now.

> [*Cindy is learning things do not always have to be perfect.*]

DR. How're the two of you faring?

CINDY. Oh, great.

DR. Really? It's continuing that way?

CINDY. Yeah. We've had a couple of setba . . . or I've had a couple of setback cases, but it's . . .

DR. What? You're going to Europe when?

CINDY. Thursday we leave town to go to South Dakota and then we leave for Europe January the second.

DR. You're going where in Europe?

CINDY. Cardiff, Wales.

DR. And what's he gonna do there?

---

* *The Confidential Clerk,* by T. S. Eliot (New York: A Harvest Book, Harcourt, Brace and World, Inc., 1954), p. 67.

CINDY. He's gonna work in the University of Cardiff at the Social Work Institute.

DR. Really?

CINDY. Yeah.

DR. I'm not too sure what he will learn there, but you ought to have a fun time.

CINDY. Well, actually we needed an excuse. That was our excuse. The college required him to have a place to go.

(Van enters the room.)

DR. This happens to be the eighteenth of December, 1972.

VAN. Three days and we leave.

CINDY. I know it.

DR. Yeah, in the year of trying to eliminate bullshit.

VAN. Something like that!

(All laugh)

DR. So you [Cindy] had a setback. What kind of a setback did you have?

CINDY. Jennifer called and I wasn't so put-together as I thought I would be. I reacted . . .

DR. Yeah.

CINDY. . . . as I was talking to Van about it, I was super cool, and then the gut level took over again.

DR. You gotta watch that down in the gut level.

CINDY. I know it.

DR. So what'd she call about? She want to have an affair with you?

CINDY. Oh, she didn't call me. She called Van.

DR. About what?

CINDY. You ought to ask Van.

DR. What about, Van?

VAN. She's getting married.

DR. So what has that got to do with you? She wants you to officiate?

VAN. Hmmmm. Wouldn't that be interesting?

DR. Hey, man, that would really be wild.

CINDY. I'll give her away.

(All laugh)

DR. So did you call her back?

VAN. No, she called, and we talked for about fifteen minutes.

CINDY. Isn't that nice? And his old girl friend [Amy Carnel], that's the fiancée he'd been with that weekend [eight years ago]; well, he came back with her address in his appointment book, so I thought, "Why can't he say goodby to these lovers, and get them out of the way, and do I have to live with them forever?"

> [*Van is able to deal easily with Jennifer's phone call, but Cindy is understandably resentful of his old girl friend's return. Does she have to live with them forever, in fact, and if so, how?*]

DR. You may have to. (Cheerfully)

CINDY. I really reacted to this business.

DR. You go bananas periodically.

CINDY. I didn't go bananas this time.

DR. You didn't.

CINDY. I didn't like the way I felt this time, but I still couldn't . . . I couldn't be the supercool woman that says, "Oh, isn't that great? I'm glad you got to talk to her again." I reacted by saying "It's not necessary, is it? Well, why is it necessary?" I got mad at him because he still has to hang on.

VAN. I didn't feel like I was hanging on.

CINDY. Ohhh; well!

VAN. I haven't seen this gal in eight years.

DR. Eight years!

CINDY. Sometime he's gonna write to her.

DR. Sounds real cosy. How do you [Van] feel things are going?

> [*I change the subject here from Cindy's comments about what's been transpiring because I regard this as an avoidance mechanism to hedge the reality of saying goodby. This difficulty in saying goodby is the issue of the session.*]

VAN. Well, we've been pretty busy, we've settled down considerably, and I've felt positive about things.

DR. How's your sex life, any improvement, or . . . ?

VAN. I think we've had better sex in the last three months than we've had in most of our married life. More frequent and more enjoyable.

DR. Yeah?

VAN. As I was saying to Cindy (Cindy giggled) the other day, I sort of discovered . . .

DR. What?

VAN. . . . that . . . I can't remember how I put it . . .

CINDY. ► ► ► He discovered that since I wouldn't go bananas . . . something about . . .

VAN. Yeah, I didn't have to worry about her . . . it doesn't make any sense to me up here (pointing to his head), but it makes sense to me here (pointing to his abdomen).

DR. Right.

VAN. And when I discovered that she wasn't gonna go bananas, when she has an orgasm; I really enjoy her orgasms.

CINDY. He really does. (Laughs with pleasure) It's almost that he's at the point now of how many times he can please me instead of his own self (giggling).

VAN. It's just . . . it's a lot more fun.

DR. How do you . . . you know, I asked you that question last time, how do you people account for . . . ?

VAN. Yeah.

DR. . . . the movement, which I think has been quite rapid?

VAN. We tried to talk about that a little when we were coming in. I didn't come up with anything . . . I really didn't . . . couldn't put anything together, except that uh . . . I think for me the discovery was, uh, what I really wanted and what was really meaningful. And in the process . . .

DR. But you thought before you knew what you wanted.

VAN. No, I don't really think that's accurate.

DR. Okay.

VAN. And, in a way we've sort of gone through another . . . I'll tell you where I'm thinking about things now, we've kind of gone through another honeymoon, or are in the process of a honeymoon. And I'm wondering if some of the same issues that got things off the track before are still there.

DR. Like?

VAN. Well, I'm not even sure. I'm not even certain what that might be.

DR. You got any idea, Cindy?

CINDY. Yeah.

DR. What?

CINDY. Well, I agree with Van that I mean, he had, I had never heard him say this before, but I again, I felt like it was a honeymoon. It was a new start for both of us. And, then I found that, like when Jennifer called the other day . . .

DR. Yeah?

CINDY. . . . and a couple of other situations on campus, that I immediately got to feeling jealous . . .

DR. Yeah?

CINDY. And I feel like . . .

DR. What?

CINDY. . . . That it's not really so much these women, but I feel that I have got to *do* something outside the home instead of just having Van my total life, because it seems to me like I'm jealous of his being in the outside world with all his relationships. When he comes home and I start asking him to account to me what went on all day long, he's not exactly wanting to, and I get really bothered by this, and I think sometimes . . .

DR. What do you think you could begin to consider doing that might give you a career or some activity out of the home, because this is what you're ultimately talking about.

CINDY. It just seems to me like, if I had somebody to talk to, and some outside relationships, that I can allow Van to have more of his outside relationships, and I can contribute more than just the soap operas and having him do all the feeding.

DR. Yeah, but you're feeding off of him.

CINDY. Right. I don't know, but I'm awful jealous of all of his relationships.

DR. Well, what do you think you can do? What do you like to do?

CINDY. Well, work part-time, but I might substitute . . . I don't want to go into full-time work, but I'd like to substitute teach for maybe two or three days a week.

> [*Cindy is now able to direct her energy to activity outside the home. Feeling more at ease with herself and her marriage, she needs to spend less time on this aspect of her life. She has a good understanding of how staying*

*at home makes her jealous of Van's activities, and she
is ready to do something constructive about it.*]

DR. Okay.

CINDY. It was fun to take this French course, and have adult con-
versations, and uh, I found that I was very much stimulated
again using the brain.

DR. But you really can't count on fucking to make a marriage
work; you gotta have something more than that.

[*Something more than the sexual act is required for a
viable marriage. This is expressed in the idea of having
"something in common." Having something in common
refers to each partner feeling that the other is interested
in him and is interesting. This interest has to be reciprocated and is shown by empathic listening—somebody
caring enough to listen to what bothers or hurts the
other or what the other has experienced. When this
listening does not occur between spouses, they feel that
they have nothing in common. The reciprocated sharing
of one's inner experience is the ultimate validation of a
person's individuality.*]

CINDY. Yeah.

DR. Right after the honeymoon bash, what else do you have going
for you? Each one's gotta take care of himself.

VAN. Hmmm.

CINDY. Yeah, and when he comes home and talks about what he
did for lunch, and like he has several students that he gets to
have lunch with, and I think . . .

VAN. What do you mean, "I get to have lunch with"?

CINDY. Well, I remember that. Six years ago, when I used to work
. . . and I'd forgotten how it feels, and so I get really jealous
of his life. I don't want to have to be a full-time career
woman, but I do want something in the outside world now.

DR. I think that, for your kids' sake, I would suggest that over time
you might do well to seriously consider a full-time career. So
that they learn how to take care of themselves because you're
then providing a model for them.

CINDY. Um-hum.

DR. Just in terms of my wife and our kids, the thing that really made our kids more self-reliant is when she went back to graduate school. And there's no question that the tone of the kids' development changed dramatically.

> [*The specific point of the tape that is to be played is the importance of partners sharing their experiences with their children and that, in effect, part of attempting to achieve a more viable, compatible marriage is to provide a healthier background for the children's development.*]

CINDY. Uh-huh.

VAN. Hm, I can imagine it would.

DR. Yeah. And, uh, you may well have to deal on some level in terms of being different from your mother, and the guilt about maybe doing something which is different from the way she spent her life. You've got to seriously think about it, otherwise, uh, maybe the marriage'll work out better, but the kids' heads are going to be messed up. I see it again and again and again.

VAN. Yeah, the models of our two families, our families of origin, are quite different, as you, I guess, know from what we've talked about. I think I grew up in a family where my mother had to work because of financial reasons, so it wasn't that much of an issue. But Cindy grew up in a family where her mother (turning toward Cindy) I don't think your mother could work, because your father wouldn't let her.

CINDY. Oh, no. Absolutely.

VAN. And that's then taking away from his masculinity, if she goes out and works.

CINDY. Right. And she . . . the only reason they allowed me to go to college . . .

DR. Yeah?

CINDY. . . . was to find a man.

DR. Yeah.

CINDY. Because he didn't want me to ever work.

VAN. It was wasting money on a college degree.

CINDY. And when I supported Van for four years, they just thought that was terrible.

VAN. That issue of dependency has been one that we've kicked around for a long time in our relationship, and I've always kinda said that Cindy's been too dependent on me, and that's one of my complaints . . . that is, she lives through me, through the stuff that I do.

> [*There is a confusion here between financial dependency and emotional dependency. Cindy is talking about one; Van is talking about the other.*]

CINDY. Yeah.

DR. That's a problem with women, and it's something that's seeded to girls, not by their fathers, primarily, but by their mothers, I am convinced.

CINDY. Yes. I am too, and in my case I am . . . And I was trying to bring home the living, and do the housework, do the laundry, and with all of this, be the wife that my mother was, plus being a career woman, and I was getting so frustrated and depressed, I was depressed all the time I remember. And finally it's when you said, I said one time, "I just can't be the kind of wife like my mother," and Van said, "Yeah, well she didn't go out and work all day and bring home the paycheck, either," and all of a sudden that felt so good. And after that I didn't care if the beds . . . you know . . . I could really let my housework go to pot after that.

VAN. Yeah. That was never an issue with me.

CINDY. No, it . . . no, thank goodness Van never cared what I served him . . . but to me it was, to me I had to have his shirts starched, and then so many shirts, and the beds changed every day, and the pillowcases starched and ironed . . . plus working. And I just thought wow, this is getting me down. And now that I, I keep thinking I'm supposed again to get to be the mother and the wife like my mother was, bake cookies and keep my kids happy all the time, and I'm finally saying, I don't like this. I want some outside excitement too.

DR. And it's not for Van to find it for you. You've got to go out and find it.

CINDY. And that's when I woke up to the fact that I was jealous of him that . . .

VAN. Well, the issue's coming up in a number of ways—like we were at a party last night, a going away party that was given for us . . .

DR. Yeah . . .

VAN. . . . And I, at about 12:00, I decided that I had had it, and I was ready to go . . .

DR. Uh-huh.

VAN. . . . And yet I thought, you know, I don't know why I was thinking these things, but Cindy was having a very good time, and really they were more her friends than mine, so I was hanging around because I thought she didn't want to go, and I said a couple of times, uh, "let's go," and then when she didn't leave, I sort of said, "Well, Cindy is a person and she needs to make those decisions for herself too," without me kind of jumping in and . . .

      [He's learning!]

DR. Right.

VAN. Part of it is a little threatening, in that I want her to be more of a person . . .

DR. Yeah.

VAN. . . . Uh, which means that I . . . let's see, how can I say this . . . it means perhaps that I face loss, I think . . .

      [It's remarkable that Van can recognize these feelings.]

DR. It's a co-conspiracy, I would say. It's not just you; it's a conspiracy between the two of you. You know, the victim victimizes the victimizer to victimize the victim to victimize the victimizer . . . it's a loop.

CINDY. Yeah.

VAN. Yeah.

(Pause)

DR. It's interesting . . . This is our last meeting, what, forever?

      [I'm trying to push the issue of saying goodby, knowing that there is much resistance to this theme.]

VAN. God, I don't know.

DR. How do you people feel about saying goodby? How gifted are you in saying goodby?

      [Saying goodby to any relationship is extremely important if a new relationship is to be formed. For example, Van's inability to say goodby to his father contaminated his ability to form a close, continuing relationship with Cindy.]

VAN. I'm not very good at it. I don't like to do it. It's one of the things that disturbs Cindy about relationships that I establish . . .

DR. Yeah.

VAN. . . . Is that I see them as continuing, as meaningful even though we're separated by distance and time. And I'm not just talking about Jennifer.

> [*Van's reaction here is part of their joint collusion in zig-zagging around the issue of saying goodby to me.*]

CINDY. No, I know.

VAN. But running into the guy, I've known him since the second grade, a good buddy of mine in Mobile, this last weekend, I really . . . I just enjoyed keeping in touch. I enjoyed . . . finding out what's happening . . .

CINDY. But you don't. You've never written . . . what do you mean keeping in touch?

DR. He does it differently, you see.

VAN. Yeah, I don't write letters, no.

CINDY. You mean in touch with your feelings, you don't let those end.

DR. Contact, verbal contact.

VAN. I found it very comfortable to go back and talk to people.

DR. Learn anything down there?

VAN. Yeah, I did. Uh, lots of stuff. In fact I got some addresses and places to write for finding out some more information. The woman I stayed with was the woman who with her husband had a boarding house that's right in front of where we used to live, and they're like second parents to me. So they're very, very nice, warm people.

DR. What are their names?

VAN. Watson, Mildred and Harry Watson. And we got to talking on Friday when I got there . . .

DR. Yeah.

VAN. . . . for about four hours, about all kinds of stuff, and I was pumping them for information. And one of the things that Mildred said to me was startling: She said, "Van, you were too close to your mother. Too close to your mother." I asked her what that meant, and she said, "Well, do you re-member the time when your dad was having all those troubles?" "Yeah, I remember them." She said, "Well, Dorothy was out of the picture, she was off somewhere, and you were right there. Your mother told me so many times how much she appreciated the fact that you were there. But," she said, "just from an outsider's point of view, you were just too involved with her problems and trying to keep her together." I can remember so well standing up in the window in their house, looking down into this little house behind, where we were living . . .

      [Verification, finally.]

DR. Uh-huh.

VAN. . . . with . . . my mother and I were standing there, and the highway patrolman going into the house, getting my father and taking him to the funny farm, to the hospital, because he wouldn't go. So (empathic sound from Cindy) it was the only way we could get him there. And I can remember my mother just breaking down into tears, and my trying to, me trying to comfort her, as I see my father with a suitcase going out of the house with this, uh, uniformed highway patrolman. And feeling . . . I got in touch with a lot of all of that stuff again, about how it must have felt for him, to be sitting there in that house, and have some cop come up and say, "Okay, buddy, we're going. Don't make any trouble, because we're going." All those kind of things. I spent about three hours at the cemetery. And I found the most difficult time was at my father's grave. And I found his grave first, and wept for a considerable length of time. I took a tape recorder and tried to put some of the stuff down. I guess the main feeling was that I never, ever really said hello to him, and that's why it was so difficult to try and say goodby, because . . .

DR. That's why you didn't have to say goodby.

VAN. That's why I didn't have to say goodby before, but it suddenly, you feel more, I felt more of a loss of what I didn't have.

DR. Uh-huh.

VAN. And all those years, I never sat down and had a conversation with that man, in my entire life, never, ever can I remember sitting down and talking to him about anything. And the loneliness of that was just incredible. In fact, I couldn't leave there for quite a while, until I then decided I'd go and find Mom's grave. And her's is not too far away, so I went and found it. And it was a much different experience. And I ran into my stepfather again. (Cindy sighs) Uh, which was quite an experience.

DR. What happened?

VAN. Well, I went to the church Sunday morning, and he goes and visits my mother's grave every Sunday morning, puts flowers on the grave, in fact, at that time I took a flower off Mom's grave, and I couldn't leave . . . I couldn't leave Dad's grave like it was, so I took a flower off Mom's grave . . .

> [*Van's stepfather must have really cared for his mother.*]

CINDY. Good!

VAN. . . . and I stuck it in the sand there.

DR. You were saying hello to him.

VAN. Yeah.

DR. For the first time.

VAN. Yeah, and I felt good. I said, "Damn it, he needs some flowers too, nobody comes to visit him." Oh, that's . . .

DR. That's still with you.

VAN. . . . still with me. In fact, I got on the plane, four hours going from Mobile to New York, I just sort of sat and looked out the window and just wept, the tears just streamed down my face. So goddamned much sadness in that family. It was just incredible.

DR. There's also a sense of outrage.

> [*I'm trying to sanction the sense of outrage which is a usual result of this kind of deprived childhood.*]

VAN. That's hard for me to get to. It's hard for me to be angry . . . all I feel is the sadness.

DR. Yeah. The anger is expressed by distancing the other, you see. Either Cindy or the kids.

> [*The anger, the distancing of his present family, represents in some ways Van's way of coping with his fear of being overwhelmed anew. The best way to avoid feeling overwhelmed is to avoid any kind of intimate relationship. Insofar as he had initially distanced his original*]

*family, he was only familiar with that pattern, even
though he wished to have intimacy with a wife and
children.*]

VAN. Okay. Or anybody, I guess.

DR. Or anybody. Which is sort of a wiping-out kind of anger. You
just deny their existence. Which is the way your father dealt
with you. ◄ ◄ ◄

[*Patterns of anger, like other patterns of relating, are
passed on from generation to generation.*]

VAN. I always saw it as fear, rather than anger, but that makes
sense to me.

CINDY. Yeah, it sure does.

DR. I want you to hear a tape because it's got . . . see, the two of
you I think have sort of worked out your relationship. There'll
be ups and downs, backs and forths, but I want you to hear
this because, you see, for me, I'm not just interested in just the
two of you working out, I'm interested in how it effects the
kids.

CINDY. Good.

VAN. That's important.

DR. And if you feel you're getting something out of something for
yourselves, then you can feel much more tuned into the kids.

VAN. That's happening. I've very much sensed that.

[*Finally, they are able to concern themselves with their
children.*]

CINDY. Uh-huh.

DR. Now, this is a tape of a guy and his wife. He's had an affair . . .

VAN. Hmm. Is this the one you played for me the first time?

DR. Is this the one I played for you the first time? No, it's another
one.

VAN. Oh, my God.

DR. This has relevance to the kids. The first one (i.e., tape) didn't
get involved with kids.

VAN. No.

DR. This guy is down in Mexico with a gal, and while he's down
there, he tells his wife when he comes back that he really
loves her, and he's thinking of her [his wife] as he's screwing
this gal down in Mexico, and he's got four boys, he's an only

child, and the oldest of whom he's distanced at the age of ten and a half, and the kid's got a lot of problems . . . reading problems, all kinds of problems. And it takes place in my home. And uh, I want you to hear it, because the last part will maybe get into the relevance of all this for your kids.

CINDY. Hmm-hmm.

DR. Okay? And I don't have a release for this one to be recorded on your tape.

      I'm still curious to find out how come you people moved that fast, because . . .

CINDY. We're just exceptional people.

DR. I don't know, I don't know. I'll leave you with that and come back.

(Plays Tracy tape. During tape Van and Cindy laugh inappropriately; she is restive.)

--------------------- **Transcript of Tracy Tape** ---------------------

DR. How did you feel about coming to my house, here?

JOHN. A heck of a lot better than your office.

PATRICIA. I felt glad because we would have been late to Cambridge. (Laughs)

JOHN. No, this seems more, I think . . .

DR. Who let you in?

JOHN. Your wife told us to come in, I guess it was.

PATRICIA. Somebody opened the window and told us just to go in here.

JOHN. This seems more relaxed; I think you can talk better here. The office seems awful cold out there. Even when it's hot, it still seems cold. And that damn hall, and that waiting room . . .

DR. Yeah.

JOHN. In fact . . .

PATRICIA. And to see those people that go up and down in the elevator all day! (Laughs)

DR. Yeah.

JOHN. It just seems more, uh, more of a strained atmosphere, let's put it that way. Of course, that may be because we like the country and don't, we just don't ever get into the city.

PATRICIA. You can look out here and see the trees.

DR. Yeah. Yeah.

JOHN. This is . . . this is more natural to us.

DR. What do you think about coming here to my home? Do you have any thoughts about coming over here? Because it has to do with me, what my home is like, what the office is like, what kind of a person I am, and so forth. Do you know what you think about that?

JOHN. You don't get any clue from the office as to what your home would be like.

DR. In what sense?

JOHN. I mean as far as I can . . . Well, as far as I'm concerned, the office down there is as near nothing as you can get.

DR. Yeah.

JOHN. In fact if I was you, I'd tell them unless I was getting my rent awfully cheap . . .

DR. Yeah.

JOHN. I'd give the landlord my notice and move somewhere else.

DR. Why? What don't you like about the office?

JOHN. It's . . . it's a reconverted apartment building, as far as I can see.

DR. Yeah.

JOHN. And it just isn't made for an office. The waiting room is too small, there's two . . . *two* little chairs in there, you sit around a corner, there's no place for a desk, there's no place for anything that looks like an office. It looks like somebody had a hall and a . . . a dining room.

DR. What do you mean, there's no place for a desk in the office?

JOHN. In the office or in the reception hall. To my mind, to my way of thinking, if . . . if I was a doctor, I'd say I'd stay there, one, because the rent is damn cheap . . .

DR. Yeah.

JOHN. . . . and if I could rent the same thing or a better place somewhere else, I'd go somewhere else. 'Cause that building is probably a professional building, that's where you have to be because of the amount of traffic you have there.

DR. Yeah. Do you share these feelings of John's?

PATRICIA. Your office doesn't bother me that much; it's always bothered him.

DR. Yeah.

PATRICIA. It doesn't really bother me that much.

DR. Does the absence of a *desk* bother you?

JOHN. Yes . . . somewhat.

DR. Why?

PATRICIA. What would he do with a desk?

JOHN. No, not the absence of a desk, but—

PATRICIA. You mean a receptionist . . . that type of thing?

JOHN. Uh, actually, you just walk into a hall there. It's, it's a nothingness to me. And you say it doesn't bother you, but you, you won't sit in that waiting room.

PATRICIA. No, I won't; I hate it.

JOHN. She wouldn't sit in that waiting room if she never got into the place.

PATRICIA. Well, there's no place to *sit* there. Who wants to sit?

JOHN. Yeah, that's it. It's so damn . . .

DR. You like wide open spaces?

JOHN. It's cold. It's the plaster of the walls. This is warm; wood is warm; this is a nice ceiling. You've got the nice floor; you've got windows. Ah, you come in, there's a warmth. You come into *there,* it's a, an absolute cold feeling to me.

DR. What, what does it remind you of? I mean "cold," . . . "rooms" . . . that's what you're talking about, isn't it?

JOHN. I don't know. Perhaps something very . . . I don't know how you'd put it. Just something very cold, something very impersonal . . .

DR. Yeah.

JOHN. . . . Just a complete lack of . . . just a complete lack of feeling. If you've got to work in a place . . . now I'm not talking for you; for me . . . if you've got to work in a place, you want it something pleasant, that you like.

DR. Yeah.

JOHN. And we do that in our own business; we do so many things and people'll come down and say, "You don't need this." Our engineers will come down, and they say: "What do you do this for?"

DR. Yeah.

JOHN. I've got to work here. I want it the way I want it.

DR. Okay, now you see, the thing I'm wondering about; here's what tinkers in my mind: uh, does it have to do with doctors?

JOHN. Yes!

DR. And your mother?

JOHN. Yes! Very much so. In fact it has to do with McCord Hospital, where my mother died. Thinking back here, McCord Hospital was the same way . . . ver-ry cold, and that same damn high ceiling and painted walls and no place to sit . . . The new, the new wing at McCord Hospital is glass, and warm, and has curtains, and when I went to McCord Hospital . . . I had an operation, oh, five years ago . . . a hernia operation . . . I was in the new part. And it was warm. But the old part . . . I didn't, I didn't tell them because I figured they were busy and they'd put me anywhere they wanted to, but I was scared to death to go into the old part.

DR. Why?

JOHN. It just seemed so cold. I can remember sitting out in the hall the night my mother died, and I sat there and sat there, and nobody paid any attention to me, and I was just sitting all by myself, and of course . . .

DR. In a cold hall . . .

JOHN. And my father was worried, of course. And I was sitting on a damn little old bench, one of those . . .

DR. Like the little old chair outside Dr. Paul's office.

JOHN. Yeah, like the little old chair outside Dr. Paul's . . . and nobody, everybody was going by, but nobody was talking to me and nobody was seeing me . . .

DR. Nobody cared about you.

JOHN. And nobody cared about me. And I can remember the high hall and the hard floors and the painted walls, and I got so upset I, I threw up, and I felt ashamed for throwing up, because I knew my mother was so sick; she needed the help, I didn't need it . . . And then somebody came over to me and said . . .

DR. What, what do you mean, she needed the help?

JOHN. *She* needed the help; I didn't . . .

[She was on heavy medication for terminal cancer.]

DR. She was out of it; you were in it.

JOHN. No, no, she was still alive then.

DR. Yeah, but they probably had her doped up . . .

JOHN. Well, I didn't know that . . .

DR. Yeah, well they probably did.

JOHN. Yeah, 'cause I didn't know that . . .

DR. And no one had you doped up; obviously you were very raw inside.

JOHN. And I was all sick, and I threw up, and uh, then I felt ashamed for throwing up. And then somebody came over, my father or my aunt, and said, "Oh, we didn't even realize you were here." And, "We should've asked you if you didn't feel good, too." And then the nurse came.

DR. But no one cared about you when you were in your real, your most intense pain.

JOHN. Nobody even knew I was there.

DR. But no one cared about you.

JOHN. I don't know.

DR. A little boy who was having a hell of a time . . .

JOHN. I would have liked for somebody to be, to put their arm around me or something, and . . .

DR. Yeah, yeah.

JOHN. (Crying) You know, you know when I talk with you like this, these things I don't even remember until I start to talk to you and now they upset me like heck. I could've gone, I bet you, fifty more years and not thought of that, until I started thinking about your office, and then thinking back about these doctors and that . . . in fact, I think that McCord Hospital hall was just exactly the same color as your waiting room is there.

DR. Did you have the feeling that if you were going to see me, initially, inside, somehow or other you might die?

JOHN. No . . .

DR. Never occurred to you?

JOHN. No.

DR. (To Patricia) Did he ever suggest this to you?

PATRICIA. No.

DR. Did you know about his feeling about doctors?

PATRICIA. No. I know he'll always say, "I'm not sick, I don't need a doctor." Matter of fact he's taken even very few aspirin since I've known him.

JOHN. When I'm sick I take . . .

PATRICIA. I always wondered why, because I . . .

DR. Can you imagine him, a little boy waiting outside in the corridor as his mother's dying . . .

PATRICIA. I can.

DR. It's really horrible. How do you feel when he breaks down like this? Does this upset you?

JOHN. This is stupid, because I shouldn't be crying about this twenty years later, twenty-five years later . . .

DR. You've been crying for it over the years . . . it's there, like a bag of pus, that . . .

JOHN. (Drawing a long breath) Yeah, but I don't like my wife to see me doing this, and I don't, I don't, it's . . .

DR. (To Patricia) Does it upset you that much to see him do this?

PATRICIA. Well, I remember what he said to me the other night, he'd just like for me to say once I needed him.

DR. Yeah . . .

JOHN. I would. That's . . . I need her, and I would like her to need me too.

DR. Do you need him?

PATRICIA. Sure, I need him.

DR. What do you feel inside when he breaks down?

(Silence. Mr. Tracy sniffs)

PATRICIA. I feel sorry for him . . .

JOHN. It seems so stupid to me 'cause I never would have thought . . .

DR. Do you think it's stupid?

PATRICIA. No, I don't.

JOHN. Yeah, but I never would have thought of this; I don't think I would've ever thought of that until Dr. Paul started working and working and working . . .

PATRICIA. I think it's probably good for you to think about it, dear.

JOHN. But it was *so long* ago.

DR. So her mother died so long ago too, so what?

JOHN. Yeah, but I can't . . . but I think how I . . .

DR. Think what?

JOHN. I can't undo what has been done.

PATRICIA. (Softly) That's right . . .

JOHN. I can't . . .

DR. Well, you're undoing some of the feelings that have been done, that you kept inside. This is what you're doing. You can't undo the fact, the event . . .

JOHN. I'll tell you what I would've liked right then now that I think about it; and I couldn't have told you this a few years ago, because I didn't know. But if my father . . . if the bench had been big enough, or we could have gone out somewhere without sitting in that damn little hall . . . if we could have been out in the . . . if my father had been able to talk to me, and maybe put me on his lap, or, or talked to me . . . or just put his arm around me and, and . . .

DR. Made you feel that he cared about you . . .

JOHN. That he cared about me . . . but he couldn't care . . . he cared about my mother, and he wasn't thinking about me right then . . .

DR. Well, you were his son; I mean, you weren't a stranger.

PATRICIA. You didn't feel that he, you know, that your mother and father were happy though, dear.

JOHN. But I can remember that he was . . .

PATRICIA. (Gently) But he still can't talk to you . . . that's the sad thing.

JOHN. But I was so lonesome that night. And I can remember that, and I can remember throwing up, and I remember the nurse coming and cleaning it up . . .

DR. All right, haven't you been lonesome since then?

JOHN. I hate to be lonesome. I can remember so clearly now, about the nurse cleaning that up, and then my father or my aunt . . . I think my aunt Mary was there too, yeah, I know she was . . . and saying, "Oh, nobody paid any attention to you." They were talking among themselves, and I might as well not have been in the world.

DR. (To Patricia) You said on the phone that you had this question as to why you ought to be coming in here because, you know, there weren't any big noises going on . . .

PATRICIA. Mmmm.

DR. But you see it's things like this in him, similar things still within you, and unless they're straightened out, they're going to take a toll. Whether you like it or not.

PATRICIA. Anything . . .

DR. You see, you can, you ought to be able to see that what happened twenty years ago, more than twenty years actually, isn't it?

JOHN. Oh, it was a lot more than that.

DR. Yeah.

JOHN. Twenty-three or twenty-four years ago.

DR. What happened then colors the way you see the hallway in Cambridge; how you see doctors . . .

JOHN. Well, I damn well would move out of there if it was mine. (Mrs. Tracy and Dr. Paul laugh.)

JOHN. I'd take care of that in a hurry.

DR. Yeah.

JOHN. No, but I . . . lonesome is a coldness . . . thinking back, when I go by the cemetery there, I *always* think of that . . . my mother in there where it's so cold and that damn, miserable iron fence, *alone*.

DR. You see, it isn't the hallway that's cold . . .

JOHN. It's my mind that's cold.

DR. . . . It's inside you. And what it reminds you of.

JOHN. And Patricia thinks I'm absolutely cotton-picking out of my mind when I tell her this. I mean if I tell anybody else, they kind of laugh at me, and they say, "Oh, you couldn't do that." But to me, our ranch is the warmest, is the most personal thing outside the home, and when I die, I don't want to be buried in a damn strange cemetery, I want to be buried on the ranch. I don't care if they just dig a hole and push me in . . .

DR. Would you want to be buried next to your mother?

JOHN. No, I'd rather have my mother come down to the ranch and be buried with me. That, the ranch, this is our la . . . The sun comes up every day on it, and it's warm, and it's the soil is warm and it's . . .

DR. Do you really feel, I want to ask you, do you really feel that these feelings are really stupid?

JOHN. Yeah. Not to me they aren't, but to say to somebody else, if I went up and said to somebody, "I want to be buried on our ranch because that's been my whole life . . ."

DR. No, but I mean these feelings of hurt, the pain that you lived through . . . is that so stupid?

JOHN. It feels stupid when I have to tell somebody else. I feel when I, when Patricia hears me cry about this . . . it's real to me; it hurts me inside, but I don't like to . . . I'm upset now, I'm nervous; I mean, here I'm biting my fingernails and pulling my fingers, thinking about that. I can see myself as a little boy sitting in that hall. And I'm *really* upset about it. I can remember that *so clearly* . . .

DR. Yeah, but you see the point about all this is: If you . . .

JOHN. But I think if Patricia is seeing me do this . . .

DR. If she can't see you do this, then your kids are not going to be able to talk about their hurts with you, because they're going to see the same way, that to do so, and to break down, is stupid.

JOHN. Hmmm.

DR. And so they're going to be doomed to keep things inside themselves, whether you like it or not. It's not stupid; it's very human.

JOHN. I see.

DR. I mean you're not a machine.

JOHN. No, no, it hurts me, inside, when I think of it. Now I don't go around . . . I haven't thought of this, believe me . . .

DR. Oh, I can believe it.

JOHN. I haven't thought of this for fifteen, twenty, twenty-four years . . .

DR. No, I believe you, and . . .

JOHN. But talking to you right now, it is so clear. I can see myself sitting there like I was there last night.

DR. And it was very real, wasn't it? I mean it wasn't imagination.

JOHN. Oh, no, no, no, this was real. But I do feel . . . Now Patricia . . .

DR. Do you know how we got on to this?

JOHN. Talking about your office.

DR. That's right. Something in 1968 moves all the way back into the forties.

JOHN. But now you see, Patricia hasn't, Patricia has . . .

DR. Has what?

JOHN. Patricia hasn't shown any hurt, really. And I feel like she's a stronger person than I am because I get all upset and I tell you what happened right to the last detail; and Patricia doesn't . . . Patricia's stronger than I.

DR. Do you think she's stronger? Or do you think she can pretend better?

JOHN. I don't know.

DR. What do you think?

PATRICIA. No, I feel that I wish I could get mine out if I could remember more vividly. I feel I must be trying to push mine back.

DR. Yeah. You see, by virtue of what you [John] are able to do, you might encourage your wife to loosen up a bit inside. You follow me?

PATRICIA. Mmm.

JOHN. It's funny though. I never thought of that until right when . . . it started . . .

PATRICIA. You still throw up when you get upset, John.

JOHN. Yes, I do; when I get upset, I throw up.

PATRICIA. When we're having a fight . . . he throws up everything, constantly, everywhere.

JOHN. I just can't keep anything in my stomach.

PATRICIA. No.

DR. See, I think that what you have to start thinking about if you want to get this thing straightened out, for yourself, your husband, and the boys, you got to think of the connection between your attitude toward Mexico and your mother. The similarities. Because I think there are similarities, important similarities.

JOHN. That seems so far away, though.

DR. Well, I mean this seemed so far away in the McCord Hospital corridor. Does that seem so far away? What in hell is far away?

JOHN. Not, not now it doesn't. It seemed before . . .

DR. But before it did.

JOHN. Oh, before it did; there was no relation at all. Nothing at all. I could've, my life could've depended on it, and I couldn't have had any relation at all between that place of yours . . .

DR. Yeah, that's right.

JOHN. And the more, the more I think of it . . . you brought it up, but the more I think of it, the closer it is.

DR. Yeah.

JOHN. But let's say, three hours ago, if you said, "Your life depends on it." I couldn't have told you that. Now I feel pretty stupid inside for the three hours of not being able to do it.

(Dr. returns.)

DR. What'd you think of that?

VAN. Cindy had some feelings, maybe . . .

CINDY. I really . . .

DR. What?

CINDY. . . . feel like getting up and walking out.

DR. Why?

CINDY. 'Cause this is my last hour with you and I don't want to hear about somebody else's problems. I thought you cut Van off when he was starting to deal with some feelings about Alabama. You cut him off and threw somebody else's tape on, and just, to me as this is our last time to talk to you, and it's more important to us to talk and get feedback from you than to listen to somebody's session.

> [*It is good that Cindy feels comfortable expressing anger at me. However, she still shows a need to be protective of Van.*]

DR. (To Van) You feel the same way?

VAN. I didn't feel it that strongly. I was trying to figure out why you played the tape and trying to get whatever messages were there.

> [*Van's reaction suggests that he was trying to distance the painful feeling that was expressed by John on the Tracy tape. I think that Van was angry at being reminded by the feelings associated with grief.*]

DR. Because the critical piece about this is that you've got to somewhere feed to the kids what's been going on.

VAN. Between us?

DR. About your life history.

VAN. Me?

DR. About you (turning to Cindy), and about you.

VAN. Um-hum. See, we were trying to talk about whether or not we distance the kids or don't allow them to express feelings. I think we've asked . . .

DR. You've asked what?

VAN. For feelings, and for communication, and for openness.

DR. It doesn't work that way; you've got to tell them, and then you get it back. You don't ask. They'll look upon it as a demand for a performance.

> [*This refers to the importance of telling children first about one's own feelings, including both pleasant and painful feelings that one has lived through, without evoking guilt in the children, and giving one's own history associated with these feelings. Children will then be able to reciprocate in kind . . . not immediately, but at some later point in time.*]

VAN. Yeah.

CINDY. Well, I thought just the opposite; like when I was so depressed and so upset, uh, the kids came in one day when I was sitting at the kitchen sink crying, and Cathy said, "What's the matter?" and I said, "Mommie's just so unhappy right now." Cathy said why, and I said, "Mommie just doesn't feel like anybody loves me right now," and Cathy said, "Mommie, I love you," and I said, "I know it, Cathy, but now I just don't feel like anybody loves me." And Mary Lee, our sensitive kid, says, "You mean you don't think Daddy likes you anymore, do you?" And I said, "You're right, I think Daddy's mad at me right now." And then I thought, that's a terrible thing to do, and I shouldn't have told her that, and I felt really bad that I let her know that. And we were having a lot of arguments.

DR. Yeah.

VAN. They pick that up.

CINDY. And Mary Lee said, uh, Mary Lee said, "Daddy, don't you like Mommy anymore? Don't you love Mommy anymore?" and all this kind of business. And now . . .

DR. Yeah.

CINDY. . . . they're seeing us kiss, and they'll say, "Oh, no, there they go again, smooching," And I said, "Well, you remember how we argued; which way do you like us?" So Mary Lee says, "Well, I like you . . . I like Daddy liking you now." But I thought that was all wrong that they saw all this going on.

DR. No. It isn't wrong.

VAN. I don't think it's wrong, either.

DR. 'Cause if they don't know, then they're responsible.

CINDY. Well, that's right too, 'cause I did find out I was taking it out on them, and I thought, Jeepers, now I've got to let them know that it's their daddy I'm mad at and not them.

DR. Well, I'm glad that you could get mad at me.

CINDY. Yeah, I don't care to hear about this guy in his office.

DR. What do you . . .

CINDY. I wanted you for myself today.

DR. And what do you want to talk about today?

CINDY. Well, not necessarily that I wanted to talk, it just . . . it's the first time Van's dealing with his Alabama trip too; I haven't even had a chance to talk to him about that, and he got . . . to me, he was really emotional, and you just cut him off and walk out. And I thought, well, that's not nice of you to do to Van.

> [*Here again, in the setting of the last meeting, with the tendency toward regression as a way of avoiding saying goodby, Cindy speaks for Van.*]

DR. Did you feel that was not nice, Van?

VAN. I didn't have those feelings, no. I tend to deal with things much differently; I tend to try to take in what I can and learn from whatever goes on, so I . . . and maybe I should get angry more than I do, but I don't get angry.

DR. Maybe she gets angry for you.

CINDY. I was just going to say that. I'm always feeling for him and reacting for him.

VAN. She's very protective in that way.

DR. Like your mother.

CINDY. Right.

VAN. In fact, during the tape, while it was playing, I reached over and grabbed her hand and said, "I love you." And I think one of the reasons . . . it came from the tape . . . but one of the reasons that I married Cindy is because she could do that for me.

DR. Yeah.

VAN. I didn't know that consciously . . .

DR. Yeah.

VAN. . . . but certainly I sense it now much more than I did before, and I think that the kind of people that I find attractive . . . the kind of woman I find attractive . . . are similar . . .

DR. Yeah.

VAN. . . . in that they're like . . . I think that was true of Jennifer.

CINDY. She's nothing like me.

VAN. In the sense that she is more expressive than I am, yes.

CINDY. Oh.

VAN. But maybe everybody's more expressive than I am, for that matter. But in that sense, uh . . .

[*Van can now see himself as others see him.*]

CINDY. (Laughing) Well I just realized I've been doing a lot of unnecessary feeling for you! (Van laughs)

[*Cindy sees through herself. Maybe this will mark the beginning of her emotional freedom.*]

DR. Maybe that's the way you got your identity. By doing that.

VAN. I can't put the puzzle together, because in Cindy's family in a way you couldn't express your feelings, so you ended up having migraine headaches. Cindy hasn't had a migraine headache since we've been married, almost, but had countless ones before.

CINDY. No, he's absolutely right. Because I have . . . you and my mother are so much alike in never showing emotions. And I was always feeling when my father would pick on mother and everything, I was always feeling for my mother . . .

VAN. Protecting her, yeah.

CINDY. . . . and taking her fight.

VAN. That's true.

CINDY. And I'm doing the same thing for you, because when my mother would get sad and so forth and I would attack Daddy, you know. And here I thought you were being sad, and I thought, well, Dr. Paul is not being nice to you. And it wasn't even feelings you're having. And like my mother used to say, "Cindy, quit picking on your Daddy. You don't know what I'm feeling. I don't care that Daddy said that to me." And yet I'd fight her fights for her.

DR. So I became whom in this triangle?

CINDY. You were my Daddy not letting him fight.

> [*In effect here, I represented Cindy's father who would not let or encourage Cindy's mother to fight and Van was in Cindy's mother's slot.*]

DR. That's right.

CINDY. (Bitterly) And not caring, and getting up and walking out.

DR. Like your Daddy would. Just like he would. That bastard.

CINDY. (Laughs)

VAN. Yeah, he is.

DR. What I wrote down here is, she married her mother and he married his father . . . next case.

(Both laughed heartily.)

VAN. Right, right on.

DR. Now, I'll tell you what you ought to do. I mean, uh, if you never come back to see me, that as the kids get older you take your tapes, you get another machine and you edit out all references to your sexual behavior, and then you'll have the process of where you came from.

CINDY. Yeah.

DR. And then you feed that to the kids. You can do it together. And they'll get a sense of your own development, as it emerged here. Not in phony terms . . .

VAN. Hmm.

DR. . . . but as it was lived out here. And you save the tapes. . . . You look sort of sad, Van.

VAN. Ah, I'm reflecting on uh, I'm doing flip-flops between what it was like when I was growing up, and what I want it to be like for my kids growing up.

DR. And the jealousy of the kids having something that you didn't have, each of you, is something you got to get riveted in your heads. And tell them, that you know, you feel jealous that they got this kind of opportunity or that experience.

CINDY. I know another thing that I'm feeling very sensitive about, that I haven't been a very good mother, 'cause I see my kids' terrible behavior, and it really scares me to be taking them to Wales, to that foreign culture where all the children supposedly there are so perfect.

> [*There's this word "perfect" again.*]

DR. They're not perfect.

CINDY. I hope they're not. But everybody's always . . . not everybody, but I get so much comment now that I'm extra sensitive about the kids because, uh, "Wait until your kids do that in Cardiff" or something, you won't be invited back for tea or something. And I think, Gee, you know, someplace, in some ways, I've gone wrong, because my kids are so . . . they don't know manners, they're so active.

DR. Well, I'll tell you how to get that straightened out with the kids. Uh, I think that Van is just about ready to move in a more positive direction with the kids. And you [Cindy] move out a bit more, and you [Van] move in, and they'll start shaping up. They have missed your [Van] more positive influence, not out of choice, but because of what happened to you as a kid.

CINDY. Uh-huh.

DR. I think you're about ready to do that.

VAN. Yeah. I think they're also getting to the point where we can talk with them about that instead of . . .

CINDY. Yeah, Cathy was exciting last night, wasn't she?

VAN. She didn't have to act out her feelings . . . we could talk to her.

CINDY. She did it for the first time.

DR. It's hard to think of saying goodby forever, here.

> [*I bring them back to the issue of the meeting. I want this pursued as much as possible before we part.*]

VAN. For me it is.

CINDY. Gee, I wasn't feeling that way, because I felt we could come back, I didn't know we had to say goodby.

DR. You don't have to say goodby; we're just thinking about saying goodby forever.

CINDY. If I think about saying goodby to you forever, I'll start crying. 'Cause . . .

DR. Why?

CINDY. Goodbys are always sad for me.

DR. It's the hardest thing for people to do, say goodby forever.

CINDY. It really is. That's why we always say, we'll write and keep in touch, and then it's a gradual . . . then we never see each other.

VAN. Yeah. My way to do it as I understand myself now would be not to feel that way now, but about two hours from now.

DR. Yeah.

VAN. I'd feel it.

CINDY. And I will cry right now, and in two hours feel so good.

VAN. Then you'd wonder why the hell I'm so sad two hours later. Yeah.

[*Two for the seesaw!*]

DR. Let me just give you a couple of inputs. In the wake of leaving here, and it doesn't have to be a permanent goodby, I'm just saying that just thinking about saying a permanent goodby, that quality of experience . . . but . . . you can be alerted.

CINDY. (To Van) I thought, you know, I was commenting to you on how I've seen real changes in the children. And I thought it was my behavior modification . . . you know, it really was your coming back to them.

[*She was trying behavior modification.*]

VAN. Yeah, I think it's both. I think you're responding to them differently than you did before.

DR. You can expect that there might be some slippage, and the slippage will be each of your ways of expressing resentment toward me, because you have to leave. Follow?

[*From my experience, slippage is in large part related to the difficulty in recognizing the existence of resentment toward the therapist. It also indicates an unrecognized desire to return to the therapeutic setting.*]

CINDY. Uh-huh.

DR. I'm still curious how you people were able to move this fast! It usually takes a little longer. This is a month and a half ago.

(Prepares to play videotape of November 1, 1972)

VAN. Is that all it's been? I'm worried that the slippage is going to happen when we get to South Dakota. I have fantasies that I'm gonna blow my cool if Cindy's Dad says boo to me. I'm gonna tell him to fuck off, sort of . . .

> [*Van is now able to express himself in an extremely loose, colloquial way. Quite an advance for the tightly proper professor in Session I.*]

CINDY. That'd be okay with me if he did.

VAN. 'Cause, going back there I can't be me. I have to be what he wants me to be.

DR. Well, so why don't you role-play it together on the way out so that you can say it to him without a big noise?

VAN. Yeah, I would anyway 'cause I'm a nice guy, he-he-he (laughs). I probably would never . . . Oh, I did on the phone when I talked to him that one time.

(Videotape playback of Van talking about walking in on parents making love.)

> [*The videotape segment from November 1, 1972 (Session V, pages 180–185) is designed to remind Cindy and Van of the beginning resolution of their problems, while Van was recounting his guilt in interrupting his parents' love-making. This is to reinforce the recognition of premarital factors accounting for their own marital and sexual difficulties.*]

DR. What do you think of them, there?

VAN. I still see him as awfully heady.

DR. Neatly verbal.

VAN. Articulate, but . . . somehow not talking about the things that need to be talked about.

DR. This is six weeks later. I want to ask you a question. How would you feel about signing a release for using this with residents or medical students?

VAN. Which?

DR. The whole works.

VAN. The whole works. Well, the only qualm would be if I had mentioned names that would be traceable anywhere.

DR. Any names other than family would be deleted.

VAN. Then I wouldn't have any qualms.

CINDY. Uh-uh. No.

VAN. Cindy's having a thing that happens to her, recently; it's that she gets a numbness in her arm that scares me a bit, I don't know what it is.

CINDY. I get like needles that are sticking in me, right here. And then it starts to go all the way down my arm.

DR. Okay. Let me see what you can do about that. When you go home to South Dakota and maybe that's why it might be a good idea if you [Van] could sort of weather the bullshit from her father . . .

VAN. Yeah, I can do that.

DR. I would make a family tree going back a couple of generations with them, find out what happened to the different people there, and you will find that you are living out in the numbness something that was nonverbally transmitted to you, but you've got to decode it. Do you follow me?

> [*Van gave me the clue to the tendencies toward Cindy's somatizing when he mentioned her migraine headaches. I took a stab at the numbness expressing some kind of internalized emotional conflict. Statistically, 80–90 percent of the complaints presented by patients are found to be functional without any organic pathological process involved. Thus, the odds are that any complaint presented is functionally rather than organically ordained. Cindy's complaint certainly could be physical but I wanted to find out what could be thrashed out pursuing it this way.*]

DR. You've gone through the business of getting laid by your father already, haven't you?

> [*The incestuous fantasy alluded to is a continuation of the strategy or technique to desensitize incestuous fantasies developed in the previous session (e.g., pages 224–229).*]

CINDY. (Nodded yes)

DR. I wonder if I told you about . . . I made reference to it . . .
did I tell you about the play, *The Family Reunion,* by
T. S. Eliot?

VAN. Yeah.

CINDY. I vaguely remember that, but I don't know what you said
about it, though.

DR. Did you read it? Did you get ahold of it?

CINDY. No.

DR. Well, what Eliot has done there in literary form is very much
like what I see myself doing here. Where the main character,
Harry, finds the piece from an aunt that resolves his head
problem.* The experiential input piece. Your body is trying
to tell you something. Let's assume it's not an organic thing.
   [*For the moment, in assuming that the pain was not organic, I was attempting to see what the sensation might
   be related to.*]

CINDY. Uh-huh.

VAN. Yeah, I was worried that it was organic.

DR. Have you seen a doctor?

CINDY. No, but it really occurs . . . like I was carrying a box up
the stairs and I was grabbed by this pain in my breast,
just . . .

DR. Crunching pain?

CINDY. Mmm. And then it, my arm just went dead.

DR. Anybody in your family have angina?

VAN. That's what I thought.

CINDY. I don't know. I don't even know what that is.

DR. When was the last time you had a physical exam?

CINDY. I think when I had my baby. Oh, physical exam, gee, I
guess . . .

VAN. You've never had a physical.

CINDY. No, I don't think I ever had a real physical exam.

DR. Well, you ought to have one, but the odds are that it's func-
tional. But get ahold of T. S. Eliot's *Family Reunion* . . .

CINDY. Uh-huh.

DR. . . . And read it, and that'll sort of sketch out in your head,

* See Introduction to this book, quotation by Harry from *The Family Reunion.*

how to find out whom you're named after, and things like that, and how do they decide, your mother and your father. You know, make use of the time that you're spending out there, and tell them . . . I would put it on tape, and take it with me, and when you're in Wales, you can review it.

CINDY. Do you think it's worthwhile for me to pursue the business of my being a . . . conceived before they got married?

DR. Certainly. Hah! Is that what you were thinking about when the thing came on?

CINDY. No. I don't think so. That was one of the questions I did have to ask you today, and I . . .

DR. Certainly.

CINDY. I kinda make questions that I wanted to ask you about.

DR. Got any other ones? I think that's an important thing to find out. It has to do with the auspices of your being.

VAN. When did those things start? I can't remember.

CINDY. The first time I told you about it was just yesterday, but about three weeks ago when I . . .

DR. Three weeks ago. Let's see what happened three weeks ago. Three weeks ago was when on the calendar? These things are very predictable.

CINDY. Is that right?

DR. Oh, yes.

CINDY. (Laughs) I can't believe it can be psychological, why it hurts so much. That's incredible.

> [*It is very difficult for people, both lay and professional, to believe that intense emotional states hidden from one's awareness can be expressed in functional kinds of pain.*]

VAN. Well, your body has always spoken for you.

CINDY. (Laughs) That's for sure.

DR. Here's three weeks ago . . . we'll work out the calendar . . . today is what? Today is the eighteenth, going back three weeks . . . do you remember the first time, precisely, when it happened?

CINDY. I was sleeping, it was in bed. I had a nightmare.

DR. A nightmare about what?

CINDY. I can't remember the nightmare, I just remember . . . I couldn't catch my breath.

DR. What night was it?

CINDY. What night was it? Oh, I can't remember that.

DR. Think hard.

CINDY. It was a Tuesday night.

DR. On Tuesday night.

CINDY. 'Cause I'd been drinking, and I thought it was the booze. Oh, I know! I know what it was!

DR. Yeah?

CINDY. Huh-huh (laughs) That was the rape scene. I was raped by about those eight men?

VAN. Was that it?

> [*Apparently, part of the dream was revealed to Van.*]

CINDY. Yeah.

VAN. Didn't you tell me your grandmother was . . . grand, great . . .

> [*Van had been told of this event.*]

CINDY. My great-great-grandmother was raped by the Indians, that's how we came by our Indian blood.

DR. Okay, you're raped by eight men in a Tuesday night dream. Now, what was that great-great-grandmother's name?

CINDY. Uh, Hazelton.

DR. First name.

CINDY. I think it was Cynthia. Cynthia. Cynthia, hmm.

DR. Wow!

CINDY. That can't be.

DR. That can't be?

CINDY. Oh, no, that's just too spooky (laughs).

DR. What do you mean, it can't be? That's how it works. It's not spooky, it just has a different kind of logic.

> [*In anticipation of this being our last meeting and the projected upheaval of being abroad, it seems that a curious dream has emerged which is related to Cindy being so named. This dream, this embodiment of catastrophe, may be viewed as derived from the nonverbal transmission of a single archetype chosen from the pool of family memories.*]

CINDY. Okay, when I die tonight in my sleep with this coronary, you gotta chalk that theory off (still laughing).

> [*Cindy certainly suggests that she's going to have a coronary because of her difficulty in saying goodby. And maybe in some ways her pain is a way of saying, "Please don't leave me, I need help," and "It's premature for me to have to part this way." Very often in the final session with clients, a variety of somatic or bodily complaints will emerge which betray their ambivalence about saying goodby.*]

DR. Well, what you do when you go out there; you do a real deep family investigation.

CINDY. I can remember, I can remember I came close to being named Ann or Cynthia because of a great-great-grandmother, but I know her last name was Hazelton. And my cousin was born a month before I was, she got the name Cynthia, that's how my mother gave me the name Cindy. There's also another . . .

DR. That scares you, doesn't it?

CINDY. Yeah, cause you just . . . it can't be.

DR. No, the thing is, it really indicates the importance of non-verbal vibes.

CINDY. Yeah.

DR. It isn't a matter of spooky or anything. It's that we are more unconscious than we are conscious.

CINDY. That's what I mean it's spooky, because you don't really . . .

DR. Know what's going on.

CINDY. Right.

DR. Okay. So you accept that, and then try to find out.

CINDY. It's so great knowing I'm not responsible for anything anymore.

> [*The theme of responsibility appears again. Since so much of our lives is beyond our control or awareness, to what extent can we be responsible? Perhaps a person can become more responsible for himself by becoming more aware of his own ability to understand his inner environment and inability to control other people.*]

VAN. I don't think that's what he said.

(All laugh good-humoredly)

DR. I want you to see yourself as you are today. What I'll do is give you a copy of a paper a friend of mine wrote, on how you get yourself differentiated out of your own family. Okay?

(Videotape playback of pages 253–262.)

CINDY. Oh. Wow.

(All laugh uproariously)

DR. (To Van) How do you look to yourself there?

VAN. I'm getting there.

DR. Yeah, I think you are.

VAN. Feels much better.

DR. Good.

VAN. Getting my shit together.

CINDY. Mmm.

DR. Well, I think you both are lucky.

VAN. Well, I guess . . . yeah, but more than that. I wouldn't like to attribute it just to luck.

DR. No, lucky was in the sense of being in the right spot at the right time.

CINDY. What was your diagnosis of us at the first session you had with us?

DR. I've given up diagnosing, because that prejudges things. Here's the paper. This is a goodby present to you. This paper you have in your hands I think will be one of the landmark papers of the century.

> [*I gave them a colleague's paper to read, "Toward the Differentiation of a Self in One's Own Family." *]

VAN. Anonymous.

DR. Well, the thing is, the guy was concerned about his family getting involved with litigation. The publisher was concerned about it. And would you just put on top, audio- and videotapes, so it's in your handwriting? All identifying data will be deleted.

> [*Here I'm asking them to sign a release for the use of their audio- and videotapes. The release is to enable others to hear in my office the selected segments of the process of the Hoopes's work with me without their tape being recorded onto someone else's audiotape.*]

* See References.

CINDY. Does this mean that people will have some of us on their tapes?

DR. No.

VAN. You want kids' names?

DR. No.

VAN. What's today, the eighteenth?

CINDY. Um-hum.

DR. Well, I think you certainly look good, I still can't figure it out. You came in here . . .

VAN. When we find out we'll let you know.

DR. Okay. Fine. I think those flicks the last time helped, those homosexual flicks.

VAN. Yeah, we never really processed that. I felt. We never really talked much about that. I had some thoughts about what all that was about.

DR. Well, it fits into what we just said before. You married your father; she married her mother.

VAN. Hmm.

DR. And on some level, that was interfering with the sexual scene.

VAN. Yeah.

DR. It couldn't help but do that.

VAN. God, it's a lifelong quest, but an exciting one.

DR. Yeah.

CINDY. Yeah, it's been exciting for me to be here.

DR. Well, it couldn't happen to two nicer people, that's all I can say.

CINDY. Hey.

VAN. Thank you.

CINDY. The luck was that we really did come to you. I think you were our turning point. I really feel it was you. Because we had just . . . if I had gone to my other therapist . . .

VAN. It would have been a bust.

CINDY. . . . we would have been dragging our feet.

DR. You would have been in a divorce court.

CINDY. You were the electric shock treatment kind of business. He was also very judgmental . . . oh, my foot's so tense.

DR. Okay, should I send the bill to where you are, or what should I do?

CINDY. Yes.

DR. It'll be forwarded on to you?

VAN. Yes. It'll be taken care of by mail.

CINDY. Oh, our tape.

DR. Did you get your tape? Well, I'm very pleased for you both. It's very nice.

VAN. I think Wales is a . . .

DR. . . . a good place to digest all this.

VAN. Yes.

CINDY. That'll be our . . .

DR. And I wouldn't worry that much about it. It'll be a good trip.

VAN. Yeah.

CINDY. Well, we need an excuse, because Van has to take a sabbatical.

DR. Thanks a lot.

CINDY. Thank you.

DR. 'By.

VAN. Thank you.

DR. You're going to go and track your father's place in . . .

VAN. Yes, I am.

DR. Okay.

VAN. I've got the name of the woman that my mother stayed with when she was in that city in Michigan so I can find out the clinic and everything through her.

DR. If there's anything that you feel that I can do about finding where your father was hospitalized, I'll go ahead with it.

VAN. Okay. Good. Thank you.

DR. Good luck. Good-by.

CINDY. Good-by.

VAN. We'll play a little bit. Have we got everything?

CINDY. Yeah. Goodby.

> You will have to live with these memories and make them
> Into something new. Only by acceptance
> Of the past will you alter its meaning.*
>
> —REILLY

* *The Cocktail Party,* by T. S. Eliot, p. 186.

Follow-up

You go on trying to think of each thing separately,
Making small things important, so that everything
May be unimportant, a slight deviation
From some imaginary course that life ought to take,
That you call normal. What you call the normal
Is merely the unreal and the unimportant.*

—HARRY

THE HOOPESES LEFT FOR Wales in January 1973 for Van's six-
month sabbatical. In May 1973, my wife and I conceived a plan
for a book using their seven interviews to illustrate a transgenerational view of marital problems. We had chosen their interviews
because the Hoopeses had asked for help in a crisis, and had only
a short period of time in which to resolve it. These factors as well
as the relatively few interviews which could be commented upon
had great appeal for us.

Besides, we had lived through some of the same things that
Van and Cindy had and had known, personally, people like them.
We, like the Hoopeses, had struggled to become aware of the historical forces dictating our own moments of dissonance, and were
also pleased when things went well. Before we started to write,
however, it was essential that we find out what had become of
Cindy and Van and obtain their permission for such an undertaking.

So, in September 1973, I, Dr. Paul, called their home and
asked them to come in for a follow-up meeting at no charge to
them. They were to come in to meet my needs to see how they
were faring and to discuss the possibility of their granting permis-

* *The Family Reunion*, by T. S. Eliot, p. 88.

sion for a projected book. They agreed to come to meet with me
in the following month.

When Cindy and Van came to my office they both indicated
that, in general, they felt fairly good about things. For Cindy, life
had become . . . *"really liveable."*

CINDY. I've been in a very peaceful stage in my life that I've never
been in before, and uh, I've been feeling good. I never had a
long period where I really felt good—I think I'm more into
reality than I've ever been before.

> *[She made it very clear, however, that Van was unable
> to communicate freely with her.* "At home he never talks
> . . . I never know what's inside him," *she said. Van
> agreed with her and made it plain that although he felt
> like a different person and dealt with things differently,
> he still held back from himself recognition of his own
> feelings. He said that he was* "ambivalent" *about com-
> ing back to see me for fear something would be so pain-
> ful* "that I wouldn't want to look at it."]

VAN. There are a lot of things that still need looking at. I've still a
tremendous amount of depressiveness to me, that gets put on
the shelf, and defended against and controlled, but it's still
there. And from time to time it pops up . . . I've still got a
lot about me that has to do with sort of a little boy in me . . .
it feels incompetent, helpless, insecure. I keep that little kid
inside. He can't get out . . . He still hollers . . . I'm also
anxious about what it is that's keeping me from getting my
father's hospital record. (See Session VII, page 288.)

> *[Van was dealing with all of this within himself; using
> so much energy to keep inner control that it was impos-
> sible for him to communicate freely with Cindy. As the
> interview progressed, it became increasingly clear to all
> three of us that there was unfinished work to be done.*
>
> *To help things along, I offered to try to find a way
> to get his father's hospital records for him, for I felt that
> they were an important key to his feeling better about
> himself.]*

DR. . . . See, the way I would sort of read it is until, on your part, you can forgive your father for whatever happened, that you're going to have some anxieties that you're going to go bananas . . .

> [*Once I had made this offer Van began to reminisce about his childhood. He speculated that once he saw the records he could more clearly sort out what it really felt like to watch his father fall apart in front of his eyes.*]

VAN. Part of my need to have things so damn controlled grows out of that [scene] where I had to support my mother and to be her somebody that cared for her while she's watching her man fall part. It just complicated the business of becoming me . . . I can remember being very embarrassed about father because of the way he spoke, because of uh, his lack of education, because of the way he looked. In particular when he'd drink wine, he'd start slurring his words, and then I just couldn't be in the same room with him, but that's when he would want to talk. It's the only time he'd want to talk. And I couldn't take it.

DR. And that's why you're so precise with words, or try to be so precise: So you're not going to be like him.

VAN. There was also a long time where I'd never get drunk; I was scared to get drunk . . . I think I was angry as hell, I can remember feeling that my mother was angry at him when he'd [get drunk] . . . I was always flip-flopping between saying, "Well, hell, he's had a hell of a rough time, why not let him drink a little . . ." sort of caring and protecting him, you know . . . and at the same time saying, "You bastard!" I was always going back and forth between those two. I never said, "You bastard," because this side always won out. I was always excusing what he was doing, what he was feeling. I think at times I hated him very much. I can remember on one occasion we started to fool around, wrestling around, and I was sort of getting big enough . . . I think this was before he had his breakdown-hospitalization, and . . . we were fooling around . . . I was about thirteen . . . and it was a strange experience to think that I might possibly, beat him . . .

It was a scary experience. 'Cause he was a very . . . well-built guy. He was a small man, smaller than I am, but uh, very muscular, sinewy. So I had more weight on him. But, uh . . . I had more strength.

> [*As Van continued to talk he explained that his father had become very depressed about the failure of his fish market in 1952.*]

VAN. His whole life had centered around getting a business—he bought it . . . and within six months it was busted . . . [At that time] my mother would say to me, "All my friends," she would say, "all my friends are telling me I should divorce your father. What should I do?" As far as I remember, I used to say, "Hell, I don't know." But . . . I don't think I ever said anything to her, but I felt the full weight of the anger she was going through. She dumped an awful lot of it on me . . . So when you say, you know, forgive, uh . . . up here, I can say, yes, I have . . .

DR. It counts down here (pointing to heart).

VAN. I know, and I don't know how to get down there, feel it down there . . . I don't know what I'm going to find out [from the records]. I'm a little bit scared about that.

DR. Whatever you'll find, it'll be real. And I think what it might help to do, is to rekindle some of the events that you lived through then.

*   *   *

CINDY. It just makes such sense, the way he has always related to me, it just makes such sense, because hearing how he was raised . . .

DR. He didn't tell you too much about some of this before?

CINDY. Oh, I never knew how he dealt with his parents and so forth, and I set the same exact stage his mother and father did, and I'm asking him to play the same exact part with me that they did. And it's so clear why he reacts sometimes at some of the things I do. You just aren't going to go to therapy by yourself. I've got to sit there and listen to what you're saying! (Laughs) It just makes everything so *clear* to me.

> [*We also talked about the possibility of using their interviews for a book. They expressed some surprise to think that what happened between them could be viewed as being valuable enough that other people would be in-*]

terested. They agreed to collaborate, however. A barter arrangement evolved wherein I would provide marital counseling free of charge on an ad hoc *basis for the residue of their problems.*

Because so much of Van's difficulty in revealing himself to both himself and to Cindy seemed rooted in his denied ambivalence toward his father, the major thrust of my efforts were to be directed toward Van. I, therefore, agreed to track down his father's hospital records if I could, make a Xerox copy for them, and then contact them for another interview.

Between the meeting in October 1973 and the next one which took place in December 1973, I was able to locate through a network of colleagues the mental hospital records of Van's father. I made a Xerox copy for Van which I handed to him when he and Cindy arrived on December thirteenth.

The following information was excerpted from the original record:

VAN'S FATHER'S HOSPITAL RECORD
FLEMING HOSPITAL
Detroit, Michigan

NAME   Hoopes, Van
DATE OF BIRTH   August 20, 1902
Catholic, Not practicing
B. baptized
DATE AND TIME OF ADMISSION   June 10, 1954
PREVIOUS ADMISSION   No
MARRIED   M
COLOR   W
SHIPMENT TO HOSPITAL BY   Ambulance—Wheelchair
ADMITTING DIAGNOSIS   Involutional Paranoid State
IMPORTANT MANIFESTATIONS, SYMPTOMS, AND COMPLAINTS   Mental
        Depression—Paranoid Ideas
FINAL DIAGNOSIS   Same
PROGNOSIS   Fair
DISCHARGED   Improved
DATE   July 15, 1954

SIGNED   David L. Fleming

HISTORY

NAME   Mr. Van Hoopes

DR.   Fleming

ROOM NO.   115

DATE   June 10, 1954

REMARKS   History from wife

REASON FOR ADMISSION   He was admitted on June 10, 1954 referred
by Dr. Herbert Fleming for prefrontal lobotomy because of
mental depression.

PRESENT ILLNESS   Patient had a failure in business two years ago,
and became very depressed one year ago. He was given thirteen shock treatments at a hospital in Mobile, Alabama. He
was able to return to work, but since January 1954, he has
become considerably depressed, sits around the house most
of the time and doesn't eat or sleep well. He has gotten very
paranoid, doesn't trust anyone including his physician and
has been very uncooperative so far as taking psychiatric
treatment is concerned. He had been crying at home, did not
care for his personal appearance. Refused to eat, thinking he
was not really sick but would eat if wife left things out.

He always has had an inferiority complex, since childhood, and never had many friends and did not enjoy social
activity.

NOTATION   Patient refuses to give any answers. Had hernia operation
several years ago.

PHYSICAL EXAMINATION

GENERAL APPEARANCE   Well developed, poorly nourished, dark com-
plexioned male. Cooperative, but not very talkative.

WEIGHT   Normal—118

PHYSICAL FINDINGS   Within normal limits except for being poorly
nourished.

IMPRESSION   (1) Involutional depression
            (2) Manic-depressive psychosis
            (3) Schizophrenia

PROGRESS RECORD

June 18, 1954:   He is less depressed since admission. However he
still resents hospitalization. Prefrontal lobotomy is to be
withheld at present. Will start on EST (electroshock
therapy).

June 24, 1954:   Patient receiving EST. Patient is pleasant and joins
the group at times.

July 13, 1954:   Cooperative, pleasant, rational. Ambitious to go back to his job and start his profession. He answers questions precisely and quickly.

July 15, 1954: 2:00 P.M. Patient dismissed today.

[*Van reacted strongly to reading this record.*]

VAN. It's amazing. It is kind of like . . . the past . . . rearing its head. I'm getting flashbacks as I read some of this about "the patient became very depressed a year about, was given several shock treatments at a hospital, was able to return to work, became depressed" and I get mental pictures of what Dad was like sitting around the house. "Doesn't eat or sleep well, has gotten very paranoid, doesn't trust anyone including his physician, been very uncooperative . . . patient refuses to give any answers."

DR. He was scared shitless there.

VAN. Yeah, well they had him, let's see June tenth it was this . . . they had him pretty well sedated when they took him on the airplane, but he wasn't . . . all too good at that point either. I still remember that, we rode from the hospital to the airport in a police car, and he was sitting in the front with me, and the whole way down he kept saying, something about . . . "Since they're going to take me away," or "since they're taking my life away, don't let them get you," something like that . . . It's really a page out of the past.

DR. He struggled his way.

VAN. "Prefrontal lobotomy is to be withheld at present." I don't know what your feelings are about that, but just reading that, I get angry. My . . . I don't know much about the operation, but what I know from what I've read is that it . . . I guess I feel protective . . . . The son of a gun, he had a hell of a tough time. He was depressed all his life.

DR. Do you feel less depressed? About your life?

VAN. Yes, I do. Yeah . . . I've been able to recognize more of what I think at least when some of the old patterns and feelings come back, and depression.

DR. Mmmm.

VAN. It feels good not to be depressed.

DR. You find Cindy to be more of a friend?

VAN. Yeah.

DR. You talk to her?

VAN. I still have trouble with that.

*   *   *

DR. So you ought to give yourself a little chance. If it's there to be flushed out, flush it out, and then move on.

VAN. There's . . . I sense less of that, uh, each time I confront it, uh, it's less heavy, than it was before. That's true.

DR. The issue is that you have, contrary to what you might feel, a right to live and feel good, even though he's dead. And the question then becomes, what kinds of experiences are going to help you feel good?

> [*So, during the following monthly (February–July 1974) interviews with Van and Cindy which included playback of both recent and much earlier videotapes, I focused on Van's continued need to distance himself from his own locked-in feelings about his father. I was finally able to prevail on him to bring in the audiotape of his visit to his father's grave (see Session VI, pages 247–249). He also brought in a blown-up picture of his father taken when he [Van] was a toddler. That audiotape was played back and Van's reaction was to cry throughout. He then indicated that he was beginning to find himself much less angry at Brian [his son] whenever Brian would hurt himself and could bear to see Brian's tears and thus was able to comfort him. He also stopped hitting Brian on the butt as his father had done to him, "to make him grow."*]

VAN. I don't know, I find that in the last couple of weeks I've really felt just great about being with the kids and with the family and all and being able to recognize in the process and say to myself, gee, this is really fun . . . this is really great.

DR. You feel it's okay to feel that way?

VAN. Yeah . . . it's something good. The heaviness, there's also the other side too.

DR. I think that if one can sort of get involved with the heaviness and get that out of one's system, then there can be a lot more joy and pleasure.

[*Cindy confirmed that Van was more responsive to her, adding that sex was freer and mutually enjoyable.*

Another important area covered was Van's new-found ability to regard Cindy's enthusiastic desire for something, such as a wish to move to a larger house as her style of expressing a fantasy, rather than as making an unreasonable demand on him. Also, a man's asking Cindy out to lunch, which she refused, was regarded by Van as a threat to their relationship. But out of all this there emerged an increased ability in exchanging sexual fantasies—a new skill.

My continued work with Cindy included helping her in acquiring more of a sense of her own person-hood. We reviewed her new feelings of fondness and respect for her mother, especially when her mother began to stand up for her own [mother's] rights vis-à-vis her father, the fun she had going out and having cock-tails with her mother, hearing her mother bitch about her father for the first time. Also, Cindy talked about the fears of having to care for her father if he should become disabled. For the first time she acknowledged her wishes that he should die because he had put so many demands on her to come and live in South Da-kota. She expressed anger at his general lack of sensi-tivity toward her. She reported a dream she had, affirming her death wish for her father wherein her mother was dating Cary Grant. That thrilled Cindy.

With this backing and filling, and especially in her beginning ability to have fun with her mother, her perception of herself and her role shifted; her tendency to become demanding lessened so that she was able to say,]

CINDY. I feel like, the first time, Van and I have, are really reach-ing a point of communication. I guess now that's why I've, I feel I want to, right now, start communicating with Cathy [*older daughter*]. I feel like she and I are kind of functioning like Van and I used to . . .

>[*We began to talk about the issue of Cindy's working part-time or doing something that belonged exclusively to herself. She began a course in public relations which interested her greatly. She was conflicted about pursuing any activity exclusively related to satisfying herself. Van added to her dilemma, for he was ambivalent about her having interests other than himself and the children. He discovered and was then overwhelmed by the realization that he felt that he wanted, and needed to be, "the only person around her who makes her feel important, wanted, loved."*
>
>*On her own part, trying to take steps to achieve a balance in her life was particularly difficult for Cindy. Her role model had been her mother, a woman who had spent her whole life at home, devoted to her husband and children who became dependent on her and, in turn, she became completely dependent on them. Cindy is now considering applying for a postgraduate degree in business education.*
>
>*Further decoding of their residual sexual difficulties developed after Van clearly indicated his escalating guilt whenever Cindy would cry, feeling responsible for anything which hurt her. Van's fear dated back to 1965 when Cindy had been in an almost fatal automobile accident. This is what emerged when I asked him how he bore uncertainty:*]

VAN. Probably very badly. Uncertainty? Oh, the first thought that pops in my mind is when you (Cindy) had a tubal pregnancy. And I wasn't sure what was gonna happen, whether Cindy would even live or not . . . At that point I was dealing with it . . . by being very religious. Part of the . . . I think I was scared then . . . But I was being very, very uh . . . I guess I distanced myself from that. I don't know why I did it.

CINDY. Well, through it all you were remaining calm, cool, collected. Because you were giving me the oxygen. If that's . . . you mean how you functioned at the time. You were functioning great.

VAN. Yeah.

CINDY. Calmly . . . Again, you did get angry, at yourself. Blamed yourself.

DR. Hard on yourself?

VAN. I can't remember it from that instant, but it certainly has been true . . .

CINDY. You were very angry at yourself. Very . . . you blamed yourself totally. In fact, we didn't have intercourse for a long time because you were scared to death that you were going to hurt me again.

DR. Did you feel guilty about it then?

VAN. Probably. Did you ever see . . . I don't know why movies keep popping into my mind. Did you ever see the movie . . . oh, *War and Peace,* I think, no . . . *Farewell to Arms.* Hemingway?

DR. Yeah.

VAN. Where the woman dies in childbirth at the end of the movie? That disturbed me no end, when I was . . . I must have been twenty years old, thinking how awful it was, uh, women to have to go through that process.

DR. How guilty did your mother make you feel about her having to give birth to you?

VAN. That's where it's from, I can remember her saying to me, uh, she shouldn't have gotten pregnant, she just had a terrible thirty-six-hour labor and finally Caesarean section for me, and then three months later she was pregnant with my sister so . . . she always talked about it as the shadow, the Valley of the Shadow of Death.

DR. So she laid that on you.

VAN. Like giving birth was going through the Valley of the Shadow.

> [*Throughout our last monthly meetings in the spring and the summer, the remaining unrecognized guilt and unresolved anger they both felt were slowly decoded. Only occasionally were they able to listen to the more recent follow-up tapes. I urged them to keep trying.*]

DR. The only way I know of nipping these things, and when I say these things, I mean these spiraling fantasies, is to review the tapes together. And it may be a bore and a pain in the ass and you might get inclined to get nauseated, but you see what gets into your head is . . . we all live according to cycles . . . I don't know how to prevail upon you people just to try and listen to some of the old tapes. I think it'll make a big difference for you. I really do. I'm especially pleased for you, Van. Because I didn't think the first time I saw you that we'd ever get this far.

> [*I emphasized over and over that however impossible and absurd reviewing the past via audiotapes seemed to them, such reviews could help them understand the residues from the past which unnecessarily were contributing to the normal struggles of the moment.*]

VAN. Yeah . . . I agree with you . . . We struggle along. Trying to make the best of the situation, and I have a very clear picture in my head about where I came from, and it feels very good to be where I am. Even though I know there's a long way to go. But . . . by contrast, uh, I, I feel damn lucky to come out of that situation to where I am.

> We shall not cease from exploration
> And the end of all our exploring
> Will be to arrive where we started
> And know the place for the first time.*
>   —"Little Gidding"

* *Four Quartets,* by T. S. Eliot (New York: Harcourt, Brace and World, Inc., 1943), p. 39.

Reflections
Ten Years Later

WE WERE CURIOUS; we wanted to know. What had happened to Van and Cindy? The years had gone by so fast. What had been the results of the interventions ten years ago? Were Van and Cindy still together? We wanted to know what had changed and what had not changed. What were the effects of that time of crisis on their children? How were their lives and those of their families progressing?

Although Betty Paul had never met the Hoopses personally, she had, when writing the book and watching them on videotape, grown attached to them. She remembered that when the writing was over, she felt much like she had lost people who had become important to her. Now she looked forward to a reunion by video.

When Norman Paul telephoned and talked with Van, Van responded most warmly saying, "What a coincidence! Cindy and I have been talking together about calling you. We have been thinking that now would be a good time to check in with you again, so I am glad that you called us first."

Then he added, "We want to share with you some of what has happened during the last ten years. Remember, I am 44 now, and I'm getting close to that significant date when my mother died at 45 or 46. Lately, my age has been triggering a reaction in me, and I am beginning to think about what she was feeling and thinking at this same age. She died of a cerebral hemorrhage, you know. I've always thought that life runs in cycles. Yes, we both would like to make an appointment."

Highlights from Follow-up Interviews with Van and Cindy

Both Van and Cindy looked very much like they had in 1972, yet they appeared more reflective, centered, and contented. In their conversation they showed a newly observed respect and attentiveness to the other's point of view.

NLP. How are the two of you doing together?

VAN. Well, we're hanging in there. We figure our relationship will be more even keeled once the children leave home.
     We were wondering if we would stir up the pot coming back to see you again . . .
     (Reflecting) . . .
     What did we do here? I, myself, put together a lot of things from my past . . . . We dumped our shit here.

CINDY. I really did become a different person. (Addressing Norman Paul) I remember now that I saw you, as a "god-figure." We felt good about sharing of our issues. I am very pleased to have added a life of my own over the years. I teach and do executive volunteer work on a national level.

NLP. (To Van) I admired your capacity to have the guts to sweat the crisis out. Most men are runners . . . their solution is to leave . . . to find somebody else.

*   *   *

CINDY. You will never believe it, Daddy is a definite alcoholic. Mother has inherited her own money which has changed her outlook on life.

VAN. I got back in touch with my sister two years ago, whom I had not seen for ten years. She has been divorced twice now, and she wondered what made it possible for us to remain married all these years.

CINDY. I told her that we found this neat therapist who helped us sort things out.

Van and Cindy talked about both Brian and Mary Lee, their children, and their general delight with their development. They added that Brian is now 17 years old, and Mary Lee is 15. They told me that they had explained to the children that they had consulted with me recently, as they had done many years ago in the past at difficult times in their lives. The children indicated to their parents that they didn't recall any turbulent times in the family's past, other than hazy recollections of "screaming fights." Presently Brian and Mary are healthy and involved with athletic and social interests at school. Brian, described as tall and lanky, is interested in competitive swimming and has won a few swimming meets for the breast stroke. He finds his junior year a breeze and looks forward to becoming a naval engineer after attending college. Mary Lee is a sophomore at the same high school as Brian. She has been excited about her recent discovery and involvement in the drama program. Last month she was surprised and elated to tell her family about her being asked to be Assistant Producer of the school's rendition of "Annie."

We discussed a minor family problem, i.e. about Brian's anger at Mary Lee for not preparing supper for everybody during the past two weeks. Mary Lee tried to weasel out of preparing meals for the family with the excuse of her involvement in the play at school. Van tended to side with her, and he expected that because of her involvement at school she would be out late, and unable to prepare meals for everyone. I offered some suggestions about how to handle the situation. All of them were to sit down and schedule who was to handle meal preparation. A written schedule could then be posted on the refrigerator for all to see. Van and Cindy thought that this format would be a good idea. A later phone conversation with Van and Cindy revealed that Mary Lee and Brian found this maneuver satisfactory. Mary Lee indicated a willingness to check with Cindy or Brian in advance if she was likely to be late.

Van and Cindy described how their relationship has matured and become more mutually supportive. There had been no recurrence of affairs, yet their sexual lives had tapered off recently. Cindy said that trips away from home tended to rekindle the "old spark." They seemed ensconced in early midlife, adding that they felt pleased to have gotten to where they were now.

A high point for the family was a visit to Mobile, Alabama to Van's parents' gravesites which took place three years ago. Cindy noted that the children were especially moved to tears at that time. They also visited where Van and his family lived and were appalled by the impoverished quarters they saw.

Over-all Impressions

It was immediately apparent that Van and Cindy were pleased to be present for "a check-in." They were surprisingly comfortable in addressing the events of 1972 as they had both apparently achieved considerable emotional distance from those upsetting times. As they reminisced together with Norman Paul about those times of turmoil and anguish, what they seemed to remember most vividly in this brief encounter was their relationship to the therapist. Cindy used the word "god-father" several times, not quite grandfather, but almost.

Van remembered Norman as a person willing to share, and as a good listener. He also said that Norman Paul's desk was "a good place to dump our shit." Norman Paul saw himself as a shepherd who had guided the two of them separately and together through an intense and potentially dangerous crisis. Now, in turn, he perceived Van and Cindy as shepherding their own children through adolescence. It was apparent to the observer, Betty Paul, that Van and Cindy had at "check-in time," both the emotional strength, and the tools to do just that. Did they gather this strength at that time in part from their work with their families, themselves, and Norman Paul? It is obvious that the Hoopses have continued to work, i.e. taking the kids to his father's grave, Cindy's reunion with 50 members of her extended family, and Van's reconnecting with his sister.

Were one intent on looking for the roots of this brand of crisis, one could conjecture and support the existence of a variety of factors;

1) Van's distancing of Cindy at the time of the affair represented his unconscious proxy effort to neutralize the emergence of images of his intense dependency needs on his mother, displaced onto Cindy.

2) The existence of Van's increasing unconscious homosexual fantasies as evidenced by a need to be involved with another woman.

3) Cindy's tendency to fuse into Van's beingness necessitating and intensifying his need to distance her.

4) Van's unrecognized discomfort in becoming a father to a son insofar as his own experience as a son to a troubled father was fearful and difficult to abide.

However, not withstanding, the above and other factors, one could state that unresolved developmental issues of adolescence seemed to have been a contextual shadow against which this family was formed and grew, unbeknownst to itself. A principal requirement for Van and Cindy's emergence from this quandry was for each to have access to what the self was doing and generating in promoting the destructive dissonance. This was achieved in large part by audiotape and the use of close circuit television thus making them co-investigators in the search for themselves.

One could say also that Van and Cindy, respectively, were acting as if each were compelled and propelled to get the divorce that their parents never got. They were both acting as an agent for the same gender parent to get a proxy divorce that the same gender parent couldn't get from his or her spouse. The process described in this book served in large substance to thwart these invisible forces.

The issue at hand, after the fact of what really happened, is to fathom some of the implications in general for a population wherein divorce continues to increase in frequency and the divorced children very often continue to exude evidence of being mortally wounded.

There is no question that we live our lives generally with no knowledge of what happened two or three generations ago, and every once in a while the results or consequences of forgotten events cascade down to our generation without our ever knowning even that this has happened. This unknown presence even cascades down to our children.

—"The Past is never Dead—It is not even past."
William Faulkner

References

Anonymous. "Toward the Differentiation of a Self in One's Own Family," in *Family Interaction,* ed. James Framo (New York: Springer Publishing Co., Inc., 1972.

Becker, Ernest. *The Denial of Death* (New York: The Free Press, Macmillan Publishing Co., Inc., 1973).

Berger, Milton M., ed. *Videotape Techniques in Psychiatric Training and Treatment* (New York: Brunner/Mazel, Inc., 1970).

Brown, Norman O. *Life Against Death: The Psychoanalytical Meaning of History* (Middleton, Conn.: Wesleyan University Press, 1959).

Choron, Jacques: *Death and Western Thought* (New York: Crowell-Collier Publishing Co., 1963).

Eliot, T. S. *The Cocktail Party* (New York: A Harvest Book, Harcourt, Brace and World, Inc., 1950).

————. *The Elder Statesman* (New York: The Noonday Press, Farrar, Straus, and Co., 1959).

————. *The Family Reunion* (New York: A Harvest Book, Harcourt, Brace and World, Inc., 1939).

Ferenczi, Sandor. *Further Contributions to the Theory and Technique of Psychoanalysis* (London: The Hogarth Press, Ltd., 1950), Chapters 4, 16, 17.

Freud, Sigmund. *On the Sexual Theories of Children,* The Standard Edition of the Complete Psychological Works of Sigmund Freud, vol. IX (London: The Hogarth Press, Ltd., 1959), pp. 205–226.

Group for the Advancement of Psychiatry. *Normal Adolescence* (New York: Charles Scribner's Sons, 1968).

Haas, Walter; Mendell, David; Mitchell, Celia; Mullan, Hugh; and Paul, Norman. *Exploring Therapeutic Encounter.* A professional discussion with LP recording of a therapy session. Audio Press, 1970, Briarwood Lane, Pleasantville, New York 10570).

Harris, Thomas A. *I'm Okay—You're Okay* (New York: Harper and Row, Publishers, Inc., 1969).

Henry, Jules. *Pathways to Madness* (New York: Vintage Books, Random House, Inc., 1971).

Lewin, Bertram D. *The Image and the Past* (New York: International Universities Press, Inc., 1968).

Novey, Samuel. *The Second Look: The Reconstruction of Personal History in Psychiatry and Psychoanalysis* (Baltimore, Md.: The Johns Hopkins Press, 1968).

O'Neill, N. and O'Neill, G. *Open Marriage* (New York: Avon Books, The Hearst Corporation, 1973).

Paul, Norman. "Parental Empathy," in *Parenthood, Its Psychology and Psychopathology,* ed. E. James Anthony and Therese Benedek (Boston: Little, Brown and Co., Inc., 1970).

————. "The Use of Empathy in the Resolution of Grief," in *Perspectives in Biology and Medicine 11,* no. 1 (Autumn 1967) (copyright 1967 by the University of Chicago).

Roth, Philip. *Portnoy's Complaint* (New York: Bantam Book, Random House, Inc., 1970).

Ruitenbeck, Hendrik, ed. *The Problem of Homosexuality in Modern Society* (New York: E. P. Dutton and Co., Inc., 1963).

Satir, Virginia. *Conjoint Family Therapy* (Palo Alto, Calif.: Science and Behavior Books, Inc., 1967).

Norman L. Paul, M.D. is an innovative family systems psychiatrist who is presently affiliated with the Department of Neurology, Boston University School of Medicine, Boston, MA. Awards have included the Strecker Award in 1966 for most innovative psychiatrist of the year. He received an Emmy nomination for "Trouble in the Family," a cinema veritas account of the resolution of a family's problem in 1966 produced by the Public Broadcasting Corporation. Between 1978 and 1981, he was a member of the Board of Directors of the American Family Therapy Association, and since 1983 has been a member of the American Association for Marriage and Family Therapy. In 1984, he received a Distinguished Contribution to Family Therapy Award from the American Family Therapy Association.

Betty Byfield Paul, L.I.C.S.W., a graduate of Bryn Mawr College and Simmons School of Social Work is an Approved Supervisor of AAMFT. She has been on the faculty of the Arlington Public School, the New England Center for the Study of the Family, and Wheelock College. She is currently in private practice in Lexington, Massachusetts. Mrs. Paul is a charter member of the American Family Therapy Association, and is a fellow of the American Orthopsychiatric Association.